BECOMING A FOOTNOTE

SUNY series in New Political Science

Bradley J. Macdonald, editor

BECOMING A FOOTNOTE

An Activist-Scholar Finds His Voice, Learns to Write, and Survives Academia

SANFORD F. SCHRAM

STATE UNIVERSITY OF NEW YORK PRESS

Published by
State University of New York Press, Albany

Printed in the United States of America

For information, contact
State University of New York Press, Albany, NY
www.sunypress.edu

Production, Jenn Bennett
Marketing, Fran Keneston

Library of Congress Cataloging-in-Publication Data

Schram, Sanford.
Becoming a footnote : an activist-scholar finds his voice, learns to write, and survives academia / Sanford F. Schram.
pages cm
Includes bibliographical references and index.
ISBN 978-1-4384-4775-9 (hardcover : alk. paper)
ISBN 978-1-4384-4774-2 (pbk. : alk. paper)
1. Schram, Sanford. 2. Social scientists—United States—Biography. 3. Political activists—United States—Biography. 4. College teachers—New York (State)—Biography. 5. Scholars—United States—Biography. 6. Social sciences—Study and teaching. 7. Social problems—Study and teaching. I. Title.

H59.S34 2013
300.92—dc23
[B] 2012041978

10 9 8 7 6 5 4 3 2 1

For

Michal McCall

My Everlasting Colleague

Exactly how you hear it, is exactly how it all went down, it was later in the evening that the facts and figures got turned around.

—John Mayer, "Stitched Up"

CONTENTS

PREFACE

In the fall of my freshman year at St. Lawrence University, my English professor gave me an F on my Mary McCarthy paper. (The war in Vietnam was in full swing at the time, and McCarthy had chosen to write eloquently on the subject. We read her as much for her prose as her politics.) That professor constantly challenged me to wake up, see what was happening in the world, and learn to find my voice to speak and write about it. The grade was its own wake-up call about my writing abilities. I eventually became that professor's colleague at nearby Potsdam College of the State University of New York where she was subsequently positioned; and she had continued to edit my writing over the years. Recently, when I saw her for dinner in Washington, D.C. (while I was in town to make a presentation at a conference), I told her that I thought I probably would have never learned to write if not for her. She responded by saying: "No, you would have learned to write…eventually." She had a point: I was not a good writer, but over time, the more you write, the better writer you become. And I cannot stop writing. I love getting to express myself in the hopes that I can contribute to understanding and knowledge. I want to make a difference. I feel strongly that everyone has something distinctive to contribute; they just need to be encouraged to find what it is that they can add. I say this not to minimize the obstacles many of us confront. Nonetheless, while social position or economic circumstance can make it harder for some as opposed to others, I strongly believe that each of us can be supported to find our voice and develop the skills to make a contribution. As an educator, this is the philosophy that informs my work.

What follows is the story about my own journey to find my voice and develop the ability to express it in writing. It is a story with a number of dimensions: the personal and the political, the substantive and the stylistic. Yet, it is primarily the story about overcoming my deficiencies to become a published scholar. Given the time period covered, it is not anachronistic to invoke that slogan from Marshall McLuhan in the 1960s: the medium is the message. I detail how I learned to write as well as report on how I came to write what I did. I guess my thinking is that if others learn that someone who got an F can do it, so can they.

INTRODUCTION

In the summer of 2000, a time that now seems idyllic, I was a member of a faculty contingent from my school (Bryn Mawr) that attended a two-week retreat at Brown University in Providence, Rhode Island, focused on issues of multiculturalism in the academy. We were assigned classes where faculty from different participating schools exchanged ideas on the topic. One day, the instructor of my class (a young but thoughtful female political scientist) asked us to engage in yet another exercise designed to get us to be more forthcoming about the issue. We were, like most students, not always quick to express ourselves. We were a diverse group ourselves, men and women, younger and older faculty from a variety of ethnic and racial backgrounds, and we needed time to get comfortable talking about ourselves to each other. We were getting better at engaging the topic and talking openly about sensitive issues, but we still benefited from these solicitations. This exercise has stayed with me: we were asked to write on both sides of blank 3x5 cards and hang them around our necks. On the first side, we were to write how we thought people saw us and on the other side how we saw ourselves. Then each of us in turn was to reveal to the group what we had written. On the first side, I wrote "New York intellectual Jew"; on the other, "former letter carrier."

When my turn came, folks were chuckling. I looked the part of the New York Jew: short, bald, grey beard, and nervous (Woody Allen without glasses). But in the discussion that followed, no one asked me about being a New Yorker, let alone a Jew or an intellectual (and this was understandable since several others in the class already, it seemed, knew way too much about these identities). What my classmates really wanted to talk about was what it was like to be a letter carrier and what were the issues of diversity in my postal workplace. While the letter carrier seemed an obscure and marginal identity in this context, I relayed that it was actually a source of some status in the post office: letter carriers spent most of the day on their own, outside, unsupervised, and they got paid slightly more than clerks. Letter carriers, in fact, had a special status in the post office.

Despite that, I was not a letter carrier for long (just a few years) before I left for graduate school (escaping the racism of co-workers, and after getting suspended for refusing to cut my hair or sign a loyalty oath during the

Vietnam War, while still under a cloud for previously being a participant in the Great Postal Wildcat Strike of 1970 that was centered in New York City and surrounding New Jersey before eventually spreading to other parts of the country—all acts performed against the wishes of my letter carriers' union local president, who was also my father). While sitting in that class with my faculty colleagues, my blue collar existence seemed in retrospect way more left-wing than teaching college. And so it was.

Years later, while out jogging, I ran into one of my doctoral students who was coming the other way, and, using the excuse to stop exercising, we started talking about prospects for a career in the academy upon completion of that student's nearly finished dissertation. The student had a business background and wanted to switch careers and become an academic, but was now getting a bit uncertain about it in the face of learning way too much about academic politics (admittedly my fault). I counseled the student not to worry, that in fact there was a big difference between business and the academy: business was cutthroat; the academy was backstabbing. Not exactly reassuring, but I would like to feel it was edifying. (The student completed the dissertation and adjuncts while keeping the business job.)

It is true that my academic career has had its own unique ups and downs. I ended up a visiting professor at Bryn Mawr College, spending sixteen years as a full-time, full professor, with sabbaticals and all, but no tenure. The American Association of University Professors (AAUP) would eventually write in complaint about this, but to no avail, as reported by the *Chronicle of Higher Education*.[1]

Nonetheless, although I struggled with what I saw as the injustice of that appointment, I have, for the most part, thoroughly enjoyed a career that has allowed me the opportunity to teach and engage in research. I have especially loved having the opportunity to combine them by bringing my scholarship into the classroom and working with students on a number of exciting projects. In fact, the oddity of my appointment has prompted me to write what I am calling an academic memoir. I want to share with others how it is possible to have a fulfilling career as a scholar in the academy, even today as it is being neoliberalized to run more like a business (where throatcutting and backstabbing are now combined). In particular, I want to convey the excitement of academic work, both the teaching and the research, but especially the opportunity to engage in scholarship. I have been fortunate to get to contribute to research in my area of specialization (social welfare)[2] and to write about the scholarly process more generally.[3] In fact, I see this memoir as being a more ambitious, if personalized, way to further the conversation about conducting scholarship in the academy today. I have had the opportunity to work with some great students and learn from the best scholars. I have had great collaborators. I want to share what my involvement in that entailed, especially for those thinking about their own engagement in the scholarly process in these changing times. Along the way, I will tell some pretty interesting stories, but my main goal is to provide a more intimate portrait of the scholarly process as I experienced it, how I affected it and it affected me. I hope folks find it, if not reassuring, at least . . . edifying.

As for the title of this book, *Becoming a Footnote,* it reflects the contradictions of my academic identity. It is a big deal in the academy to be cited; it can be the basis for keeping your job (if not tenure, as in my case). It can suggest that your work is valued, that it is contributing to scholarship, that others rely on it for laying a foundation for their own work, either as something to build upon or something to tear down. Yet, it also implies that in spite of all your efforts you are reduced to a footnote, a mere afterthought.[4] The contradiction that lies at the heart of my becoming a footnote reflects the same ambivalence I expressed in the 3x5 card exercise: I think people tend to see me as some kind of intellectual, but I still know that I came from far less rarefied circumstances. While I like to think I am intelligent, I am still often haunted by this inferiority complex. I have always felt an outsider inside the academy.

In fact, writing this memoir at all is its own contradiction: simultaneously self-indulgent and self-effacing. On one hand, it implies that I think my personal story is noteworthy enough that people would want to hear about what I did, how, and when. On the other hand, it involves revealing that my work was largely enabled by other people, especially colleagues and students. In fact, people who know me well know I am a ball of contradictions. I am just as described on that 3x5 card: somewhat brash on the outside, but insecure on the inside. No matter how you look at it, for me, becoming a footnote says a lot. It is a significant accomplishment of the most humbling sort. What follows provides details on how I have lived that contradiction.

ONE

HOW I HAD FOUR MAJORS IN COLLEGE

At both Bryn Mawr and neighboring Haverford, there is Customs Week (elsewhere this is often called freshman orientation). Why these schools persist in using such an anachronism is surely subject to question. I suspect it is because Bryn Mawr and Haverford are proud of their traditions and want their incoming students to develop a sense of respect both for the institutions and themselves: they are being acculturated to the folkways of a very special place and should feel special about being included. It turns out what is customary at each school is not really what students are being introduced to as much as what are the rules and regulations regarding their conduct as students taking courses and living on campus. Looming large is the honor code at each school.

It is all part of keeping up appearances and projecting the image of an elite institution. Both campuses at Bryn Mawr and Haverford are laid out and groomed to imply privilege and status in ways that unmistakably suggest that the opportunity to study there is a special one. It can make students feel they have been anointed, but then again, that itself can also be intimidating. Bryn Mawr's campus in particular is stunningly misleading in its magisterial facade. It is a women's college that was started in the late 1880s by a man from Haverford who felt his sister and women like her should be able to get the kind of education that men at Haverford had been getting since the 1830s. In order to suggest that women were not being shortchanged, the buildings, as they were erected one after another over the course of the first century or more of the college's history, seem to have been intentionally designed to mimic the architecture of schools such as Oxford or Cambridge in England, to imply a much older institution with a more august lineage. Smoke and mirrors seem to be involved as much as bricks and mortar. The visage was and still is overwhelming. Bryn Mawr has buildings with turrets and flying buttresses.

In fact, Bryn Mawr is very serious about keeping up appearances, especially when it comes to those flying buttresses. The exterior of the major auditorium on campus was refurbished back around 2000, and that included repairing the many flying buttresses that adorn the outside of the building. When the restoration was ongoing, I expressed concerns to my dean about the cost of maintaining such anachronistic architecture, saying we could better spend the money on other things, such as hiring more faculty or raising our pay. (Flying buttresses might have been necessary to support walls propping up roofs of some windowed cathedrals, but this one had very small windows and the buttresses clearly served no real architectural purpose. Their value was, in my mind, strictly symbolic, connoting the idea that Bryn Mawr should be seen as a much older institution than it actually was.) My dean responded by saying, yes, the college's administrators were well aware that the Gothic-looking flying buttresses on our medieval-looking auditorium were a major expense of questionable architectural value, but she nonetheless insisted they were necessary because it had long ago been proven that flying buttresses keep away evil spirits! It was a joke, to be sure, but one that was taken seriously by those responsible for maintaining the image of the school. The college did not hesitate to spend huge sums of money to restore its flying buttresses. Bryn Mawr tells itself many stories to justify its commitment to its customs, traditions, and even its anachronistic architecture.

Customs Week is another relic, no less durable than those flying buttresses, equally symbolic in value, if less physical in appearance. Part of the ritual of Customs Week is the opportunity to hear from faculty about what they expect from students and what they think it is it like to be a student at that school. More generally, it is simply an opportunity to hear a professor speak about something other than one of the subjects in the courses offered. It is part of the process of humanizing the institution for new students.

I have given the same talk at customs for both Bryn Mawr and Haverford. It is entitled "Why I Had Four Majors in College." Like a lot of my titles and pronouncements, it is supposed to be somewhat misleading in order to make a point. Students often think that because I am a professor, I must be smart or some kind of academic whiz. So the assumption is that I simultaneously had four majors while breezing through my studies as an undergraduate. This could not be farther from the truth. I tell them that I did not have four majors in college at the same time (something that is actually prohibited at most schools), but instead I had four different majors in serial fashion, moving from one to another as it became clear that my grade point average (GPA) would suffer if I continued with my current major from that point on. In other words, I was not a whiz.

I tell the story during Customs Week to reassure students that they need not overstress the issue of having to choose a major, that they can switch majors as they go, that this is not unusual, and that it can all work out in the end (even if you are not an academic whiz). If a non-whiz like me, who was a serial major, can make it as a professor, then they can probably plan on doing just fine during and after college. I am not sure if the story calms all fears among the first year students who hear it, but it gets laughs, and for that moment the levity must defuse some tensions felt by these newcomers to a very proud and possibly intimidating institution. Some students might actually start to feel they belong and deserve to be there.

My story begins at the end of my first year at St. Lawrence University, 1967–68. How I ended up attending St. Lawrence is its own story. In the spring of 1967, I had gotten a full scholarship to attend Butler University in Indianapolis, Indiana, where my family had taken me on a visit the previous summer. Probably because of the scholarship, my dad tried to tell me Butler was the Harvard of the Midwest; but that did not work since our neighbor, who was a year ahead of me in school, was finishing his first year at the University of Chicago. (I remember at the time thinking it odd that a city had a college all of its own, but my friend was to quickly school me on the established fact that Chicago was where it was at academically.) I told my father that Butler had a great basketball team (that I would never get to be on), but it was supposed to be my backup school, according Mr. Mazzone, my guidance counselor. The plan was that I was going to go to Brown University with my friends and we were all going to play soccer there, or at least try. (Two of my friends did in fact go to Brown and play soccer there on a team that was usually in the national championship tournament.) St. Lawrence was to be number two. I got a partial scholarship to St. Lawrence and was waitlisted at Brown. I sent in my deposit to St. Lawrence, honored to be partially subsidized. (It was not much money, but what it symbolized to my feeble brain was huge.) Subsequently, Brown admitted me, but I turned it down because I had already submitted my deposit to St. Lawrence. (It was not that much money, but to my feeble brain it was hard-earned money that I refused to give away.)

Subsequently, in my senior year at St. Lawrence, during what was called inter-term, I spent time at Brown, attending some philosophy classes with my friends and thinking I would have flunked out if I'd gone to Brown. When I returned years later as a professor from Bryn Mawr for a multiculturalism seminar, I was haunted by the fact that I had stupidly chosen not to attend Brown, as well as the idea that I probably had made the right decision because I was in all likelihood not good enough to have finished there. This ambivalence continued to haunt me more recently when the economist Glenn Loury invited me to speak there but then had to cancel when the more preferred speakers on his list agreed to present. Ever the ball of confusion and contradiction, I could never sort out my feelings about Brown.

My first year at St. Lawrence, though, went well. Located in remote northern New York just south of the St. Lawrence River and the Canadian border, St. Lawrence is a beautiful residential campus in the small town of Canton (population six thousand). This sort of remote campus does leave a student often with very little to do other than to trudge to the library to study with friends. In the winter, this was likely to be one of my longer trips outside. The result can be, at times, higher grades than might otherwise be the case. As a freshman, I declared myself a Physics major. (I was academically strong in math and science in high school, and there was of course the whole Sputnik craze.) In my first year, I aced both semesters of introductory Physics and did the same on the labs. I was evidently a physics whiz. When I went to meet my advisor, Professor Lufburrow, he wanted to know how I did it. Lufburrow was the quintessential physics professor, grey hair, moustache, wire-rimmed glasses and a bit of an accent (vaguely European). He seemed approachable up to a point. More importantly, he was delighted to have such a promising student under his wing and was curious to know how I approached my studies. In particular, he was especially interested in how I scored perfectly on those labs.

I told him I treated them like my Bar Mitzvah. This was not helpful on several levels, especially since Lufburrow was not Jewish. Professor Lufburrow looked at me like I was a dog barking and asked me what was I trying to say. I said that in order to become a man in the eyes of the Jewish religion, a boy had to read from the Torah in Hebrew during the Sabbath service on Saturday morning in front of the whole congregation, at the age of thirteen. (It seems in retrospect cruel to make young kids do this in order to be pronounced the man they still are yet to be—but this is not my point.) I told Lufburrow that in order to be able to prepare for your reading the rabbi gave you a 33 1/3 phonograph record with a recording of someone reciting your assigned passage in Hebrew. I took it home and proceeded to play it over and over until I memorized the singsong recitation. And here is the important point: I never for one minute knew what the Hebrew words meant. Sure, I went to Hebrew school twice a week for years and learned some Hebrew, but not nearly enough to speak it fluently or to translate passages or do anything that would approximate being literate in Hebrew. I knew next to nothing about Hebrew. I memorized the sounds so that I could emulate the recitation, regardless of my ignorance of what it meant about God, being a good Jew, or anything else. This of course raises profound issues about whether I deserved to be recognized as a real man in the eyes of the Jewish religion. And it evidently, upon this telling, raised real issues in the eyes of Professor Lufburrow as to whether I should be recognized as a real Physics major. He suggested I might want to think about another discipline in which to concentrate my studies.[1]

Lufburrow's suggestion was most appropriate. His point was that lab writeups reported on what you actually did, not your idealized understanding of what you thought you were supposed to have done. You were supposed to conduct an experiment, record the results, and write up the report. I conducted the experiments (rolling metal balls down inclines and other exercises), but I really did not understand what we as students were doing or why. What I did know was that there were equations for everything and I could memorize them and write out the calculations. I went through the motions of the labs and then just plugged in the numbers to the equations and wrote out the results. I was a zombie Physics major. Lufburrow, like most physics professors, believed in the importance of labs as an opportunity to learn by doing. The fact that I was not learning while not actually doing was in direct disregard of this whole pedagogical approach. I was sleepwalking through the labs and relying on my mathematical abilities to get me through. I was no real physicist. At this rate, I would never be able to conduct my own experiments. It made sense that I should look into other majors that did not require learning by doing.

This would eventually prove to be most ironic, since a part of my scholarship years later would come to be about promoting this very approach. I have been a big promoter of experiential learning at all levels of higher education and especially in the curriculum at the particular schools where I taught. I have published articles and books about this issue. I have been cited as an authority. I became a footnote on the basis of that which I had failed so miserably. My past evidently did not deter me. With never a reference to my youthful disregard for learning by doing, I spoke forcefully about breaking down barriers between theory and practice, student research and faculty research, the classroom and the community.[2] As if it were something I always embraced, I have expressed my heartfelt belief that students learn best when they get to be active participants in the research process. Eventually, I went farther, conducting research that featured being connected to the community as a better form of social science because we all learn from each other by being actively involved in the research process.[3] With time, I could understand why at the time Lufburrow was so disappointed that his prize pupil only existed in theory, because that student at that point only relied on theory and never got his hands dirty applying theory in the lab in a thoughtful and attentive way. One way or the other, I eventually felt his pain, took it to heart, and tried to make amends. Yet, back then, it was too soon for me to know why it was such a big issue for my advisor; instead, I just looked for another major.

Major number two was then not a surprise but in fact a full retreat back to theory—Mathematics (which I had been taking as part of my prerequisites for Physics). I had taken Calculus I and II my freshman year and aced both. Yet, I should have known that my new home would prove to be only a temporary haven. At some level, I had already realized that I had aced both Calculus I and II because they never got beyond the calculus taught to me back in high school by the amazing Mr. Fife, a gangly Ichabod Crane of a teacher who was a bit eccentric, but boy could that guy teach. My high school was actually great in mathematics and perhaps only okay in the natural sciences. We had not only Mr. Fife but also Dr. Kambor, who, if you could believe it, was a high school teacher with a PhD in his area of instruction. Kambor may have been a roly-poly guy with a tendency to mumble clichés, but he, too, was an excellent instructor. But it was Fife who made calculus essentially a gut for me in college. But how long would that last?

I did not let any doubts deter me as I sought a new major at the start of my sophomore year. Yet, coasting through calculus started to end in the middle of the fall semester in Calculus III with Professor Van Dyke. Van Dyke was very formal, constantly writing theorems on the board, spending most of the class with his back to us. I was getting worried, and not so much because I was not developing a connection to this man I knew only from his back. Now we were in new territory, and deriving the proofs was proving difficult. I ended up with a B in the class (my perfect record in math was gone). I pushed on, hoping I would adapt to now actually having to learn new things. In the spring, I enrolled in Boolean Algebra. I was about to learn what I did not know and never will. To this day, it remains a mystery to me what exactly Boolean Algebra actually is. I got a 36 on the first test. I went to see the instructor, Professor Simpson, whom I had had for Calculus II. I asked Simpson: "Thirty-six out of what?" I was thinking it must have been scaled on some kind of curve (it was math, after all). No luck. Simpson responded: "Thirty-six out of one hundred, you idiot!" (Back then, professors were not so well schooled in nurturing students.) Simpson was like a friend or an uncle; in fact, he had an avuncular demeanor and a wry smile, with a tendency for bad jokes. He always joked with me in particular in Calculus II, like the time one day in class when he made fun of a song I had requested for my girlfriend the night before to our student radio station. (What he was doing listening to student radio that night I now consider just something odd.) I was not offended by his way of talking to me, but I was chagrined that I got such an abysmally low score. Simpson tried to reassure me by saying: "Don't worry, you did better than most in the class." Wow, we all flunked! This was not reassuring, but instead totally frightening. What was I to become as a Math major now that there was no more calculus that I could take that rehashed what I learned from Fife in high school? And who could I rely on if we all sinking together? I decided to switch majors again. I dropped Boolean Algebra (the only course

I would ever drop as an undergraduate) and went straight out of the hard sciences altogether, determined now to seek shelter in the supposedly more nurturing humanities.

I had been taking German along with Physics and Math (I think I imagined myself as a budding Jewish Werner Von Braun). So German was now my new refuge as my career in the hard sciences bottomed out in the middle of my sophomore year. I had studied German in high school with Herr Kerr, who called students "Chico" if they switched from German to English when speaking in class. Years later, my anthropologist son relayed to me that another anthropologist had made a study of what she called "mock Spanish," as in "hasta la vista, baby," ala The Terminator, suggesting that white Americans used mock Spanish in a racist way to imply a macho, tough-guy type of posture.[4] That was Kerr to a T, who could be tough, but was a very effective instructor nonetheless. I ended up scoring high on the German SAT test, and I think it helped me gain admission to colleges. I continued with German in college, acing courses as I went, and by the second semester of my sophomore year I was in an advanced German literature course with Herr Bühler.

Yet, German literature with Bühler would soon prove to be not the humanities haven I sought. My problems in Physics and Math actually intensified. My strengths in German were similar to those in Physics and Math: I was good at memorization and bad at creative application. I had a rich German vocabulary and could also strictly follow the rules of grammar, composing my own German prose in precise fashion. Yet, translation required creative leaps of interpretation. It was the language equivalent of applying theory to practice in a hands-on way inside a story rather than a lab—already proven not to be my real strength.

The fatal story I had to translate came late in that spring semester seminar. It was *Die Panne* ("The Breakdown") by Friedrich Dürrenmatt who was heavily influenced by Franz Kafka.[5] At the time, the title did not alert me to what was just about to happen to me as a German major. Ever the naive one, the warning staring me in the face was hidden in plain sight. Part of the reason was that I idolized Kafka for his dystopian perspective on modernity, and, given Kafka's influence, I was excited to read the lesser-known Dürrenmatt. Yet I ended up having a breakdown over translating "The Breakdown." In spite of how the story resonated for me, I could not muster a credible translation. Bühler in fact decided it was so bad that he should read it aloud in class. As I said about Simpson, back then professors were not as versed as now in being nurturing educators. In fact, Herr Bühler was not really what I would call a real professor; he was just some fairly literate guy who knew a lot of German, probably because it was his first language, and he was hired to teach us. Bühler neither looked like a professor nor acted like one; but he did indeed speak German fluently. Everyone laughed when Bühler read my translation, and I remembered sitting there frozen with fear that people would turn around and look at me. Fortunately, that did not happen (probably out of sympathy more than lack of ability to figure out who had blown the assignment).

After the laughter died down, I stopped by to see Herr Bühler in his office and we talked about what was lost in translation. Evidently, a lot. And so I quickly decided I was probably done with my third major. I did not panic, but things were now looking bad. Time was running out. I still had a decent GPA, hovering around 3.3 out of possible 4.0 (making me a B student). But that average was inflated by my early A's in Physics, Math, and German, all garnered before the roof fell in each major. Where could I go to sustain my GPA? Who would take me in and give me a place where I could shine? Given those collapsed roofs, I was now without a home, academically speaking.

I was unsure where to turn. At the time, I was profoundly distracted, but this actually was to prove to be my salvation. In the fall of 1969, President Nixon's plan for the Vietnamization of the war was not going well. Mai Lai was about to become the scandal that turned so many Americans against the war. I was already attending meetings of the Students for a Democratic Society (SDS); people were planning demonstrations, including a mass vigil in front of the ROTC (Reserve Officer Training Corps) building on campus. The killing of student protesters at Kent State would happen in less than a year, forcing campuses to close just about everywhere, but even before that we were increasingly mobilizing against the war. We rallied, we marched, we protested, just as they were to do at Kent State. We kept signing pledges to resist being drafted. One day, walking in line up to a large steel receptacle with flames rising, I burned my draft card.

Around that time, the protesting and the schooling merged. I thought about it and decided that my main extracurricular activity should become my major. Politics was already in the classroom. I would go to the library at night and it seemed as though everyone was reading C. Wright Mills's popular book *White Collar*.[6] We were discussing in class SDS's Port Huron Statement (in part inspired by Mills's critique of American society).[7] We talked as if we ourselves could become agents of change who merged intellectual and political work, just like Mills.[8] We were living *The Strawberry Statement* in real time even as we were reading it.[9] The table was set for me; all I had to do was sit down. I switched to Government in the History/Government Department. It was made easier by the fact that we were required to take History as part of our general education distribution requirements. I had already taken U.S. Government as well. I signed up for a course on the war in Vietnam. At some point in the fall of my junior year, my avocation became my fourth major.

It turns out that St. Lawrence was a great place to focus on politics as an undergraduate major. We had wonderful professors such as Bernie Lammers, Ansil Ramsey, and Victor Wallis. Ansil taught the Vietnam course and was knowledgeable about South Asian politics generally. Victor was a charismatic, if soft-spoken, professor who motivated me to embrace radicalism. He had us read edgy stuff about the student protests of May 1968, about *favelas* in Latin America, and critiques of mainstream political theory. Bernie was an incredible force; he was full of life in the classroom; he made studying politics exciting. He adroitly combined theory (Hannah Arendt was one of his favorites) with concern for civics education in order to promote a more thoughtful democratic citizenry. (Years later, when I taught at Potsdam, ten miles from St. Lawrence, Bernie would run for Congress and I would be his campaign manager. We drove all over the North Country continuing the dialogue that had begun years before back in his classes. We lost the election, but I learned a lot.)

St. Lawrence also had a great speakers series of politically noteworthy people coming to the campus. It was remarkable for a small college in remote northern New York. When I think back to this series of prominent and politically relevant speakers, I think that it must have played a major role in my political education and an even greater role in my budding political consciousness. It would have been difficult not to become a politically aware citizen while being exposed to such a star lineup of important political thinkers.

I remember that in my first year we heard John Kenneth Galbraith, the great economist (who had been ambassador to India), speak about his writings, including *The Affluent Society*,[10] which I had read just the week before (probably as assigned). Not long after that, Ralph Nader, the then very young consumer advocate came and spoke about his concern for corporate malfeasance. His book, *Unsafe At Any Speed*,[11] about the Chevrolet Corvair, had been published in 1965. Saul Alinsky came and was hysterically funny describing the various tactics he used to trouble the people in power.[12] Michael Harrington, the author of *The Other America*,[13] spoke and was magisterial, though his explanations of his fallout with the New Left and SDS were not entirely convincing to us young leftists. (With Harrington, I committed a *faux pas*, when in a small group discussion I asked him, in mixed company with some older women present, to explain more about his disagreement with the New Left activists, including especially Tom Hayden and others in the leadership of SDS. I made the mistake of specifically asking him to amplify on what he had said in an interview in *Playboy* magazine.

Harrington pointedly noted that people could read his assessment of the disagreement in a number of magazines other than *that* one. I slumped a bit in my chair when he said "that one"!)

Yet the speaker who had the greatest impact on me was the political scientist Charles Hamilton, who came later in my junior year just before Kent State and spoke about the book *Black Power*[14] that he had co-authored with Stokely Carmichael (Kwame Ture). I sat with my Black History professor William Mallam, who was a great influence on me in spite of his rather droll sense of humor, which sometimes was at my expense.[15] I think sitting with Mallam really motivated me to engage Hamilton. I was about to get my wish. Hamilton spoke about the inner city as colonized by the white power structure and how decolonization via community control and self-help initiatives in the form of black capitalism were the appropriate responses. Black separatism would be the best route to realizing the fruits of black power. The black folks left behind by white flight needed to take charge on a neighborhood basis, go their own way independent of white society, and forge a black capitalism that would vault them to an independent existence of self-determination and self-sufficiency within but apart from white society.

I understood some of what Hamilton was saying, for personal reasons. I was born in Newark, New Jersey, but grew up in the suburbs. The issue had troubled me for some time. My family was part of the great white flight to the suburbs that had accelerated rapidly in the 1950s in metropolitan areas of the Northeast and the Midwest. That may explain why I was intensely interested in the issue of race relations throughout my college days and beyond. Having professors that urged me to think about it, given my background, undoubtedly helped. Admittedly, it was not something I came to on my own, but confronting this issue had become an important challenge for me by the time I attended Hamilton's talk.

My personal relationship to the issue, therefore, might explain what I did that night. Impulsively, I just got up and spoke during the question period, without really knowing what I was getting into. I had evidently just learned (or perhaps invented) the phrase "economic distributive justice" and blurted out a question using that cumbersome term, asking Hamilton how could we realistically expect black separatism to ensure that African Americans would be able to get their fair share of the broader economic pie if they cut themselves off from the economic engine that white capitalism had become.

Hamilton treated the question as an assault on his dignity (or so it seemed to me). Upon reflection, I can see why. In any case, still burned in my memory is how he proceeded in animated fashion to mow me down in no uncertain terms about how deluded I was in thinking that whites would ever allow blacks to get their fair share if they pursued strategies of integration. (Years later, Charles Hamilton would head a Ford Foundation project to fund research on poverty, and in 1986 he approved a small grant for me and helped me get on a panel he organized to present a paper at the American Political Science Association's annual meeting in Washington, D.C. I asked if he remembered our encounter and he said yes. He told me he had mellowed since then and had come around to my side of the argument. I told him I did not even know I had a side in the argument at the time and my question was something that just popped into my head and got spoken thoughtlessly.)[16]

Shortly after my encounter with Hamilton, we heard of the shootings at Kent State, and the semester ended prematurely (probably out of fear that something like that might happen on our campus). We all went home with incompletes and worked on term papers over the summer. I had a chance to get further into the study of movement politics, the war, and race, my three main areas of interest. Given everything that was going on, majoring in Government at St. Lawrence was starting to make a lot of sense.

So Government was a good choice for my fourth major. And the fourth time proved to be the charm. I did all right as a Government major. I ended up maintaining my 3.3 average. I was less than a great student, however; I continued to rely on my strengths and did almost nothing to try to correct my deficits. I could retain large amounts of information, but processing it was always a challenge, whether it was in a term paper on John C. Calhoun for American Political Thought, an analysis of the causes of the Russian Revolution in a course on the History of Communism, or an annotated bibliography on some now forgotten topic in Political Science. I was a mediocre student, underperforming and underachieving.

When I think back, I see that I could have done much more. I tended to coast. I was diligent about attending class, taking notes, doing the reading. I was a real student in that sense. (A couple of preppy fraternity underclassmen befriended me in my communism class, calling me "the scribe.") Yet the idea that I would somehow work hard to synthesize what I was learning and then present it in a lucidly written analysis that demonstrated some level of reflexivity was something that was just beyond me. There was too much other stuff to do, like hanging out, listening to music, smoking dope, debating the true meaning of Marxism, protesting the war, or chasing girls. Those things had higher priority than working on my intellectual deficits. I see now that it was good that I stayed in school all my life, so that I could finally get around to this issue. Slowly over time, first in graduate school, then when trying prepare courses as a young instructor, and then most critically while trying to become a published scholar, I found I could not delay addressing my limitations any longer. Slowly, I learned to resist the atrophying of consciousness and to try to think critically. At some point, it started to kick in. I started to look beneath the surface to analyze what made something out to be a knowledge claim that deserved to be taken seriously. After a while, it became second nature, something I just did, without saying it or thinking it. You just do it. Yet it is still a work in progress. Writing this chapter has been its own opportunity to realize how I have continued to carry around unquestioned misunderstandings about how I think about these issues. And then there is the writing. Writing has proven to be its own learning by doing. So this chapter has been, for me, quite therapeutic, if anything. In the least, I hope it will enable more of us to choose a major a little more thoughtfully and then maybe stick with it.

TWO

GOING POSTAL, GETTING DRAFTED

How I Ended Up in Graduate School

My mother was a great person. She was probably the kindest person I ever knew. She was so upbeat; she always saw the positive side of things. She did not like to hear bad news. She always turned it around into something positive, if she could. One time, however, she was challenged in a fundamental way—when her husband died.

My father was a great man. He died too young (at fifty-three years of age). The morning my mother called me when he did not wake up, she was crying like I have never heard anyone cry, before or since. She was never the same; she always seemed more vulnerable after that. We (my wife and I) were more attentive to her in the years that followed. She lived twenty-two more years after my father died. She had a good life. His was tougher.

My father did not graduate from high school. He was born in 1920 and was in high school when his father died (also prematurely at forty-five years of age). (Yes, the fact that both my father and my grandfather died so young has obsessed me for my entire adult life, but now, at sixty-three, I just keep jogging to stave off the trend.) When my grandfather died, my dad had to drop out of high school and join his brother in trying to keep my grandfather's gas station going. In 1937, in their hometown of Newark, New Jersey, the Great Depression had hit businesses very hard and customers were dwindling. They lost the station pretty quickly.

My father ended up in the army, getting shot by accident by one of his fellow soldiers while in the Pacific and not having to do much more after that as World War II ended. (He got a small check for his injury from the government that came in the mail each month.) When he came home to Newark, he met and married my mom. Two great families were joined at that point, it always seemed to me. They tried to run a candy store (but that failed too). My dad ended up in the post office, where my mother's brother worked. Eventually, one of my father's brothers also joined the post office. (My dad's other brother owned a popular luncheonette where I eventually worked as a soda jerk in my teenage years.)

My father was a letter carrier. We moved to Livingston, New Jersey, a growing suburb of Newark, when I was six. It was 1955. Not long after that, my father got transferred to be a letter carrier in his new hometown. With my mother working as a bookkeeper for a small insurance firm in nearby West Orange, my parents could afford a single-family home in the suburbs. Working-class people could live like they were middle class back then.

There was a twist to this egalitarian society. The affordability of the suburbs intensified segregation.[1] By moving to Livingston, we had become part of the great white flight. Newark in the 1950s was the poster child for white abandonment of the city. In fact, as time went on, the rush to the suburbs contributed mightily to five decades of population decline, depopulating Newark at a breathtaking rate, from 438,000 in 1950 to 274,000 by 2000. From 1950 through 2000, Newark was losing whites at a rapid rate while it gained blacks almost as fast, but not enough to make up the loss. From 1950 to 2000, Newark's white population declined from more than 350,000 residents to just above 50,000, while during the same time its African American population increased from slightly above 50,000 to approximately 150,000, and the Latino population increased marginally from about 50,000 to approximately 52,000. The increases in the African American and Latino populations could not make up for the decline in the white population that was fleeing to the suburbs.[2]

More than population decline affected Newark. Businesses and the jobs they offered were moving to the suburbs along with the white families. This intensified especially after the Newark Riots of 1967, which turned out to be just a prelude to the waves of rioting that swept through cities all over the country the next year, in the wake of Martin Luther King's assassination (during my freshman year of college). As a result of the 1967 riot, Newark quickly started to hollow out: it got less dense, with fewer people, fewer taxpayers, fewer businesses, and it also got more black. (I did not know it at the time, but being part of this sea change shaped my intellectual and political orientation for the rest of my life. I was learning while doing, without even knowing it.)

Growing up on the South Side of Newark, and living on Peshine Avenue for the first six years of my life, afforded me an opportunity to see white flight firsthand. My neighborhood was predominately Jewish but also already partly comprised of African Americans and others. We had old European-style peddlers with trucks that were more like carts. We had older women with long blue numbers tattooed on their wrists, indicating they were from the Nazi concentration camps. We had fights break out in front of the apartments that could only be stopped by police cars pulling right onto the sidewalks. We thought it was fun as kids under six to join with older boys and burn stuff in the large metal drums behind the apartments. (Perhaps it was a dress rehearsal for burning my draft card in a flaming metal receptacle years later.)

My best friends on Peshine Avenue included an Orthodox boy named Moshe, who had to wear a yarmulke all the time and came to my house on Saturday morning to watch the Lone Ranger (with his mother's permission) because his father would not allow the television to be on during the Sabbath. My parents attended the neighborhood Orthodox synagogue but did not keep kosher or practice Orthodox in any way. They were secular Jews who dutifully attended temple. Being a Jew for me was largely an ethnicity. Other best friends were brothers who lived next door, named Peter and his younger brother Pot (short for what I did not find out), who were African American.

The neighborhood was in transition. I thought it was normal that large moving vans were always in the driveways of the apartment buildings on our street. You could almost never see to the end of the block. White people (Jews) were leaving in droves, moving to the suburbs. Even the letter carriers were leaving. White flight was fueled in part by an economy that allowed working-class people to make a decent living and be able to afford single-family homes in the suburbs. A more equitable economy, ironically, created the basis for more racial segregation.

The non-letter carriers were leaving Newark, too. My uncle and his family followed us out to suburban Livingston a few years later. My uncle's luncheonette—Seymour's—was in our new home town. My father and his siblings all had what I thought were Jewish names: my father was Harold Harvey Schram, his brothers were Melvin and Seymour, and his sisters were Adele, Ruth, and Sylvia. Years later, I came to the conclusion that these were not Jewish names (except Ruth): how many people in the bible are named Seymour? Instead, these were British names Jews gave their children to facilitate assimilation into an English-speaking culture.

Seymour's was a popular hangout for older men associated with sports (like my dad, who was active as a coach for guys older than us kids in Little League). The high school football coach, the coach of the nearby Seton Hall basketball team, and other sports figures would come to schmooze and debate sports. By the time I was fourteen, I was one of the young people behind the counter who made their drinks (milk shakes and such) and served them their food (pie). The place was two blocks from my parents' house and I could walk there. (Sunday mornings, very early before any traffic, I walked down the middle of the main drag—Northfield Avenue—to bring in the fresh baked goods and the newspapers that had just been delivered. I felt like I owned the town.)

Moving from Newark to Livingston was moving from blacks to whites. In retrospect, it was how Jews would finally actually become white, by moving to the suburbs.[3] Livingston was less than fifteen miles from Newark, but the entire time I was growing up there, never once did an African American student attend any of my schools, and I never saw any African American residents in town, ever, at all. The greengrocer in the small supermarket next to my uncle's luncheonette was a very polite, African American, Albino man who was passing but did not live in town. One day, when it was finally revealed that he was African American, a bunch of people felt betrayed, and expressed their dissatisfaction to him personally. It was that kind of town, in the mid-1960s, in suburban New Jersey.

There were no laws prohibiting African Americans from living in Livingston, as far as I could tell. And by the mid-1950s that was probably illegal. Livingston had its great growth spurt during the 1950s, when its population rose from just under 10,000 in 1950 to just over 23,000 by 1960. Yet, none of this rapid population increase included any African Americans, even though 100,000 or more African Americans lived just down the road in Newark. By 1967, when I graduated from high school, the civil rights movement was at its peak, but there were no African Americans residing in the town. By then, Livingston's population was about 28,000, but still no African Americans.

It was like magic. Just twelve miles from Newark and no blacks. It was a mystery of sorts. Well, not quite; as I grew up, I learned that Livingston, like all New Jersey townships, had zoning ordinances that allowed for different types of buildings to be built in different neighborhoods. Yet one consistency across the zones was a prohibition against multi-dwelling buildings, i.e., no apartments. Only single-family homes were allowed, and in some neighborhoods the lot sizes were substantial, sometimes as much as a quarter-acre or even, in the pricier neighborhoods, a half-acre. This made it extremely difficult for low-income families to reside in the town. That would automatically exclude many African Americans. But not all. Plus, my family was by no means rich. If a postal worker from Newark could move his family to Livingston, that meant that African Americans as well as Jews ought to be able to live there. But as it turned out, that was true only for Jews, not African Americans. Still today, Livingston has almost no African Americans (2.3 percent according to the 2010 U.S. Census), but approximately half the suburb's population is Jewish, making it the most Jewish town in the United States.[4]

So there had to be something more at work than just zoning ordinances. I never found out what it was. By the late 1960s, civil rights legislation was outlawing discrimination in housing as well as employment and education. There was time for Livingston to better reflect the racial composition of the metropolitan area. Yet that never happened. I think I would need to ask realtors if steering blacks away from Livingston was an accepted practice even after housing discrimination became illegal. You would think that some people might have been concerned about this issue even before the U.S. Congress passed the Housing Act of 1968 banning discrimination in the sale and rental of housing. Yet I never, ever, remember reading a single newspaper story about the extent to which this common practice was actually occurring in my home town. Then there were those pesky mortgages. How many banks made it more difficult for African Americans to get mortgages for homes in Livingston? Were African Americans being systematically denied mortgages for housing in Livingston either before or after the 1968 legislation? The record is again silent. I checked in vain. In fact, as I recall, when I was growing up there, no one in town ever seemed interested in this issue. It just was not discussed. So, in retrospect, you have to wonder: How did they do it? How did they get away with never discussing an issue that was staring them in the face, as if hidden in plain sight?

I am sure there was discrimination against Jews in housing as well. Yet that did not stop them from coming to Livingston in large numbers. For African Americans, the story was different. They never got to buy homes in Livingston when I was growing up there. And, back then, it was never considered an issue in school, at work, in the community, as far as I can tell. In fact, the law books suggest there was never any litigation decided or legislation passed to open up Livingston so that nonwhites could live there.

Race, therefore, was a huge issue of non-discussion growing up in Livingston. Whites moved away from blacks and that was that, as if it were the natural thing to do. Yet, moving to the suburbs involved another undiscussed issue. For almost all Jews, moving to the suburbs involved moving away from Orthodoxy.[5] The suburbs mostly had Reform or Conservative congregations with very few Orthodox ones. Conservative Judaism had developed in Germany in the nineteenth century to create a path between Orthodox Judaism and the Reform movement that broke with fundamental Jewish Orthodox practice. Conservative Judaism tried to find a way to keep Orthodox Judaism alive while adapting to modern society. Given this focus, it is not surprising that its greatest growth period occurred when Jews began moving to the suburbs in the United States during the post–World War II period. It was as if Conservative Judaism was explicitly provided as the solution for integrating into New Jersey suburbs so that Orthodox Jews could be more assimilable, acceptable, and presentable in the Christian world of neatly manicured suburbia.

Actually, in most cases, switching to Conservative Judaism was the default option for Orthodox Jews who moved to Livingston, for one simple reason: the only synagogue in town was Conservative. There are more Reform (more liberal) congregations in the United States than either Conservative or Orthodox, but there was no Reform synagogue in the Livingston at the time. It was as though the housing developers made us Conservative when they built a development and then helped finance a Conservative congregation's synagogue right next door. Then, just about everyone had to become Conservative. With our working-class income, we lived on the less Jewish side of town and not in the Levin-Sagner development, where the synagogue was located next to the bigger homes professionals were buying for their families. Nonetheless, we immediately joined Temple Beth Shalom, the Conservative synagogue on the edge of the Jewish development. We became Conservative overnight. It was not an agonized conversion. All we had to do was move to the suburbs.

Years later, I would learn what I lost by our switching from Orthodox to Conservative. When an elder in my family died, we went back to temple in Newark. It was Orthodox. The service was different. In the Orthodox service, the whole congregation had an obligation to pay attention and to speak out and correct mistakes made by the rabbi (who was not seen as having some special authority, say, like a priest in a Catholic church). The responsibility fell to the whole congregation to keep the service perfect and consistent with the Word as originally intended (which came from He Whose Name We Cannot Speak). It was so communal; it was so egalitarian; it was so political; it was so Orthodox. The Conservative service, in comparison, was so bureaucratic and hierarchical. No one would dare disturb the service by interrupting our rabbi. It would have been the biggest affront imaginable. Like a suburban front lawn, everything was prim and proper, everything in its place. By comparison, the Orthodox service was an informal, hurly-burly of corrections. I learned to think about community as something we co-create the day one of my grand-uncles died. It was the only time I regretted not still being Orthodox.

This is to say that I knew even then that Orthodox Judaism undoubtedly had its limitations. The service was sex-segregated (with the women sitting upstairs, in our congregation). Actually, it was socially, culturally, and politically conservative in many ways. Yet when I was six years old, I knew nothing of these things and was not prepared to criticize them even if I had known. When I came back, years later, I noticed the difference with Conservative Judaism, but by then I was not just moving away from Orthodox

Judaism but actually well on my way to becoming an atheist, so the difference for me was noteworthy only as an observer, not as an observant Jew.

Regardless of these changes, Livingston suited me just fine in most respects. And by the time I could walk down the middle of Northfield Avenue in the mornings when I worked at my uncle's luncheonette, I really felt I belonged. I do remember walking home from high school with two friends one day when one of them indicated he really did not like Jews, to which the other gently responded that he was pretty sure I was Jewish, whereupon the guy who had just expressed his distaste for Jews immediately apologized and I automatically responded: "Don't worry about it." That was it. This was the one and only instance of anyone ever expressing any dislike for my family's religion or ethnicity. It never seemed to be an issue. On the less Jewish side of town, most of my friends were not Jewish, and that was fine by me.

Working in my uncle's luncheonette had its own attractions. Lots of people knew who I was (though many people thought I was my uncle's son, which seemed incredibly odd to me). I also got lots of free food. Yet as time went on, I was still only getting paid one dollar an hour, and after just a few short years that was getting old. I asked my father if I could join the post office. He found out when the test was being held, and a friend and I went one morning to East Orange and took it. I passed; my friend just missed. (I guess some of the family's postal knowledge had rubbed off. While I do not think much of the test was actually about postal matters—it was more like general knowledge, as I recall—it makes you think how families pass along knowledge almost surreptitiously.) So I told my uncle I was taking off my apron and going across town to unload parcel post. (He actually was mad at me for a while for deserting him to go work with my father, if you can believe it; but he got over it fast, and we were all close again soon.)

I worked mostly mornings 4:15 till 8:15 a.m., unloading trucks and sorting packages; then I went to school. I slept through homeroom often, and even took another nap in Senior Math, which I had first period. (It was good that Calculus came in the afternoon because that was where you had to pay attention). Those mornings ruined my track times running the two mile. I remember our coach Mr. Berry saying I had to choose between my job and my sport. I didn't, and he accepted my nondecision but ended writing something a bit wistful about it in my yearbook at graduation. I delivered mail as a letter carrier on the weekends, summers, and holiday breaks. I continued to deliver the mail during summer and holiday breaks through my college years and eventually went full-time at the post office after college in 1971. I had become an employee of the newly created U.S. Postal Service (the quasi-public corporation created to replace the U.S. Post

Office, originally launched by the U.S. Constitution in 1789). I had gone postal, in one sense.

Being a letter carrier was cool; well, at least that is how I saw it. Like most people my age, I wanted to be different than my dad, whom I did not think of as cool necessarily—nice maybe, but not cool. Yet me being a letter carrier just like him; *that* was cool. It was the job that was cool. You got to be on your own for most of the day. You got to be outside. You got exercise. You got paid decently, fairly. It was real money for a blue-collar kid.

But there were other parts I did not like. They did not really train you. You learned by mistakes, sometimes costly ones, like when I wrote the forwarding address on someone's specially purchased first-day letter with a new issuing stamp. Oh well. (Not all learning by doing is good.) I got written up a ton; memo after memo in my file said what a schnook I was. I learned to be intimidated by the bosses. (It did not help that the postmaster was a crook, who eventually got sent away to prison with a sentence of five to eight years for stealing stamps and selling them on the black market. I know it is hard to believe, but evidently stamps are used to launder money.)

Being a letter carrier definitely had its downside. Some people got really mad if you "cut" their lawn (in the sense of walking on their grass to get to the next house). One day, a woman who lived on a route where I was substituting for the regular carrier, who was on vacation, called the office to complain about my cutting her lawn and asked: "Who was that Spic delivering my mail?" I was a substitute carrier at the time and did not wear a uniform. Admittedly, I was not the best-dressed postal employee. Plus, I was starting to grow a beard (which would soon prove to be a source of conflict with my bosses). Yet none of that excused my dear postal patron from using such an epithet. I learned that day a little too much about her. Not everything about being a letter carrier was fun.

Then there were the dogs. I got bitten multiple times in just a few years while delivering the mail. Most bites were nothing. The positive was that sometimes, if you needed it, you only had to report you got bit and you got the next day off to go to the doctor and get a shot (which did not hurt). No rabid dogs or anything like that; all suburbanites had inoculated their dogs. Most dogs were in fact pretty small; I even, sometimes, felt bad when I batted them on the nose, redirecting them away from my legs with a rolled-up newspaper that I was about to deliver. It was really nothing, or at least that is what I thought. Then one day, there was this gigantic Great Dane, who pushed the screen door down, knocking me off the steps and strewing the mail for that house on the lawn. I hightailed it out of there. I was not bitten, but something worse happened. The residents of that abode complained that they were missing a check that was to be delivered. (How lame is that? They could get it reissued.) Nobody wanted to mess with them; I got written up again, this time with a super-stern reprimand.[6]

The post office was starting to look like one of my majors in college; the clock on my time there was running out. It could be very poorly managed. My supervisor only knew how to yell at me. For instance, he once tried to get my attention when I was starting my Jeep by shaking the vehicle until I almost fell out onto the ground. He lacked etiquette. The post office was becoming a storm waiting to happen. And there was nothing perfect about it.

Eventually, I went postal in that other popular colloquial sense of going off on people. Between my times spent at college, I was a part-time employee. After college, I was back at the post office, now full-time, not sure what I was doing there other than making good money and treading water while feeling uncertain about my future. It was a crazy time. I knew a bunch of the guys (we even had a woman younger than I was delivering mail by then). Some were friends, some were scary people, and one was my father, who also happened to be by then the president of our letter carrier union local. Several guys were out and out racists; and now several other guys were African American. It could be a bit tense. It did not help that on right side of my desk was this white guy who tried to educate me on the evils of black people while we sorted the mail for our routes in the morning, and on the left side was this much nicer, new guy who was black. It helped less when one day I came back in the afternoon from finishing delivering the mail for my route and the new guy on the left side was nowhere to be found. It turned out he had lied on his application and in fact had been convicted of a crime, having served time for armed robbery. I could not believe it; he was a great guy. The racist was very happy, thinking his outlook on life had just been permanently vindicated. (He had never seemed all that interested in evidence before and now seemed too willing take this incident as definitive proof for the Aryan view of life.) I started to think I needed another job.

A bunch of the sane people hung out with my father. They would come to the house and talk about politics and of course the post office (we still called it that). I know it seems crazy, but we were very interested in the post office, how it was or was not managed, and what its future was. For some, the mail is a precious commodity, not quite on a par with gems, but close. (My mother's father—my other grandfather—had been a jeweler, so the precious stones contrast has always been a touchstone for my family. My father was, for instance, always worried about protecting the family jewels. This concern about his family jewels was, I think, due to the fact that he had been a semi-professional baseball catcher.) I respected, even revered, many of the people who worked at the post office. (My father's best friend, Bobby Bellelo was, in my mind, the most kind and polite person I ever met—other than my mother. I was very proud that he was my father's best friend.) Yet there were others who made me think that the post office was not the best place to be.

In any case, events were conspiring to limit my time there. The year before, the Great Postal Wildcat Strike of 1970 started in New York City and spread to the surrounding metropolitan area before engulfing more than thirty cities across the country. The strike was in reaction to the plan to abolish the post office and create the United States Postal Service, a quasi-government corporation that would run on a profit and loss basis. We joined with other union letter carrier locals in New Jersey in what became a nationwide strike in opposition to aspects of the plan. President Richard Nixon called up the National Guard while his administration quickly negotiated an agreement with the unions. The result was pay raises and improved working conditions, along with collective bargaining rights in the wake of the shift to the U.S. Postal Service.[7]

My father actually opposed the strike, creating a division between us. My dad always worried what people with power over him might say or do. He worried about this and life in general too much, or so it seemed to me. (I inherited some of this, but I also ended up being more of an outspoken-critic type, for better or worse.) My father was a super worrier in general, and I think it shortened his life greatly. In any case, he was reluctant to oppose the Postal Service plan even though he knew it threatened the job security of letter carriers (though clerks more). He wanted my friends and me to keep our mouths shut. He also wanted me to agree to conform to the rules, to sign their disgusting loyalty oath, and to adhere to the dress code by cutting my long hair and shaving off my beard.

On the dress code, he was probably right—hippie letter carriers look silly. On the loyalty oath, well, that was different. The loyalty oath in place was the result of Executive Order 9835, issued by President Harry Truman on March 22, 1947, as part of anticommunism hysteria led by attempts by U.S. Senator Joseph McCarthy and the U. S. House of Representatives Committee on Un-American Activities (HUAC) to root out communists in government agencies and other major institutions in our society. The oath was designed to prevent the "infiltration of disloyal persons" into the federal government.[8] The Truman loyalty oath read:

> I, _____, do solemnly swear (or affirm) that I will support and defend the Constitution of the United States against all enemies, foreign and domestic; that I will bear true faith and allegiance to the same; that I take this obligation freely, without any mental reservation

> or purpose of evasion; and that I will well and faithfully discharge the duties of the office on which I am about to enter.[9]

The oath became an issue between my bosses and me in the wake of the agitation about the war in Vietnam. I was switching from being a temporary, part-time employee to a full-time probationary employee. Given my opposition to the war, I refused to sign.

Loyalty oaths in the post office had been a flashpoint for African American and Jewish postal employees in particular going back into the 1930s and 1940s, which had resulted in mass firings that seemed to various observers at the time, including the editors of the *Chicago Defender*, to be targeted at "Negro and Jewish government workers."[10] The issue was even explicitly called out by W. E. B. Du Bois, the leader of the National Association of the Advancement of Colored People (NAACP) as primarily one of selective enforcement that saw African American and Jewish workers being dismissed for their alleged political affiliations while members of the Ku Klux Klan were getting a free pass.[11]

In any event, I was suspended in 1970 for not signing the loyalty oath. Out of work, I took a job at a White Castle (in Millburn, near Short Hills, just one town over, where Philip Roth grew up a few years ahead of me after his family also moved from Newark). I was now flipping burgers, but mostly mopping floors and washing the dishes on the overnight shift. My boss actually told me he thought I had a future in the food industry (as he called it). Yet this job would prove to be a short-term appointment. There was a frequent customer who was very eccentric, or so it seemed. He finally lost it, when he came in early one morning during the breakfast hour at the end of my shift, wearing a bright yellow hardhat and banging two big baseball bats on the floor. The cops showed up fast, with sirens blaring and lights flashing, to haul him away. I decided to rejoin the post office. But it would be not for long.

By then, I had been drafted. Now I really wanted to go postal in that other sense. My father wanted me to just do what they commanded; he said something about patriotism. I almost choked on my vomit. But we talked this one through and basically agreed I had to decide it for myself. (It was one thing to go along with a dress code; it was entirely other matter to just up and agree to go to Vietnam when they called your number.)

The draft had been in existence since 1940. During my junior year of college, in 1969, the federal government instituted a lottery for processing the draft and abolished the student exemption for graduate study. The draft was officially known as the Selective Service System—though, with the lottery established, it was not clear to me what was so selective about a system that was now basically taking us at random. The lottery was based on birthdays. To start, all male U.S. citizens born between 1944 and 1950 would face induction in order of their birthdates, as drawn from a glass bowl. (It seems in retrospect nothing less than hysterical that such a momentous life-changing decision for so many young people would be executed as if it were a stunt on a television game show. Then again, it was the sixties.)

With these changes, we all became way more interested in the war and who was going to be required to wage it. One night in 1969, during my junior year, my friends and I sat in front of a television and watched as our futures were drawn from a slightly larger than normal sized fishbowl. My birthday was January 18, and according to the lottery, the corresponding number for the draft was 140. During the rest of that year, the government would call up guys with birthdays ranking well above that. Things were not looking good for me. As I would soon find out the next year (my senior year of college), 140 remained a bad number. During the first month of my last semester in college in January 1971, the draft called up everyone up to 60 or something like that. By March, they were at 125. They had another whole nine months to go through another fifteen numbers and then my magic number would come up. I figured I was screwed. All that protesting, even burning my draft card, now seemed to have done no good. We were going to war, whether we thought American imperialism was a good idea or not. I was treading water in the post office. It was like the frying pan instead of the fire.

Earlier in the year, back at college, I had been thinking I might go to law school, but I decided instead to get drunk the night before the law boards exam, because by then I had already concluded that, given the way things were going with the good ole U.S. of A., I very much did not want to be a lawyer—I was thinking I wanted to be a revolutionary. I had served as a chaperon, with five other guys, for Jerry Rubin when he spoke on campus in 1970. Rubin was one of the Chicago Seven, who had been tried for allegedly fomenting a riot outside the 1968 Democratic presidential nominating convention. At that point, it seemed like being a radical was going to be a full-time job. Disappointingly, Rubin's speech was a bunch of hot air, but I was by then committed to working to end the war and transform society, and was not about to let one bad speech stop me. (Yet I evidently knew down deep inside that the revolutionary thing was not going to work out, because I did in fact go ahead and take the law boards the next day, probably mostly out of curiosity, and scored rather poorly, as I recall.)

Instead of the law, my backup for being a revolutionary was graduate study in Political Science. (It was silly, I know, but at the time I did not know how far from political radicalism was that academic discipline.) I had applied to a few schools for graduate study in Political Science, one in the town where this beautiful girl I had just met was living (we ended up falling in love, getting married, having two kids, and making a life of it). Yet, at this point, these applications and exams actually seemed irrelevant; I assumed I would be inducted and sent off to Vietnam.

In the spring of 1971, in my senior year as an undergraduate, I had to forego my presentation in Victorian Literature on John Stuart Mill's *On Liberty* because I had to fly home and go into Newark for my induction physical (which I passed with flying colors, unfortunately, in spite of the efforts of my pediatrician, who passionately opposed the war and had written a letter of woe about my childhood convulsions and other maladies that had complicated my development into a fully grown human being). I had wanted to present on Mill very much. I was trying to combine my coursework to free up more time for protesting and other pursuits. You could say I believed in creating a certain type of synergy in my courses. (You could probably also say this reflected some other things about how I approached my schoolwork.) Yet the irony that I had to skip out on my *On Liberty* presentation for my induction physical was lost on me at the time. I thought about Arlo Guthrie in the big movie the prior year, *Alice's Restaurant*, and how the people in the film were just like us going crazy protesting the war and trying to get out of the draft. It was profoundly mortifying, as well as freaking crazy. (A friend of mine lost so much weight, he became very ill. I am not sure if he ever fully recovered, but he did get out of the draft.)

My induction physical was a zoo. It was, most ironically, conducted upstairs above the post office near my old childhood neighborhood in Newark. I am pretty sure this was a coincidence born of nothing other than that was where the Selective Service office for my county (Essex) was located. Nonetheless, I was still in the post office even as I was upstairs being inducted into the army. It was as if I was just changing uniforms. I remember being fascinated that the African American soldier in charge of our group of inductees wore a spanking pressed uniform and gleaming shining shoes, but with the cuffs of his shirt stapled together. I was learning quickly about the army. I was about to learn a lot more five minutes later when we all stood in a line in our underwear and the solider was walked past inspecting us. He stopped and started talking to an African American recruit just three guys away from me. He leaned into my fellow recruit's ear, whispered something, and then all of a sudden hauled off and decked the guy with a right cross to the chin. The recruit dropped to the floor like a sinking stone. Oh shit, I thought, what is he going to do to me? (I guess that was the idea, i.e., to let us know, subtly or not, who was in charge and to what degree.) I now so wanted to be downstairs back in my old post office uniform.

The exam doctors were not like my pediatrician, who was still looking out for me, even though I had not talked to him for years until I asked him for that letter. Yet, they were not like our chaperon either. Still, they laughed at my pediatrician's letter and marked me down as 1-A (fit for service). So much for the Hippocratic Oath! These doctors were there to make sure I would get in harm's way.

The draft then started to turn into the military equivalent of choosing a major. I next turned to the reserves. I signed up without thinking, right on the spot—it was a lot like how I chose Mathematics as my second major. The math in this case was simple: six years in the reserves versus two years in the army. But there was a qualitative difference. Back then, we did not fight our wars using the reserves; they were reserved for other, more domestic, things. The six versus two calculation was actually the difference between staying out of the war versus going off to fight in Vietnam. The reserves seemed like the preferred alternative even if it meant longer service. Yet the only thing about my signing with the reserves that I remember was the guy who took my application saying at the end: "You know, you will have to cut that hair before you show up next time" (meaning when I went to basic training)! The hair was a big thing back then; it was a flashpoint; it was a political statement. They desperately wanted me shorn of any indication of political resistance, whether it was in the post office or the military.

Yet I switched again before I could hear from the reserves. Through the antiwar grapevine, I heard that if I went to Columbia University (ground zero for the antiwar movement), I could speak to an antiwar counselor who had the inside story on how to resist (or dodge, depending on your politics) the draft. I left school again, went home once more, took the bus into New York City, and met with this guy who might have been younger than me. I was chagrined, and thought there is nothing like the blind leading the blind! As it turns out, he had the real scoop. He said all I had to do was appeal on psychological grounds to admit to my drug use and I would be declared 4-F (not fit for service).

This had not always been the case but had recently become so. It seems that the top brass waging the war had decided that too many frontline soldiers were overmedicating themselves with illicit drugs, thereby making military discipline that much harder to enforce just when they needed it in battle. Reports were filtering back from the front lines that as many as 15 percent of the U.S. servicemen in Vietnam were addicted to heroin. In just a few months, President Nixon would hold a very public press conference about this issue and announce the creation of the Special Action Office of Drug Abuse Prevention dedicated to fighting the evils of drugs. This was the beginning of what became the War on Drugs. A part of the response was to have the military prevent the druggies from going to the front lines and, in fact, to weed as many of them out upfront through the selection process.[12] The system, it seems, was becoming more selective even if it processed us at random. I immediately went back to school and appealed my 1-A status. (I finally saw the beauty of the law: due process is such a wonderful thing, I thought.)

A few weeks later, I was back in Newark above the post office talking in a dimly lit, private room with an older, African American psychiatrist. He was very soft spoken and seemed much more understanding than the other folks I had had the pleasure of meeting during my induction physical. He asked me why I wanted to appeal on psychological grounds. I told him I used drugs. He asked me which ones and I said mostly marijuana. He wrote something in the book on his desk and said I could go. That was it. I got a letter a few weeks later; I was declared unfit for service on psychological grounds (the letter said nothing about drugs). I was out. (Curiously, the reserves never called me; maybe it was the hair. I used to worry they would call and I would have to put my studies on hold, but it did not happen. I kept my hair long just in case. Eventually, though, I went bald, probably due to worrying about that and other things such as getting tenure. My worries varied in size.)

Yet the war went on. At least for a while, anyway. I decided to join my girlfriend in New York State's Capital District and attend the Graduate School of Public Affairs in the State University of New York at Albany with the idea of getting a PhD in Political Science. Maybe I wouldn't be a revolutionary or even a political activist, but I could study it; at least I was willing to give it a try.

In other words, I chose to pursue a doctorate in Political Science for the least scholarly reasons possible: to get out of the post office, avoid the draft, escape mainstream society. Actually, I would bet many of my generation were in a similar situation. Many hippies from the sixties did not want anything to do with "the system." Antiwar activists had burned through a variety of commitments to established institutions quickly in just a few years of reading and talking about how America was a flawed project insisting on its privilege and power in all the wrong ways, domestically as well as internationally. The ivory tower was allegedly removed from the real world, a haven where we could contemplate a better life for all. It was the logical repository for a dispossessed generation of political refuseniks. I was probably not alone in choosing graduate study over law school for just these reasons. As to how many of my cohort chose their particular graduate school based on love is another story, but if I had to, I'd guess the percentages might be similar.

As the years went by, as a faculty advisor, I was struck by how many of my students were much more thoughtful than I had been about deciding whether to go on for further study, in which disciplines or fields, at what schools, and with which professors. They all seemed so rational compared to me. I am very proud of my students, and many of them have had great careers inside and outside the academy. Their planning and foresight about next steps has probably helped them in many cases. Yet, in some cases, even with all that forethought, students had to go to Plan B.

Still, it is nice to have the luxury to plan. When I was leaving college, it was not a time for planning, more like plotting, plotting how to escape the horrors of the war in Vietnam or the cruelties of the post office. It was a crazy time. Under those circumstances, any graduate school sounded good, especially one near the love of my life. I am delighted it accidently turned out to be such a good place for me to learn about Political Science.

THREE

HOW I LEARNED TO READ

Given my tussles with the draft board, I did not arrive in graduate school until mid-year (January 1972). All the assistantships had been allocated, and students were already finished with the fall semester. I had to take out a student loan in order to start graduate school. It made me an odd duck right off the bat. I was like a stranger in a strange town. I had to learn fast how to play the game. Compounding my confusion was the fact that Political Science at Albany was in the Graduate School of Public Affairs (eventually renamed Rockefeller College of Public Affairs and Policy), along with Public Administration and a few other smaller programs. I was interested in making political change but I was to learn how to do it in a school of public policy. (It was here that my interest began, by what seems total accident, in crossing disciplinary boundaries, relating theory to practice, mixing methods, etc.)

Running to catch up, I took courses on Jurisprudence (we read John Rawls's recently published *A Theory of Justice*),[1] Theories of Marxism (I wrote a term paper on Gabriel Kolko and the critique of corporate liberalism),[2] and the Politics of South Asia (I wrote a psychological analysis contrasting the leadership styles of Nehru and Jinnah). At some point early on I took a course on political behavior and learned to analyze the National Election Studies from the University of Michigan. I was no longer sleepwalking through school but I was still very naive. I did not read actively or critically yet. I could read, yes; I was not illiterate, obviously—I had graduated from college! Yet I was not an active reader. I did not read critically, reflecting on the process by which any text created opportunities for me to make meaning of what I was reading. In this sense, my reading stayed on the surface of the text, oblivious to the underlying discourse or what I would call the structure of intelligibility that informed the text.[3] Without being curious as to how a text was framed or structured, I was unable to critique it, except maybe to point out contradictions that were visible in the surface narrative (which would be rare in published scholarship, if you stop and think about it).

I went to class and listened to students talk about what a particular assigned text lacked or how it elided certain issues. Rawls evidently feared politics and sought to make it unnecessary. (This was Spring 1972 and that was said by a doctoral student. Years later, I would remember reading critiques of Rawls's by then much-heralded book and hear similar analyses being offered, and thought that my fellow doctoral students had been really insightful critics who had anticipated the critiques of the major works in the discipline.)[4] We had to write term papers on our own theories of justice and I, still finding my way, chose a conservative course of action and wrote in agreement with Rawls's idea of justice as fairness. I was not yet a critical thinker as much as I was an alienated youth of the sixties who wanted to overthrow "the system" (and not just the Selective Service System that wanted to pick me at random and send me to Vietnam). Yet, without critical reading skills in my chosen field of study, I risked becoming politically aligned with the most recent piece of scholarship I had read. (This type of "empty" pluralism was something I knew I had to reject in order eventually to come to a more thoughtful, critically reflective pluralism, which I did not yet know how to practice.)[5]

I remember distinctly the moment when I finally started to appreciate what it meant to read critically. It was not, as I recall, the most theoretically sophisticated piece, but the issue of theoretical abstraction finally broke through into my consciousness as a key to unlocking meaning from the text. I forget which course it was in, but the text was an article concerning Philip Selznick's argument in *The TVA and the Grass Roots*,[6] where he explicates his concept of co-optation. Selznick showed that in order for the Tennessee Valley Authority to enlist the support of local Appalachian communities in its development projects it needed to allow itself to get co-opted into going along with prevailing racist hiring practices and other local forms of discrimination. (I ended up relying on Selznick's concept of co-optation in my dissertation on community planning for the elderly via the Older Americans Act of 1965. Using Selznick's concept of co-optation was, it turns out, very popular in my Graduate School of Public Affairs.)

I remember reading the article in question and realizing that its beginning quickly rose up to a level of abstraction for purposes of framing the analysis that followed, and that it was my job as a critical reader to follow that ascent while critically maintaining my own perspective even as I was being drawn into the vantage point that was being offered by the text. As I tracked the framing of that analysis, I felt as if I had just learned to speak another language or to ride a bike for the first time without training wheels. I also felt I had just stumbled into the secret entrance my fellow graduate students already knew about for unlocking the mysteries of a text. It was very exciting, even if late in my academic studies.

HOW I LEARNED TO THINK

Learning to read scholarly work made graduate school a lot more interesting. Now I knew what the game was. My job was to be like other graduate students and come to class prepared to question each and every reading for underlying assumptions regarding how it framed its analysis, how it presented that analysis selectively, how it traded on those assumptions to create a willful suspension of disbelief among us members of the reading audience. There was a theatricality of research and scholarship, was how I saw it. I saw it this way probably because for me everything was still way too dramatic and way too staged (even the war in Vietnam was staged on a theater, the theater of war, as they called it). My lapsed interest in acting or writing fiction or even poetry and music was the basis on which I approached social science—it was its own theater of performance. I was now totally into performing, but performing in the sense of demonstrating proficiency as a student, scholar, and researcher.

Yet figuring out my particular stage on which to perform was still a ball of confusion for me. I was taking courses in quantitative analysis in the study of political behavior, even as I still pursued the issues of political theory and public policy implementation. My vexed status was reflected in the fact that my Rawls term paper got me nominated for a university fellowship, where my job was managing the data tapes from the University of Michigan's Institute for Social Research, including, most especially, the National Election Studies. I was a theorist with data tapes—go figure. It was all happenstance. My interest in mixing methods, combining theory and empirical analysis and other transgressive practices in the increasingly specialized world of the social sciences was in part an artifact of my naïveté, my ending up studying political theory in a graduate school of public policy, and my inability to choose my own specialized way to approach the study of politics.

In part, my confusion was the result of not even knowing that we were supposed to specialize or that specializing was a good thing, or even what the specializations were. I noticed, though, that some faculty hardly talked to other faculty, and that was related to what they taught. My cluelessness was prolonged by my never, ever once attending a graduate student association meeting, where, I heard once, indirectly, divisions in the school were discussed (and probably a lot more). This lack of interest in the student association reflected another one of my contradictions that goes to the core of my schizoid academic personality: as much as I was a radical who wanted to overturn the system, I was always a very obedient student who dutifully followed along, doing what was expected of students in a largely unquestioning way. (I eventually grew out of this persona as a faculty member, for better or worse.)

There was another reason I never attended the student association meetings. It reminded me of my letter carrier union. It was a union of academics (mostly theorists, no less); this struck me as incongruous. Letter carriers in the union were all united in seeking a pay raise at the same rate. It seemed to me that academics were supposed to be about each person going off in their own way to make their own distinctive contributions to the field. Here I was trying to get away from the post office and the student association was reminding me that graduate school was not all that different. No matter how painfully true that really was, I did not want to hear it; I did not want to be drawn back into fighting over work conditions. I wanted now to experience a more independent existence concentrated on my studies, not the bureaucratic politics of running the school.

Don't get me wrong. I am still as much as ever pro-union. Remember, my father was a union local president, and I actively supported the Wildcat Strike of 1970. I would later help organize faculty colleagues at the first college that hired me. There, we became the Nasson Faculty Guild (if you can believe it), because some faculty had such an aversive reaction to being in a union that they would rather be in a medieval guild (as if that was better). A few years later, I was a union officer on the faculty at the State University of New York College at Potsdam. I was pro-union always, even in graduate school. It was just that it seemed to me back then, at that point in my budding career, that joining the student association would be missing the point. It seemed not right to be getting together with other graduate students to discuss our working conditions while I was busy trying to prove I was good enough to become a professional political scientist. Years later, I would support graduate student associations and even efforts by graduate students to form unions around the country. Yet the fact of the matter is that when I myself was a graduate student I was not focusing on whether I was being exploited; I focused on whether I was succeeding. Exploit me! That was my position then. It's just the way it was. Perhaps, it was ambition that was starting to lead me in a careerist direction; or perhaps it was just that I was running scared just trying to prove I belonged. I was preoccupied with succeeding in graduate school and that meant focusing on my coursework and my research assistantship responsibilities.

As a result, I remained basically clueless as to the politics of my school and of the discipline. Yet my ignorance became its own sort of bliss. I was free to think about Political Science in my own inchoate way. The *methodenstreit* in Political Science, however, would eventually capture me and become a topic I took seriously as a political scientist (although I have approached it, consistent with my initial ambivalence, as one who has tried to find a way to move beyond the deeply embedded divisions between positivistic (scientific) and interpretivist (humanistic) approaches). Yet, at the time, as a graduate student still in interested in promoting political change, arguing over methods seemed to me to be an example of how academic debates were beside the more important point of trying to use politics to change society for the better (in fact, my later work focused on taking a more problem-driven, rather than theory-driven, approach to studying politics, so that our scholarly efforts could relate better to ongoing political struggles).[7]

My reluctance to engage in this debate about methods and my cluelessness about the need to choose a specialization were demonstrated quite starkly one day in class in a course on political gerontology. We were asked by our professor, Roy Speckhard, to contrast the methodological approaches of a statistical analysis on the causes of crime and a prison memoir. (I do not think I got the idea for an academic memoir from reading that prison memoir, but the parallels between physical un-freedom of a prisoner and mental un-freedom of an academic are sufficiently intriguing.)

My fellow students were quite sure how to distinguish the utility of an autobiographical interpretation of a life of crime from a statistical analysis of the most significant factors that generally cause people to commit crimes. And they seemed to know why they preferred either the positivistic approach that offered causal explanations or the interpretive approach that provided understanding of what a life of crime meant for that serial perpetrator. I could not be so sure. In fact, I tried to suggest that both approaches had real value. I admit I took this position because I still was basically clueless about the whole methods debate; however, my refusal to choose continues to this day. The big difference is that at some point I started to stop worrying about my inability to choose and started to learn to insist on the refusal to do so. (I ended up doing a mixed-methods dissertation on citizen participation in the implementation of community service programs for the elderly under the Older Americans Act.)[8]

The day when I finally stopped worrying about my schizoid methodological orientation was not yet to be. I had to first learn how to think. I was learning to read Political Science literature but I needed now more than ever to learn how to think like a political scientist, whatever that was. As in most doctoral programs, we were required to take a course in the scope and methods of Political Science. Ours was a year-long in-depth survey. It was not some mere requirement, but instead was the course at the center of our doctoral curriculum. The two-semester course was taught by Jack Gunnell, who already at a relatively young age was making a name for himself as a leading scholar of Political Science as a discipline. Gunnell, basically, studied how we studied things (his was a meta discourse.)[9] We met for a year on the top floor of Mohawk Tower, at night once a week. Sometimes, when there was a storm, I was convinced the end was near, but the drama of the course came from how Jack challenged us to think. The course was an incredible intellectual experience. It changed me on many levels. When it was done, I went to Gunnell and expressed an interest in pursuing this kind of meta-theory. He was sufficiently concerned that I had such a naive perspective that he recommended I take a tutorial with him. I eagerly agreed, not knowing what I was getting myself into.

The tutorial was its own initiation into the life of the mind. Jack would propose a book to read, then I would come the next week to his office to ask him questions about the book. His responses were often other questions. (This reminded me of my grandmother, who invariably answered questions with other questions—I think it was some kind of Eastern European Jewish vernacular that she practiced. Jack's question-for-question technique came, I suspect, from somewhere else, the Socratic method perhaps, though the goal may have been the same.)

We read some of Jack's favorite books on a set of related issues. We started with William Connolly and the debates on the structure of power.[10] Connolly examined the mid-range theories of power that were so popular at the time, but from a more critical and philosophical perspective. It provided an opening to thinking at a meta level about the underlying discourse that each perspective employed. We then moved to Peter Winch and his use of the philosophical orientation of Ludwig Wittgenstein to question the underlying assumptions of the idea of social science.[11] Next was Thomas Kuhn's *The Structure of Science Revolutions*.[12] As the books piled up, I noticed how our meetings changed. In the beginning, I would ask a question and get challenged as to the premise of my question. Then I would ask another and the same thing happened. The initial meetings were painfully short. I asked too few questions and could not sustain the conversation. As time went on, I started to come more prepared to continue the dialogue, such as it was. I was taking baby steps when I should have already reached at least adolescence intellectually. Yet, at some point, Jack thought we had met enough and I could start talking to myself and others without his prodding. I felt as if I had been affirmed without Gunnell actually saying so. I was starting to learn to think like a critical-minded political scientist. I felt as if I should go buy new clothes but could not afford to. Yet it was a great feeling nonetheless.

Once again, my moment of relief was short-lived. My comprehensive exams brought a challenge to my eleventh-hour affirmation. In our doctoral program, upon completion of coursework, we crafted proposals for how we should be examined in each of three subfields we chose. American political systems was my major field, political theory and public administration were my minor fields. My political theory proposal was concentrated on what I called contemporary political theory, and within that it focused on the meta issues I had started to study with Gunnell. Unfortunately for me, the year I took my exams, Jack was on leave, living in a remote village somewhere in Southeast Asia and writing a book. He was unavailable to chair my theory exam or to even consult with the department chair about my proposal. The chair of the Political Science department at the time was not a theorist and was suspicious of my proposal. He waited until the night before my exam to call me at home to say that he had approved the committee to examine me only by adding an outside person to ensure I was tested in a way reflective of the major concerns of the theory subfield. The next day, I arrived unsure what would happen in the room where we were sequestered for the exam. I think my professors felt sorry for me and passed me with distinction as a protest against the way my proposal had been treated. The lesson I learned was that even my approach to theory was transgressive and disrupted normal expectations. The takeaway message for me was that I remained the odd duck in the highly specialized Political Science pond; a proverbial black swan, swimming upstream against the tide of conventionality.[13]

HOW I LEARNED TO WRITE

As time went by, I enjoyed my coursework, but most especially working as a research assistant, in particular for Leigh Stelzer, who studied school board politics. He was a quantifier from the University of Michigan and he taught me a lot about how to do empirical research. His courses on community power structures, political behavior, and research methods were great as well. Yet he was eventually not tenured, due to lack of publication. I turned to Joseph Zimmerman, who was chair of the department and who offered to take me in when I got left out in the cold just when it was time for my exams. Joe was already one of the leading scholars of U.S. federalism[14] and he had liked that I had conducted my own empirical analysis in a term paper in his federalism course. (I actually forget what I did but it had something to do with testing a hypothesis about communities in California, I think.) With Zimmerman's tutelage, I prepared for my exams and passed them. Next was the dissertation.

Yet, in the interim, I had been hired by Governor Nelson Rockefeller's new think tank, the Institute for Public Policy Alternatives. (Roy Speckhard brought me on board to promote more research on the elderly in New York State). We applied to the Hess Foundation (of Hess Oil) because our boss Joseph Swidler (formerly a member of the Johnson administration in energy regulation) knew Leon Hess. We got a major grant for over $350,000 (which in 1975 was not chump change) to focus research on the needs of the elderly. (Swidler put a toy Hess Oil truck under the office Christmas tree that year.)

We then created the Aging Research Coordination Project, or the ARC project as it was called, working in conjunction with the New York State Office of the Aging and writing policy briefs to serve as support for legislation proposed in the state legislature. Our briefs supported the property tax circuit-breaker for elderly homeowners, by which they got state income tax rebates for a portion of their property taxes. We also backed legislation allowing elderly tenants to keep pets in public housing, expansions in home health care, ombudsmen for nursing home patients (in wake of the scandals in the homes at the time), and a variety of other bills that got enacted into law.

The bills would stack up like a logjam until the budget negotiations were resolved between the governor, the speaker of the Assembly (who was a New York City Democrat), and the majority leader in the Senate (who was an upstate Republican). Then the logjam could break and the bills could pass if they were part of the compromises and deals associated with the budget negotiations. You have to wonder how much the research affected all this.

The younger Republican staffers kept telling me that if their party could come to power big changes would happen. They all were reading a new journal, *The Public Interest*, out of Harvard, which was bringing liberals and conservatives together to move social welfare policy in a rightward direction. (James Q. Wilson and Daniel Patrick Moynihan, along with Nathan Glazer, were leading the charge stage right.) Based on what they read, failing schools would get less money, not more; students would get to move elsewhere from those schools. For-profit providers would provide charter schools. Home health care, welfare-to-work programs, and other public services would also be privatized. Businesses would get tax breaks to move into the state. I thought all of this marketizing of the state was just plain crazy. Years later, however, it became the reality of social welfare policy in the United States. We did not call it neoliberalism yet, but that kind of thinking was incubating in the Republican Party in the New York State Legislature in the 1970s. When I think about how prophetic those young people were, it shocks me still. I remember it as if it were yesterday.

Some of the Republican staffers were classmates of mine at St. Lawrence. If you can believe it, they had been with me as strike leaders against the war in Vietnam; now they were touting the neoliberalization of social welfare policy. Go figure. It was scary to see them turn on a dime. Yet I also thought they were on the losing side. And at the time, that was correct. I, however, was busy deluding myself that we were connecting research with policy in influential ways, not appreciating that with time they would overtake these incremental efforts and turn social welfare policy discourse in a heartless direction.

Yet, even if my new-found optimism for conventional public policy-making was misplaced, it was exciting nonetheless to be involved in relating research to policy, and it furthered my interest in pursuing a Political Science that connected to ongoing political struggle. I might have hoped it was associated with a more radical politics, but I was settling for any connection at that point.

It was, however, so not what I was supposed to be doing. I had forgotten about the dissertation. I remember even thinking that maybe I would not write it. I was making money promoting better social policies. Zimmerman called one day and basically said: "What the hell are you doing?" (He would never say it that way; but I knew what he meant.) He then arranged for me to leave the Institute and receive funding while I wrote my dissertation—something that was not usually done.[15]

Back as a student, I proceeded to pursue a dissertation researching whether citizen participation in federally funded Area Agencies on Aging (AAAs) allowed the elderly to influence community programming on their behalf. I did a mixed-methods study of twenty-eight county AAAs, visiting the offices, interviewing the directors, attending the advisory board meetings, where the local elderly clients were allowed input, and having the board members complete a questionnaire. I acquired all kinds of data that provided strong triangulation for the idea that Elliot Krause had developed that citizen participation was basically a "bureaucratic ideology" designed to co-opt the community into going along with whatever the officials in charge of the program basically had already decided to do.[16] One of my main findings was that a nontrivial proportion of the elderly members of these AAA boards who were chosen as "consumer representatives" were not even real clients but often former service professionals and politicos aligned with the AAA director as part of a political coalition of sorts. These boards, in a number of cases, operated as a symbolic gesture to ratify the agency's policies, legitimating them as blessed by clients when in fact that was not really what was happening; or so it seemed.

I was fortunate to get a job interview while writing my dissertation, or so it seemed. I presented my results at my first job talk for a position in the Department of Political Science at Northeastern University, where Elliot Krause was a sociologist. Krause had been told about my research relying on his work and he attended my talk. I was a bit nervous given it was my first job talk and knowing he was in the audience. I suggested that while I agreed with Krause for the most part I thought his argument was overstated and that citizen participation was potentially a good thing. I believe this still, but back then I probably should have not stated it so bluntly, recognizing he was in attendance. He got up and left, saying something about how he did not need to sit there and take it from a nobody or something like that. He overreacted. But I should have been more careful in my wording. The chair of the department later counseled me about being more politic when interviewing for a job. It was an understatement. I did not get the job (probably for a bunch of other reasons) and went back to finishing my dissertation.

Writing up the dissertation would prove to be another trial by fire. My writing had been up and down in graduate school (continuing my struggles from my undergraduate days). I had my moments, though. One time, when writing a paper for Stelzer on the myth of community as a prevailing force in American politics, I stayed up late laboring over each sentence. When I read it over, I was thoroughly dissatisfied. I ripped it up and decided to start again from scratch even though it was already way past my bedtime. The rewrite flowed much better. I should have learned something from that, but I am still not sure what. By the time I started submitting chapters to Zimmerman, he already knew I had writing issues from my dissertation proposal. His first comment on this was something like: "What happened? You wrote well for my course." I changed constantly, writing better some times than others. I had no clue why.

I ended up learning to write while composing my dissertation. Zimmerman taught me by editing line by line. It was a grueling process. Four times he made me rewrite the pivotal chapter 6, where I turned from the all the prefatory chapters (background, theory, method, etc.) to analysis of my data. Just before the last rewrite, I asked if he thought I would ever finish and he stated quite honestly that it was entirely up to me. I finally finished and knew at least how to work on my writing. (A few years later, when Joe was the person who presented me with the distinguished Political Science alumnus award for that year at the school's annual banquet, I talked about how he taught me to write during my dissertation. I said I learned to write as if he were looking over my shoulder advising me on each word and sentence. And that when I wrote now, I still sensed he was looking over my shoulder surveilling my writing and correcting my lapses. I then turned around and looked at him standing behind me just off my shoulder and we smiled, as the audience laughed. I think he took it well.)

It was pretty late in the day to learn to write, but it was great to get the help. I was now moving toward a career as a teacher and a scholar and there was no denying the fact that writing was an important part of the whole process. Yet writing is a lot like riding a bicycle; you learn best by doing it over and over, improving through a growing familiarity with that practice. It is its own learning by doing. It is, however, probably best to get started practicing well before you have to write chapter 6 of your dissertation four times.

FOUR

I WENT DOWN TO THE CROSSROADS

Activism and Scholarship

During my graduate school days, I still envisioned myself a political activist of sorts. Doctoral study had made me stop thinking about being a revolutionary; more and more I just wanted to change society for the better rather than keep believing that I could be part of a movement to overturn the structure of power. Cut off from campus activism, I drifted away from Students for a Democratic Society (SDS). It is not that I came to reject the cause of revolutionary change (though I knew I was not about to join the Weather Underground faction with their willingness to use violence, let alone become a member of the Symbionese Liberation Army and kidnap Patty Hearst).Yet I still wanted to make a difference.

After just one semester in graduate school, I had returned to Newark, not to organize the poor for more radical efforts at promoting social change, but to work on the presidential campaign for George McGovern.[1] McGovern was inspiring. I remember that whenever he spoke it sounded different than other politicians. In fact, when he spoke, I eerily could hear nothing else. It was like he had this direct line to my ears that filtered out all noise. What McGovern said made so much sense to me. What he said sounded straightforward, unadorned by political varnish. I remember feeling that what he said was exactly what needed to be said for our times and that he said it honestly and courageously, regardless of the consequences. In my mind, he was speaking truth to power. I would never hear another politician the way I heard him. Maybe I was still very naive, or maybe he was really different that way. In any case, I really wanted to work for him.

I became Newark's South Ward coordinator for the McGovern campaign in the 1972 New Jersey Democratic presidential primary election. I am not sure why I got the job, but it was my old neighborhood. The campaign was being run by a bunch of young people who had worked for Bobby Kennedy previously and were from Massachusetts (i.e., the "Kennedy Machine," as it was called, had been imported to steer the McGovern campaign in New Jersey). This redheaded Irish guy with a strong Boston accent was in charge of Newark. This made almost no sense since Newark was already increasingly largely African American and almost nobody had a Boston accent of any kind, let alone the kind this guy had. I forget his name, but he was, regardless of being totally out of place, nonetheless inspiring. He was so upbeat. We can do this! He was the first person to tell me that "we are about hope and the other side is about fear." Barack Obama would revisit this theme when he rode to the presidency in 2008.

I admit I like politicians who are positive, who emphasize hope over fear, who believe in people, who think we are basically good and want to do good, and can and will do good, if we are given the support to do so. Politicians like that are consistent with my pedagogy. Yet, back then, I had no educational philosophy, let alone a pedagogy, so that is not why I was a good fit for the campaign. Instead, it was probably something much more pedestrian. If I had to guess, I got the job as the coordinator for the South Ward because these folks desperately needed locals to legitimate their efforts and most party activists in the neighborhood were already committed to working for the local party establishment, which was backing Hubert Humphrey. (There were some young African Americans from the neighborhood who volunteered to help out but they had day jobs, leaving the coordinator position open for a white guy from the suburbs.)

It turns out I was not entirely a foreign element. Our offices were not more than five blocks from my family's old apartment building. I went back there immediately as soon as we settled in. I was shocked. The first floor of my old building was now partially gutted, right where the grocery had been located on the corner of the building. There were gigantic weeds growing out of demolished buildings across the street. I did some canvassing in homes on the street only to find that in an apartment in the building next door, where my friends Peter and Pot had lived, now there was a dirt floor. (Years later, visiting friends in Havana, I learned that many people there also had dirt floors). A dirt floor in my friends' old house was almost too much. I wanted to cry. The neighborhood had really gone downhill. My immediate reaction was that I was mad that the racism of white flight had left my old neighborhood without the resources needed so that the people still there could create a decent life for themselves. All the money and jobs had left along with the families that fled to the suburbs. Now, in the early 1970s, the jobs were gone, the schools were underfunded, the crime rate was increasing rapidly, and all the whites were gone. White flight over the years had left Newark with fewer and fewer resources and had taken my neighborhood and thrown it away. I had gone back home only to find it was not there anymore.

Our campaign had an uphill struggle—McGovern was fighting the Democratic Party establishment for the nomination. Most folks in Newark were loyal to Hubert Humphrey. McGovern did have the support of the newly elected first black mayor of Newark, Kenneth Gibson (himself an insurgent and a reformer whom I deeply admired). Most of the party leaders, however, were with Humphrey.

We had other challenges that were more neighborhood-based. Another person from the South Side was politically active at the time—Amiri Baraka, formerly LeRoi Jones, the Beat poet and playwright. Baraka had just changed his name in 1968, and performed a play as "now Amiri Baraka" at St. Lawrence University when I was a student there. (It was not normal for people from Newark to congregate in northern New York at St. Lawrence, but there he was on stage that night.) He used a gun in the performance, which shocked some faculty.

To say that Baraka was controversial is no overstatement; he already was practicing his penchant for saying things that made white people uncomfortable. In 1992, he would come to Macalester College in St. Paul, Minnesota, where I was teaching, and in the middle of a thoughtful presentation about his concept of "Pan-African Americanism," he would digress into suggesting it was time to violently overthrow the white power structure. Whether he was right about this was beside the point; it was a hiccup in a thoughtful presentation that seemed to just pop out without warning. He seemed to do this a lot; he would become most notorious in 2002, when, as the poet laureate of New Jersey, he wrote something profoundly outrageous in his poem *Somebody Blew Up America*: "Who knew the World Trade Center was gonna get bombed/Who told 4000 Israeli workers at the Twin Towers/To stay home that day/Why did Sharon stay away?"[2] Questions without answers, but incendiary, to say the least.

Yet, in his hometown of Newark in the late spring of 1972, Baraka was just being difficult for me in the most querulous way. He was causing trouble by having people take down McGovern posters we had put up all over the neighborhood. Why? I have no idea. There was no evidence I could find that Baraka was a Humphrey supporter. (In fact, just the suggestion seems odd.) His people met with staff from our campaign; we worked out some understanding and the posters could stay up. We went back to trying to win the nomination.

The campaign was a frenzy. Baraka was our local celebrity, but others came through, in serial fashion, and they added real luster to our pedestrian efforts to mobilize support for McGovern. I remember thinking that Arthur Ashe was incredibly informed when he gave a talk in Weequahic

Park, at the tennis courts. I also remember that he was less than impressed with my inability to engage him sufficiently about McGovern's proposal for a guaranteed income. In retrospect, this was ironic, since I ended up years later writing about the whole push for a guaranteed income by the National Welfare Rights Movement during the late 1960s and early 1970s.[3] Yet, in the heat of the moment, my lack of knowledge about this issue prevented me from effectively engaging a prominent person about whether this proposal was a good move for a presidential candidate who was already seen by most American voters as way too liberal. There were other encounters that were less embarrassing for me. Marlo Thomas gave a great talk to supporters and did not seem disappointed in my lack of policy knowledge. Eddie Hinton of the Baltimore Colts was a friendly, witty guy who seemed to enjoy our exchange after he gave a good talk that helped energize support for McGovern in the community. My main job was arranging events such as these, along with making sure our basic canvassing and mobilizing got done. In the campaign, my main strength was keeping everyone on task. I left the policy debates to others. It seems ironic, since I was hired in part because I was a graduate student in Political Science who allegedly knew about public policy (but actually not so much).

At the end, we won the South Ward, but lost the city, even as McGovern took the state. We got the job done in the South Ward. The party establishment held the city. Yet what mattered most was that the bulk of the state's delegates were going for McGovern. It looked as though he would get the nomination. The primary system that he had championed in the preceding four years had opened up the nomination selection process and he was the first beneficiary (though I would like to think that we the people in the long run were the real primary beneficiaries). I went back to graduate school in the fall hopeful about change. Unfortunately, McGovern's candidacy never caught on with the general electorate; he was too liberal about ending the war in Vietnam, redistributing wealth, and a whole bunch of other issues.

AN ACADEMIC CROSSROADS: FROM POLITICAL GERONTOLOGY TO WELFARE POLITICS

I continued to be active in politics as the years went by, sometimes more inside the policy process and consistent with conventional politics, sometimes more outside the bounds of the interest group system and focused more on radical political change. I would eventually write about the importance of connecting political science to politics[4] and even about rethinking how research is done so that it can better serve social justice efforts.[5] In the process, I tried to become more up to date on policy deliberations, so that

I was not left without something to say when important people expected it from me. But after the McGovern campaign, back in graduate school, I was increasingly focused on succeeding in the academy. I know I got there by accident, but now it was like my job. I also discovered that I was ambitious. I wanted to succeed in my chosen career (even if I never really consciously chose it). This was a conservative influence in my life. I focused on fitting in more than trying to overturn the applecart. It was as if I had gone down to the crossroads and made my pact with the devil. In exchange for giving up my activism, I could acquire the skills necessary to be a professional political scientist. I made the proverbial Faustian bargain without really knowing it. My cluelessness was my enduring consistency.

Yet I rationalized things in my mind such that I did not see the contradiction staring me in the face as I stood at this avocational crossroads. I envisioned myself fitting in in a particular way, as a credible scholar who would make real contributions to knowledge that could change society for the better. As time went on, I struggled with the tensions between trying to be a good scholar and developing the ability to impact politics via that scholarship. My ambition, though, did not let me ponder this dilemma too much. I wanted to make my scholarly mark. I gave talks about my doctoral research before it was done. I presented papers at the Gerontology Society meetings. I published several articles before I finished my dissertation. (This is normal now, but at the time I was told I was putting the cart before the horse.)

The whole process of conducting research and writing it up for publication was something that required a lot of time back then, especially for someone with as few skills as I. In those days, it took great effort for me to write. And not just because my prose was so forced. The actual operation of producing a manuscript was something that I labored over tremendously. For instance, I could not really type much at all. (I had gotten a D in typing in high school.) In fact, I wrote with paper and pencil, using an eraser, scissors, and staples to edit. Yes, that's right, I often cut out sentences and moved them around, stapling them into the paper to change their order. It was a laborious process, to say the least. On top of that, I had to pay others to type my papers once they were completed. I wrote my dissertation that way, and my early articles were all composed in this primitive fashion.

Yet I kept at it. For some ill-apparent reason, I never tried to publish from my dissertation research. My dissertation advisor persuaded me to have multiple copies of it printed when I finished and they just stayed in my basement for years. I never really thought about trying to publish it as a book. I did think a bit about an article or two that could derive from my dissertation, but somehow it did not appeal enough to me to follow the normal course of action for doctoral students and enact a research agenda from my dissertation research. I continued my own haphazard way of pursuing my scholarship as if I wanted to intentionally make it more difficult to be a published scholar. (In retrospect, I wonder if I would have stayed a political gerontologist if I had stayed on the worn path of publishing my dissertation research first.)

I started to publish about related issues of intergenerational conflict in social welfare policy. I was still a political gerontologist, but I was collecting new data. I had in fact published multiple articles before I finished my dissertation, without touching my dissertation research. I was ambitious but definitely following my own poorly thought-out path to making a scholarly contribution. For no reason in particular, I scored some early success publishing articles in social work journals. (This undoubtedly helped me later to begin teaching in this field.) Between 1978 and 1983, I published in the *Social Service Review,* a leading journal in the field, once before completing my dissertation and then twice afterward. (Years later, I would be appointed to the editorial board of that journal.)

I argued that the elderly were reluctant to coalesce with other social welfare constituencies for fear that they would be tainted as seeking handouts like those who received public assistance. I examined the new social services block grant at the time (Title XX of the Social Security Act) and found that the elderly were not being proportionately served, in part because they shied away from being associated with welfare programs. They practiced "elderly policy particularism."[6] I had coined a phrase. I did not know it then, but naming something is a very important dimension of the research process that I actually think is still underemphasized in our technique-driven social science mentality about what research entails.[7] For some reason, this article caught on. I got requests to reprint it in two different edited volumes on the politics of old age; I was notified that it was required reading in Social Work courses in a number of schools across the country. I even made royalties from the reprints. Somebody was paying attention. It was all happening fast.[8]

By the time I started submitting articles to the *Social Service Review,* I had my first teaching appointment, as an instructor in the Department of Political Science at Nasson College in southern Maine. I must have really wanted a career teaching college: I passed up an interview for a job doing research for Mary Jo Bane, the Harvard professor of social welfare, who had just been appointed to a major position in the New York State Department of Social Services. I turned that interview down and packed up to leave Albany with my wife Joan for southern Maine, even though my contract had been held up because Nasson was undergoing financial difficulties (which would soon prove to be a massive understatement). What was I thinking?

Nasson was originally founded 1912 as a school for what were then called "wayward" women, to rescue them from a life of prostitution in Boston and send them to remote southern Maine where they could learn alternative trades of a more acceptable sort. It went coed and became a liberal arts college starting in 1935. By the time Joan and I got there, Nasson was not the strongest school, academically or financially. As it turned out, I started teaching at Nasson in 1977 just before it went bankrupt, and it finally closed in 1983. Think about it: most colleges never go bankrupt. This would always be a big reminder to me of the marginality of my career at this stage.

Yet we loved living in southern Maine and being part of the Nasson community. We made many fast friends, young couples starting out together seeking lives in the academy. It was a lot of fun. We loved living so close the ocean, the Maine coast in particular. What a beautiful place! We lived in Kennebunk, about fifteen miles toward the ocean from the college. (I carpooled with two historians and learned a lot listening to them talk day after day about history, politics, the arts, teaching, whatever.) Our favorite thing to do was to drive five miles to the ocean at Kennebunkport after dinner and walk on the rocks while trying to avoid getting splashed by the waves. Our favorite spot was an incredibly beautiful jagged ledge called Walker Point. There was a compound of black houses, including a mansion, next to it. The local rumor in 1977 was that it was owned by someone in organized crime. It came out about a year or so later that it was owned by George Herbert *Walker* Bush (who was the director of the Central Intelligence Agency [CIA] at the time, and eventually would become the forty-first president of the United States). My response was: "Well, the rumor was partially right!" (If you go to Walker Point now, Secret Service officers in yellow jackets with the agency name plastered on the back walk around and greet folks and ask them how they are doing. So much for them being the Secret Service! Now it is not a secret who lives there; and the rumor is gone, if not forgotten.)

I taught at Nasson for just one year before the husband of my freshman English professor called me and asked if I would consider returning to New York State and agree to teach at Potsdam College of the State University of New York, just ten miles from where I did my undergraduate work. I had actually applied for that job earlier in the year, but I received word at some point that I had been eliminated in the search. Then, evidently, the person who was offered the job turned it down at the last minute, throwing the search into a scramble for a replacement. I am not sure how far down the list I was, but I got called, went on the interview, accepted the job, and my wife and I moved to Potsdam one month after we had moved into town to be nearer to Nasson for the start of what was supposed to be our second year there. Joan was by then six months pregnant with our first child, adding more excitement to the confusion.

I guess I got the call to come to Potsdam because the chair knew me a bit. His wife was the inspirational freshman English professor who had motivated me to take my studies seriously and make them relevant to what was happening in the world. While in graduate school, when I was the data tape person for the SUNY schools in the region, I had had to travel to Potsdam to meet with faculty, at a dinner held at my English professor's house. It was a happy surprise to arrive at the house and find her there. I reconnected with her then and got to know her husband a bit. A few years later, he called me to come for the interview. I ended up becoming chair of the department myself a few years later, after finally finishing my dissertation, publishing a few more articles, and getting tenure. (They made me chair like five minutes after I was tenured.)

By the time I completed my dissertation at Potsdam, I was already moving away from political gerontology. Someone had said something to me. A friend in graduate school took me aside one day when I was visiting my dissertation advisor about finishing my dissertation. He told me I should switch sides in the generational social welfare conflict I was studying. The elderly had it good and the non-aged poor were getting marginalized in the process. The elderly were benefiting from what I would eventually come to call the "deep semiotic structure of deservingness."[9] While older people who received social security were seen as having earned their benefits, the non-aged poor who received welfare, mostly single mothers, were seen as being dependent on assistance from others that they did not necessarily deserve and definitely had not earned.

I thought about it for a long time, several years actually. Should I shelve all the hard work of trying to become a political gerontologist with in-depth knowledge of that area of focus? I was hoping to be someone whom people could turn to for informed recommendations on how to address public policy for the elderly. To give that up, after all that work to specialize in an area of study, seemed like a bad career move. Then again, I had already, just a few years later, thoughtlessly left copies of my completed dissertation in my basement never to be sent to publishers. I obviously was not pursuing an efficient strategy. And what was all this strategizing about? Since when was I a careerist? Maybe the academy was sapping me of all my remaining activism. I stopped and thought some more. I remembered that that the only reason I got into studying the elderly for my dissertation was funding. I enjoyed studying the elderly; and helping to improve public policy on their behalf was fulfilling. Yet, it was not really my first choice for a focus. I was worried most about the fundamental axes of oppression, the race-class-gender system that social scientists euphemistically called the socioeconomic order. Maybe now was the time to focus on what I was really concerned about.

Shortly after I finished my dissertation and the articles I had written on old-age social policy had been published, I decided to jump ship. It was time to start speaking truth to power by switching sides and focusing on antipoverty efforts for the non-aged poor. I had already drifted into criticizing "elderly policy particularism," so for the next step it was not all that difficult to focus on what I saw was an invidious distinction embedded in public policy that disadvantaged the non-aged poor as less deserving than the elderly, who were exalted in policy as having earned their benefits. It was time to take seriously the deep semiotic structure of deservingness as a focus of research.

One reason I was ready to make the move was that in my dissertation I had relied on the work of Frances Fox Piven and Richard Cloward, in particular the book *Poor People's Movements: How They Succeed, Why They Fail.*[10] To this day, Piven and Cloward's work towers over the social sciences, and the study of social welfare and poverty in particular. At the time when I was writing my dissertation, in 1977, their book had just been published and was already causing quite a stir for suggesting that the poor lacked the resources to engage effectively in interest group politics, and that their ability to influence politics was in large part manifested when they practiced a politics of dissensus, disrupting the normal state of affairs with protest. The poor were better off not organizing in conventional ways that would only lead them to be more easily co-opted. Instead, they should organize in ways that facilitated their ability to be activated for protest politics when the time was right.[11] Piven and Cloward's prior book—their first—*Regulating the Poor: The Functions of Public Welfare* had been published in 1971 and already provided an enduring assessment of the politics of welfare policy for the poor. It ended with this conclusion, which summed up their understanding of the political potential of the poor: "The moral seems clear: a placid poor get nothing, but a turbulent poor sometimes get something." [12]

Piven and Cloward made me think more critically about what it really took for politically marginalized groups to exercise influence in the political process. They made me think more critically about how social welfare policy was not necessarily simply altruistic efforts to aid the disadvantaged. They made me think more critically about how to conduct research and engage in scholarship that would actually help inform meaningful change. I ended up including them in my discussion of how citizen participation programs could operate to co-opt clients into going along with what the limited existing social welfare programs offered rather than actively pushing for more dramatic change. I ended up considering the efforts of Maggie Kuhn and her leadership of the Gray Panthers as a more activist alternative for pushing onto the public policy agenda the concerns of the elderly, the low-income elderly in particular.

Yet, by the early 1980s, I decided that, rather than trying to bring Piven and Cloward's thinking into examination of the politics of the elderly,

I would switch to studying the politics of the non-aged poor itself. The elderly were largely assimilated to the existing political system, given that they stood to benefit from being seen as deserving beneficiaries of Social Security. Yes, many older people needed assistance of various sorts, and many concerns of many older people were being neglected by the policy process, but I wanted my work to be associated with more dramatic political efforts to challenge the established understandings of how the policy process worked to (or not to) provide assistance for the poorest people in our society. I wanted to be on the right side of challenging the deep semiotic structure of deservingness that for so long had made it seem that the poor were cause of their own poverty and were somehow not deserving of government assistance.

I remember the moment when I made the decision to switch. I was in my office in Potsdam reading an exchange in the *American Political Science Review* (the lead journal in the discipline) between Piven and Cloward and Robert Albritton over what was at the time called the "Piven and Cloward thesis."[13] In *Regulating the Poor,* Piven and Cloward had upset the established understanding of social welfare policy by arguing that welfare was not simply an altruistic effort to aid the disadvantaged. The issue of whether the poor were deserving of assistance was actually beside the point. Access to assistance was tied to the real underlying economic and political purposes of providing welfare. For Piven and Cloward, welfare was a secondary institution calibrated to serve political and economic functions on behalf of the primary institutions of the polity and the economy, the state and the market.[14] Welfare served an economic function by providing assistance to the poor in ways that enforced work and compelled their willingness to take available low-wage jobs. It did this largely by making welfare hard to get and by keeping benefits below the wages of the lowest paying jobs. This was consistent with the principle of "less eligibility" from the British Poor Law of 1834, which required that the conditions in the workhouses (where the poor went if they could not support themselves) had to be below those of the worst available jobs. Yet, for Piven and Cloward, welfare also served political functions in that it provided enough assistance to gain the acquiescence of the poor to go along with the existing political economy, even as it failed to afford them a decent life.

For Piven and Cloward, welfare policy alternated in giving more or less emphasis to either of the competing political and economic functions, depending on circumstances. In this way, welfare policy changed in cyclical fashion, as it shifted from imposing more, then less, emphasis on its political or economic functions. They argued that in the 1960s in the face of civil disorder in the cities, welfare was made generously available to quell the dissent. This development was consistent with their thesis that when the ruling coalition was disrupted, say, when elites in the governing coalition are divided, or when there is instability in the majority electoral coalition, political leadership would encourage policymakers to make welfare more generally available as a concession to the poor, if support from them facilitated the elites retaining power. This was true for the Democrats and the Johnson administration in the 1960s. As a result, one hypothesis one could postulate from the Piven and Cloward thesis was that the number of poor people on the welfare rolls would rise more where there was greater civil disorder.

This thesis was profoundly controversial. First, it implied that welfare was surreptitiously designed in part to co-opt the poor rather than simply aid them (i.e., it had ulterior motives behind its provision of aid). Second, the poor could gain improvements in aid by being disruptive, practicing a politics of dissensus, protesting, and even rioting. Social scientists in multiple fields heaped scorn on Piven and Cloward for allegedly denigrating attempts to aid the poor and for inciting violence.[15] I read these criticisms as yet another instance of the proverbial blaming of the messenger, this time for highlighting how welfare politics actually operated.

Piven and Cloward were, to be sure, the model for activism and scholarship. They not only chronicled how protest politics in the 1960s had energized welfare policy liberalizations, but they also were active in helping the National Welfare Rights Organization (NWRO) push for improvements in social welfare policy, including being part of the campaign for a guaranteed income. They had famously published an article in *The Nation* back in 1966 that highlighted the distinct possibility that as many as one-half of the people who were eligible for welfare were in fact not receiving it and that if they did the system could well be thrown into a crisis that would make moving to a guaranteed income more plausible.[16] The "Crisis Strategy," as it came to be called, spread through the efforts of NWRO, and the numbers of recipients on the welfare rolls did increase dramatically duc to these efforts and the increases in civil disorder in the later part of the decade. President Richard Nixon, of all people, did in fact propose a guaranteed income, and Congress twice voted on it.

Yet the plan ultimately did not gain passage. Nixon's plan was not as generous as liberals wanted but too generous for some conservatives. By 1972, Nixon himself had lost interest in the idea. It no longer was consistent with his "Southern Strategy" to build support for himself and the Republican Party in the South. The guaranteed income as proposed was set at a level where Southern states would not need to contribute to its financing because its benefit levels would exceed the low levels of welfare payments in those states. States outside the South would in many cases, however, have to add to the guaranteed income to avoid seeing declines in their own benefits to recipients. The plan was patently biased in favor of the Southern states; however, by the time it came up for its final vote in 1972, Nixon had already made major inroads in gaining Southern support, and he lost interest in the guaranteed income as part of that strategy.[17] In the end, Nixon's "Southern Strategy" was successful in moving the South into the Republican column; and while Piven and Cloward's "Crisis Strategy" might not have led to a guaranteed income, it did lead to massive numbers of poor families that were eligible finally getting access to assistance. For instance, in 1960 there were 745,300 families receiving cash assistance in the main welfare program for poor families with children, Aid to Families with Dependent Children (AFDC); by 1975, there were more than 3.35 million families on AFDC.[18]

Although Piven and Cloward were scholar/activists whose research directly contributed to the campaign for a more just system of social provision, they were not guilty of the most outrageous criticisms made against them. While cognizant of the underlying political and economic dimensions of welfare policy, they were not suggesting that the people who strove to provide assistance to the poor were malevolently focused on keeping the poor oppressed. Instead, their argument suggested that welfare's limitations were an artifact of the structural necessity that it serve political and economic functions to buttress the existing political-economic system, irrespective of the intentions of the people who administered the program.

Piven and Cloward were also not guilty of the charge that they were purveyors of violence. Their argument that a disruptive poor sometimes got something, but a placid poor got nothing, was a scholarly assessment based on in-depth historical research. This scholarly finding also did not imply that violence was a necessary component of a successful politics of dissensus. In fact, Piven and Cloward's work with NWRO and the "Crisis Strategy" pursued a politics of disruption by peaceful means and did not help instigate the riots that swept over U.S. cities in the 1960s. Their activism in general during this period and their "Crisis Strategy" in particular was focused on a politics of disruption that did not involve violence at all. Instead, being politically disruptive was successful by making conventional politics unworkable most often without resorting to violence.

It is true that riots were additional sources of disruption during this period that could not be ignored: between 1964 and 1971, hundreds (perhaps as many as seven hundred) of riots occurred in the cities of the United States.[19] An important question, to be sure, is to what extent the riots independent of the "Crisis Strategy" efforts affected the expansion of the welfare rolls during this period. Yet, neither Piven and Cloward's theory nor their activism was focused on instigating rioting.

Instead, they emphasized that political instability, more than social instability, was what could at times force elites into using social assistance to regain the acquiescence of the poor to the existing socioeconomic order. Their analysis and activism were focused on how political disruption (as in the disruption of the process of securing and maintaining political power) leads to the state's expanding assistance to cool out the poor and recommit them to the political order. A politics of disruption for them was focused largely on disrupting coalition and party politics, such that those in power could not continue to assume that they could continue to ignore the needs of the poor, for fear of losing important bases of support that were enabling them to stay in power. Protests, demonstrations, civil disobedience, and various other actions short of actual violence were the primary ways in which this kind of dissensus politics could be successfully practiced.

Years later, misunderstanding of Piven and Cloward's "Crisis Strategy" and its focus on political disruption went viral with the misplaced vilification of Piven and Cloward by Glenn Beck, who used his show on Fox News to demonize them as the evil geniuses whose "Cloward-Piven Strategy" was consciously intended to bankrupt America and force it to adopt a communist government.[20] Beck, and others, not only conflated a strategy to promote political disruption with one that promoted violence, he went further to say that Piven and Cloward were intentionally seeking to bankrupt society. Incomprehensibly, Beck actually claimed that President Barack Obama was an acolyte of Piven and Cloward and had been using their ideas from the "Crisis Strategy" to intentionally destroy the American economy so that the public would have no choice but to accede to adopting a communist form of government.

For a time, it seemed to me that the leading voices on the Right in United States were competing to see who could outdo the others in making the most outrageous claims about Obama. It was as if the person who made the most over-the-top assertion would be the winner, by giving voice to the outrage many on the Right felt when Barack Obama, a black man, became President of the United States. Suggesting that Obama was secretly enacting this more diabolical version of the "Cloward-Piven Strategy," as Beck and others called it, was the ultimate version of this kind of ever-increasing acceleration of irresponsible claims. Boycott campaigns in reaction to Beck's rantings about Piven and Cloward, the Obama administration, progressive activists of all sorts, and Jews, too, ultimately led to his show getting cancelled. By then, more than three hundred existing and potential sponsors had chosen to not buy advertising time on Beck's show.

Back in the late 1970s, Albritton's criticisms were muted compared to those others made. He was a scholar, not a fearmonger. His main point was that Piven and Cloward simply lacked sufficient evidence that civil disorder in the 1960s had led to increases in the welfare rolls. He presented evidence indicating that the cities that had the greatest amounts of civil disorder did not have the largest increases in the welfare rolls. Piven and Cloward responded by criticizing his characterization of their argument and the evidence he presented to refute it. Then, in a passage that was immediately and forever burned into my mind, they wrote:

> To test the relationship between civil disorder and the welfare explosion obviously requires that riots be correlated with post-riot welfare increases; instead, Albritton mainly used a pre-riot measure of changes in the AFDC rolls. Roughly three-quarters of the riots throughout the decade occurred just in 1967 and in 1968. . . . We hope Albritton will perform his correlations again, using appropriate post-rioting caseload measures. . . . Even with the depressing effects of . . . errors, he obtained a correlation which moved in a direction consistent with our analysis. With the errors corrected, the correlations could turn out to be statistically significant.[21]

I circled the passage, Xeroxed it, posted it on the board above my desk, and for the next year treated it as my marching orders into a new research project. I was going to switch fields by starting to test the Piven-Cloward hypothesis the way they themselves said it should be tested. I felt I had just signed on to become a quantitative researcher who examined the most politically controversial of topics. My hope was that my empirical efforts could provide evidence that supported a better understanding of how we treated the poor, and did so in ways that helped us think more clearly about how to get real change on behalf of the poor. It was as if I had gone back down to the crossroads (this time by switching from political gerontology to the study of welfare politics). I had switched once again from careerism to activism, now by seeking a better way to combine research and politics, all in the name of trying to do scholarship that could help challenge the existing structure of power.

I definitely wanted a correlation I hoped to prove the Piven-Cloward hypothesis right. But I was not about to lie about it. I wanted sound empirical research to demonstrate the plausibility of their hypothesis. This meant a major research project with next to no funding. That required teamwork. I then went and convinced my good friend and colleague, Pat Turbett, in the Sociology department at Potsdam, to join me in this endeavor. He agreed. We immediately recruited Anne Hildreth, an excellent undergraduate student, to help collect the data. (Anne eventually went on to become a tenured Political Science professor in my alma mater, the Graduate School of Public Affairs, at Albany University of the State University of New York.) We collected data on the riots in the 1960s from a variety of sources, including newspapers. We collected data on other variables, such as the number of recipients on the welfare rolls, from government sources, including the *Statistical Abstract of the United States*. It took more than a year to collect and manage the data, which were on punch cards back then. It was as laborious a process as writing. Everything back then took way more effort. Yet, in the end, we had a dataset. We conducted statistical analyses. Our results strongly confirmed the Piven-Cloward hypothesis.

We first sent our paper to *Social Problems*. It was rejected. It probably deserved to be rejected, because, as you might guess, it needed a rewrite. Yet, what really stood out was that the editor at the time was Malcolm Spector, who told us explicitly that he was suspicious of quantitative analysis, along the lines of "anybody can lie with statistics," though he stated it a little less bluntly. I felt like writing back that that was indeed true (anyone *can* lie with statistics), but in this particular case we definitely were not lying! I still think this was one of the greatest examples of methodological bias I would ever encounter in all my years of submitting scholarship for review. Yes, years later it would seem to many social scientists that the leaders in their disciplines had a quantitative bias that led them to look down on qualitative analyses. Spector's assertion, although it was in the other direction, was just as obtuse as some of the methodological snobbery you can hear about today.[22]

Next, we sent the article to the *American Sociological Review* (the main journal in that discipline). We were, once again, not following the script. The normal course of affairs is to go to a less prestigious journal after getting rejected, in hopes of finally getting an acceptance. Yet, we had heard from mentors that the *American Sociological Review* was open-minded. So we gave them a try. What our mentors said turned out to be true. What good news it was, then, when we read in a letter that the *Review* was not just open to quantitative analysis, but that they accepted our article.[23] We then completed another analysis using the same data and published that in the *Social Service Review* (where I had previously published on the elderly).[24]

The conclusion in the *American Sociological Review* piece summed up our major findings:

> [T]he general pattern in our data is consistent with the idea that the relationship between civil disorder and welfare growth in the late 1960s and early 1970s was the product of a two-step process. Rioting by the poor exacerbated a volatile political climate com-

> pelling national liberalizations in welfare policy, which in turn were most actively implemented by the most riot-torn states. Our findings offer support for the Piven and Cloward thesis that welfare largely operates as a form of social control and in the late 1960s it expanded as part of government efforts to recommit a rebellious poor population to the existing social order. These findings also complement a growing body of literature on the role and function of welfare in capitalistic, industrialized societies which argues that welfare performs a social-control function for the state.[25]

Our work was quickly noted. For instance, in the popular textbook, *The Politics of Power,* by Ira Katznelson and Mark Kesselman, in 1987, it stated:

> Thus, the most compelling explanation of the welfare explosion from 1960 to 1970 combines an emphasis on mass insurgency with an analysis of why politicians in some states were prepared to change the rules to permit an expansion of AFDC. In one of the best treatments of these issues, Sanford Schram and Patrick Turbett argue that in the states where rioting was most severe AFDC caseloads increased the most, but only after changes in national and state public policy facilitated this growth.[26]

Our research would get cited frequently over the years as this work joined with that of many others who also tested the Piven-Cloward hypothesis. We had become a footnote, in some small way another brick in the wall of scholarship on welfare politics. This was, however, not always an affirmation of our work. Even our political allies would raise issues about our work. Sometimes the criticisms were on methodological grounds. Yet we were never accused of being incompetent quantitative analysts (though I always thought somebody would say that). No, it was, again, that kind of expression of distaste for quantitative work as not grasping the subtleties of social relations. It was frustrating that the penchant to prefer one or another type of approach to the study of society would crowd out consideration of our empirical findings. The great social welfare historian Michael Katz is the most prominent example of this. In his book *In the Shadow of the Poorhouse,* Katz wrote about our and others' statistical tests of the Piven-Cloward hypothesis:

> All of these quantitative studies seem shot full of weaknesses. For one thing the debate does not distinguish between the extension of

> welfare by the federal government and the liberalization of procedures by local welfare bureaucrats who retain considerable discretionary authority. Different dynamics, certainly, must apply in each case. Even more, statistical correlations between riots and welfare in individual cities are weak evidence, especially in the age of instant news. For they do not measure the anticipatory reactions of other cities. Who can tell, even with multivariate analysis, the impact of a riot in Newark on, say San Jose? The Piven and Cloward thesis, it seems to me, can only be tested through individual historical case studies that try to find out not only what happened but why it happened. From the evidence I have seen, the impact of militant protest is indisputable, though certainly, not the only important factor. Nor do Piven and Cloward say it is. In fact, most critics ignore their careful specification of the circumstances in which protest has been effective.[27]

While I agree that understanding the relationship between civil disorder and the welfare explosion of the 1960s requires attention to what people were thinking and experiencing, examining systematic patterns across the states and communities is something Piven and Cloward themselves endorsed (that is why I got started on this; because they told me to do it, or at least that is how, back then, I read that pivotal passage I quoted above). For me, a variety of different types of studies were needed to get a robust understanding of the relationship of the disorder of the 1960s to the growth in the welfare rolls. I remained reluctant to choose one method over another. Not choosing seems to me the road to a better scholarship that can better relate to ongoing political struggle. I felt that way then when I read Katz's passage and I still feel that way. On some things, I don't budge.

Regardless of the criticism, our research was to be part of an effort to question the more complacent understandings of the role of social welfare policy in our society. It was nice to be included in that conversation. Eventually, our work became the basis for more sophisticated and nuanced analyses that provided even better confirmation of the Piven-Cloward thesis.[28]

At the time, I felt I had completed my transition back to a more radical stance, this time still in the academy. When I think about this transition in my scholarship, I see how my childhood transition from Newark to Livingston really did shape me. I remember the Newark riots, how a relative's music store (Kirshner's) was burned to the ground in 1967. I remember talking to a cop in Livingston who told me they were on alert, ready to put up roadblocks (twelve miles away, mind you), as if hordes of hopped-up have-nots were going to come streaming up Mt. Pleasant Avenue and overrun the town center. I remember my freshman English professor that fall being stunned that I seemed nonchalant about the fact that Newark had been burning. Now, by studying the Piven-Cloward hypothesis, I was engaging in empirical research that tried to shed a better light on why the riots in cities such as Newark had occurred, how they affected our politics, and how they shaped welfare policy. It was as though I was trying to make up for being part of that white flight.

FIVE

STANDING ON SHOULDERS

Scholarship as Networking

By 1986, I had been tenured and chair of the Political Science Department for one year and was now going on my first sabbatical leave. I was very excited. Teaching at Potsdam was extremely fulfilling but grueling. We were an increasingly underfunded state college where faculty normally taught four courses a semester with large enrollments. As chair, I got released from one course for the year, so I taught seven courses while tending to the administrative responsibilities of the department. I enjoyed serving as chair: you got the immediate gratification of being able to do something small (such as direct funding toward a project) that could facilitate other people's work. Yet it was time consuming and could be boring. The teaching was even more demanding: two sections of Introduction to U.S. Government with forty students each and two upper division electives in the fall with twenty to twenty-five students each (e.g., Urban Politics, Power and Democracy in the U.S., etc.), and then two sections of U.S. Government in the spring with one elective. It was a ton of class time and several tons of essays and papers to read and grade (without teaching assistants). There was no time for scholarship. It felt as though I would never learn anything new the rest of my life. Yet the sabbatical was my big chance to continue to keep on learning and studying so that I could make a contribution to my field with new research (which, hopefully, could have political impact beyond the academy).

Potsdam had its moments. Or should I say it had its movements. Grassroots activism abounded, especially about preserving the rural environment in the face of the juggernaut we now call "global warming." The back-to-the-land people who dominated the left-wing culture there were prescient. They saw where our pollution was taking us thirty years before the rest of us. We ate dinner in houses built by friends who used no electricity . . . either in the building of the house or in the living in the house. Spaghetti never tasted so good! I started a bimonthly tabloid, funded from donations (we took no advertisements), about the issues of concern in the North Country (as it is still called). We focused on the environment, but we also published a How to Apply for Welfare article (my idea). We were out there. The paper was called *Current: The Journal of North Country Action* (North Country Action would today be something like a 501c3 for leftists, or something like that).

I became a point person for people trying to do good. My friends made it happen. I love them still. One day, the idea that I was the go-to guy was driven home while I was taking a shower and the phone rang. Dripping wet, wrapped in a towel, I answered the phone assuming it was someone trying to meet a deadline. I said: "Hello, Sandy Schram." The response: "Hi Sandy, this is Abbie Hoffman." I retorted: "No way! Who is this?" The answer: "No really, this is Abbie Hoffman!" He wanted to show slides of his trip to Nicaragua and the good work of the Sandinistas, who had finally won power there.

But I should have known. The notorious hippie of the 1960s had by 1973 gone underground, eventually assuming the identity of "Barry Freed" while living in the North Country and hiding out to avoid the feds, who pursued him on a drug charge. He had become the head of Save the River, the main environmental group working to clean up the St. Lawrence River, which divides Canada and the United States. I had always thought he was a peculiarly frenetic person whom I knew (only casually) as Barry. It turns out that Hoffman was bipolar, and ended up allegedly committing suicide for related reasons down here in Pennsylvania years later. By the time he called me in 1984, we had heard who Barry Freed really was and that he had copped to the drug charge, done some time, and was now back, but as Abbie Hoffman. Still, I was in shock that another one of my idols would call me now that he was out and about. So actually I was delighted he called. I had not seen him since he went away to prison. I'd always wanted to ask him what it was like to be posing as someone else for seven years. When he called, though, I did not even know he had been released from jail, let alone gone to Nicaragua now as Abbie. Ever clueless, I of course helped arrange his slide show.

We definitely enjoyed living in northern New York. Yet, most of the time at Potsdam, it seemed like I was sitting on my couch at home grading papers. I was starting to go nuts reading endless repetitions of what I had said in class. This was partially my fault for not pushing students more, perhaps out of fear that I would be seen as too hard on them. Yet, in any case, the crush of class-related work that was less than intellectually rewarding was starting to weigh on me. (It did not help that one administrator berated us department chairs in a meeting once, stating that the higher-ups saw us as teachers, not professors who were scholars. I wanted to cry.) I desperately wanted to be a scholar or at least have the luxury to spend more time working on improving my scholarship.

Just when it was starting to seem too much, my sabbatical got approved for the 1986–87 school year. I knew right away what to do. I wrote to Sheldon Danziger, who had just become the director of the federally funded Institute for Research on Poverty (IRP) at the University of Wisconsin-Madison.

Madison has a great tradition—the "Wisconsin Tradition" of trying to support scholarship that makes a difference in the public sphere and can help shape public policy. John Commons, the economist of the Progressive Era in the early twentieth century, was a forerunner to the great Edwin Witte in this regard. Witte, another Madison economist, was the chief of staff of the Committee on Economic Security, headed by President Franklin Delano Roosevelt's Secretary of Labor, Frances Perkins (the first female cabinet secretary, and a social worker). Witte successfully pushed the committee to rely on the Wisconsin Model for creating the Social Security system that got enacted in 1935.[1] In the 1960s, the administration of President Lyndon Baines Johnson turned to still another economist from Wisconsin, Robert Lampman, to help form the brain trust that informed the Johnson administration's War on Poverty. Out of those efforts came the creation of the IRP to create a place to promote more scholarly research on the poverty issue.

I wanted to go on sabbatical to work on my research. But I most especially wanted to go to Madison to pursue research that could be relevant to efforts to improve public policy related to fighting poverty. I wanted my scholarship to matter politically. Yet I increasingly recognized that this meant raising troubling issues about both research as it was conventionally done and politics as it conventionally avoided the difficult questions about the structural impediments for attacking poverty. I wanted to politicize research in ways that would make it more politically relevant. This was my evolving understanding of how I would get to be a radical, this time in the academy rather than in the streets (though my research was about the relationship of the two). I wanted to do research that addressed the fundamental concerns that antipoverty protesters were raising, and that meant being a protester against conventional poverty research.

Sheldon was great; he arranged for me to come to IRP for the year by helping me get two courses to teach, one each semester at the La Follette Institute of Public Affairs and Political Science. The spring course was in Political Science, on the U.S. Presidency, which I taught in Science Hall to

114 students (with a teaching assistant). Science Hall was where a bomb had killed a graduate student during the anti–Vietnam War protests on campus in the 1960s. The guy who planted the bomb did not know anyone was in the building when it went off that sad night. After he got out of prison, he sold jewelry in front of Science Hall as a street vendor, and he was there as I taught my course. I bought some jewelry from him one day and we chatted about my course. There was actually a lot to talk about. I taught the course during the spring semester of 1987, when the Iran-Contra affair was being investigated and hearings were held in Congress. Each student was required to write a term paper on a particular issue of presidential power raised by the controversy.

As much fun as that that course was, I was mainly in Madison use the resources of IRP to make progress on my research. And IRP was great. The staff was incredibly helpful. The seminars were highly informative. My colleagues were immensely supportive. I loved being there and benefited from my time there immeasurably. Yet, as is my tendency, the experience was quickly becoming its own contradiction. As I was just settling in, I was increasingly questioning whether the mostly-economists' IRP approach to antipoverty research was really the right way to go. I knew I was committed to promoting radical antipoverty politics and wanted to find an alternative approach to research to support that.

THE THREESOME

We came to Madison just when a new governor was about to be elected who would eventually make his name politically as the governor who first successfully got welfare reform enacted in a way that became a model for the entire country. The idea of welfare reform was starting to receive serious attention nationwide, but especially in Wisconsin. The Democratic governor, Tony Earl, was getting into trouble for being too liberal and coddling the poor and the criminals. He had proposed building a new prison near Milwaukee on the grounds that it would be closer to the hometown of many of those who were imprisoned. There was quite a stir over that; many people thought that was too liberal, too understanding, and just plain too much. He was up for reelection, and it was starting to look less than a sure thing.

Earl's opponent was a long-time state representative that many people never could see as governor—Tommy Thompson, who would eventually become U.S. Secretary of Health and Human Services under President George W. Bush. He would defeat Earl, shortly after I arrived there for my sabbatical. It seems in retrospect that the folks at IRP and La Follette were attuned to how things were shifting when they chose to bring three very different welfare scholars to campus for the year.

The folks at Madison originally were planning to bring just two scholars but then added me. Based on what I eventually heard, I think they wanted more balance than the two gave them. They were Michael Wiseman, the economist and welfare policy expert, from the University of California, Berkeley, and Lawrence Mead, the political scientist, from New York University. Both were well published and widely recognized as experts on the topic of welfare for the poor. Michael was pretty much a conventional, mainstream, moderate-liberal economist who approached the study of welfare policy in ways entirely consistent with the way the folks at IRP did. He was already affiliated with IRP, and at the end of the year accepted an appointment to become a member of the Economics Department at Madison so that he could continue his work at IRP. Larry was the author earlier that year of the much-discussed book *Beyond Entitlement*, which spelled out that he was a very conservative critic of welfare.[2] Adding me as a leftist balanced the team a bit, and so, when I offered my name, the folks at IRP were glad to accommodate me.

It was exciting to be involved in discussing, researching, and even collaborating about welfare policy research all year. Michael and I ended up co-authoring an IRP discussion paper based on conversations we had.[3] Larry occasionally drove me home from work, and we talked then and other times. We were not, however, to write anything together. I am sure both of us preferred it that way. (We still exchange ideas all the time.) There were some interesting things that happened, from the trivial to the serious. For instance, Larry showed up with a Macintosh computer, making him different than all the liberals and leftists in another way. In fact, he told us that he had decided to get that Apple computer because Charles Murray, the most prominent conservative critic of welfare at the time, told him that all the conservatives were using that model to distinguish themselves from the liberals.[4] I thought that was just so funny.

There were other differences. Several of us got to hang out with Governor Earl (his wife Shelia held an administrative appointment at the La Follette Institute). Larry was advising Tommy Thompson. And over time, Larry ended up continuing to offer his opinions to Thompson when he became governor, including when Thompson enacted the Wisconsin Works (W-2) program that became the model for national welfare reform, which would be enacted in 1996. Larry would write a well-received book about how Wisconsin's effort was that model program.[5] Larry became dedicated to championing this get-tough approach. I eventually co-authored a book with Joe Soss and Richard Fording designed to counter Larry's argument that the get-tough approach was the way to go.[6]

Yet there were also some shared concerns that reflected why we were in Madison at the same time. While Larry and I have profound differences about how to look at welfare policy and the poor, we have shared an interest in making political science move toward being more connected to political engagement and less obsessed with its own internal arguments, especially its preoccupations with refining method at the expense of saying something substantive that matters to ordinary people and their struggles and concerns.[7]

GETTING MENTORED

Being in residence at IRP, I started thinking more about challenging the political biases in mainstream antipoverty research. I was applying Piven and Cloward's radical critique not to social welfare policy but to the research that was being promoted by the government to inform social welfare policy. I was trying to be a radical critic of research as opposed to policy (though the idea for me was that the research and policy were related, both emanating from the centers of power both inside the government and outside in the private funding sources, and both tied to the same embedded biases about the poor).

My turn to using Piven and Cloward in this way was not an accident. I had started communicating with them, and they advised me on how to proceed. I met Frances Fox Piven and Richard Cloward at the annual meeting of the American Sociological Association in August, 1986, in New York City, right after my wife and our two kids had moved with me to Madison for my sabbatical. Frances and Richard expressed interest in staying in contact. Next, they sent me the page proofs for their next book, co-authored with Fred Block and Barbara Ehrenreich, *The Mean Season: The Attack on the Welfare State*.[8] The chapters by Piven and Cloward focused on the history of U.S. welfare policy and the role of welfare policy research in not always helping to understand the limitations of welfare policy. I wrote extensive marginal comments, while finding almost no typos. It was an exercise in learning for me more than proofreading for them. Richard told me later that I should publish my comments. Eventually, by 1993–94, when I was back in Madison for my next sabbatical (this time on leave from my new school, Macalester College), I did in fact finally complete the first full draft of a manuscript based on that very suggestion.[9] I was seizing my opportunity to learn from Piven and Cloward and apply their perspective to welfare policy research.

Another person who helped me think critically about the embedded biases of welfare policy research was Murray Edelman, the great political theorist and critic of American politics who held an endowed chair at Madison. Murray took me under his wing, educated me on the ways in which research was an artifact of discourse, and encouraged me to examine the prevailing economistic way of talking about welfare and poverty had come to influence the way most research on the topic was conducted. Murray was a mild-mannered dissident within the poverty studies community who happened to be located at the citadel of poverty research.[10] I learned so much from Murray. And he knew it; he encouraged me to stay on for his National Endowment of Humanities (NEH) Summer Seminar on symbolic politics in 1987, and it was in that seminar that I was able to greatly accelerate my attempts to apply discourse analysis to social welfare policy research. The seminar was a tremendous opportunity to learn from other, more knowledgeable colleagues and apply their insights to my own work. Thanks to Murray, I had become a government-funded guerrilla boring away from the inside at the unchallenged assumptions of mainstream antipoverty research.

Another Madison icon was Linda Gordon, the prominent scholar of women's oppression, who also encouraged me to question how poverty research had become by then the thoroughly economics-dominated field that it largely remains today.[11] Linda in particular was keen to support my efforts to highlight the fact that political biases embedded in antipoverty research stemmed from its funding ties to the government and foundations, and that this led researchers away from studying the possibility that many women on welfare were relying on it not because they were lazy but because they were trying to extricate themselves from abusive relationships.[12]

Piven and Cloward, Edelman, and Gordon all became my mentors, teaching me to think more critically, helping me to become the radical critic not so much of welfare policy but of the research that the government was funding to inform those policies. They helped me find a niche where I could make my own specific contribution. Together, they made the perfect combination for me to fashion my critique: Piven and Cloward provided the model of consummate scholar/activists, Edelman supplied the mode of analysis in questioning the discourse of poverty research, and Gordon was a font of ideas on the specific embedded race, class, and especially gender biases in this area of research.

I cannot put in words how much I benefited from their insights and how generous they all were with their time. And I could be needy. Lunch every Wednesday with Murray, coffees with Linda, and constant communicating via email with Frances and Richard. Their support, commentary, and criticism were incredibly helpful.[13]

The contact with Piven and Cloward increased after I left Madison and for years to come. In many ways, their support made my career. Without their help, I would have remained woefully ignorant of many important issues. And without their support, I would have been unable to complete a number of the projects on which I worked. The letters of reference and the help networking were important as well. (Once, I got a job interview largely because the department chair wanted to ask me how well I knew Piven and Cloward and what they were like—or so it seems, especially after I did not get the job, though a number of the faculty complained about my being passed over—academic searches can be very confusing. Even after I got a job and Frances came and spoke at my new school, later, at dinner, the dean wanted to know—asking in what seemed a disbelieving way—how it could be that we were friends.) What luck to be chosen to be someone that these giants in my field were willing to support and help in such an intensive way. I was standing on their shoulders.

As the years went by, these mentors continued to advise me, particularly Frances and Richard. Frances and Richard became special friends as well as mentors. Yet before I got to be someone who would benefit from all this support and advice there was an issue that had to be addressed. Really only one, it seems. One point that needed special examination was the fact that I had published some articles with Theresa Funiciello, a former single mother on welfare who became an activist.[14] I had enjoyed working with Theresa; she taught me a lot about how women on welfare experienced the welfare system. Her husband, Tom Sanzillo, was also informed about policies for the homeless, which were starting to get increased attention. This unproblematic collaboration with Theresa was a source of curiosity for Frances and Richard, since Theresa had had a falling out with them. Theresa herself admitted in her book that she had a tendency to fall into biting the hand that feeds her. (Given her own realization of this tendency, it is somewhat ironic that her great memoir is entitled *The Tyranny of Kindness*. Once again, hidden in plain sight is the truth we refuse to see.) Theresa evidently had turned on a number of her supporters, Richard and Frances most especially, when they disagreed over strategy during welfare rights campaigns. Yet I knew nothing about this; and once that was clear, the issue was put aside. (I did go back and read Theresa's book more closely to find out what I had stepped into.) From then on, Frances and Richard saw me as another younger person whom they could reliably encourage and support. And that they did, to an extent that you could never imagine.

It remains to me a mystery that such prominent and accomplished people can be accessible and available to help others without asking for anything in return. When people such as they offer to help you conduct your research, it can mean so much. I was very lucky, to be sure. Yet the larger point is that we all depend on others as we conduct our work, and mentors are critical in this regard. Some mentors are better than others, though, and I had the best. I was standing on the shoulders of giants.[15]

IT TAKES A VILLAGE

Madison was proving to be the ideal place for me as a young scholar trying to develop my craft. Yet I was not yet ready to use my time efficiently. I still had writing issues, even with the advent of personal computers. I could now, finally, type and compose, because I could correct mistakes easily with a computer keyboard. But having something to say was still a challenge, and figuring out how to say it well remained a mystery. After that glorious NEH seminar led by Murray Edelman, as my sabbatical ended, I came up with an idea for a book that would critique the dominant discourse of poverty research, but at that point it remained just an idea, which I was not ready to realize.

I returned to Potsdam focused on seeking another job, where I would have time to write. Madison had seemed like the big city it really was not, but Potsdam was Potsdam—a nice small town. (A colleague once applied for jobs elsewhere, saying that as much as he liked the North Country, he considered it the academic equivalent of internal exile. That pretty much summed up my new perspective. I had seen the bright lights of the big city—i.e., the enchantments of a university town.) I now knew what was possible elsewhere and I very much wanted to be part of it. I wanted to be involved and engaged intellectually and politically in ways I could not at Potsdam. It took a year, but I got a chance to go to Macalester College in St. Paul. It was only a two-year visiting position, but I took it, desperate to move my scholarship forward. My formal research presentation was on the ways social welfare policy discourse reflected embedded biases of the prevailing power structure in our society, which had infiltrated even how researchers approached the topic. It was my book project summarized. I got the job based on the book project, and I worked on the book every chance I got. I was finally getting the time for my scholarship and using that time to talk explicitly about the limitations of poverty research, mortgaged as it was to the deep semiotic structure of deservingness, even though I had not yet explicitly named it that.

It was a risky venture, and living in the upper Midwest took some getting used to. One attraction that we hoped would smooth our transition was that St. Paul was the city where Garrison Keillor performed his immensely popular weekend public radio variety show *A Prairie Home Companion*. But by the time we moved there in the summer of 1989, Keillor was in transit, taking his show to New York City, in the very state from which we had just moved. We were ships passing in the night (or on the Interstate). In the fall, he came back to St. Paul to perform his show in its old location. Now that it was based in New York City, interest in the show had increased, and the local public radio station had a call-in interview with him. I picked up the phone and asked Keillor to comment on our being ships passing in the night, and whether he had any tips to help a New Yorker like me get acclimated quickly to the Twin Cities and its seemingly more reserved style of interpersonal relations. I wondered if I should form a support group of exiled New Yorkers. The program's host asked Keillor if he had formed a similar group of Minnesotans in his new home town. Keillor responded by saying the last thing people do when they move to New York City is want to spend time hanging out with people from Minnesota. It was said in jest, but for me it was in no way reassuring.

It was a time of personal challenge. We had moved as a family so that I could take a temporary job just to pursue my career. I had to make good on that opportunity. I remember the first night we were in our rented, college-owned house, right next to campus. I sat in front of my personal computer, which was propped up on still-unpacked boxes, staring at the bright blue screen of the monitor. I had to write a paper for the American Political Science Association meeting that would occur in about a month. I thought about what I had agreed to write. I knew that being at Macalester was my chance to start a career in which I could have time for scholarship. I wanted to be better as an academic, but I wanted more. I wanted to be a real intellectual, who had studied his topic such that he had something worthwhile to say to people, including students, colleagues, policymakers, the general public. Remembering what my freshman English professor had told me, I decided that the only way this was going to happen was if I started to speak in my own voice, think for myself, write and research things the way I thought they should be done, not necessarily the way others expected me to think, talk, and write. I started writing. The paper addressed the extent to which research on requiring work from the poor who received welfare was shot full of political biases that distorted the significance of the empirical findings. The paper would subsequently get published in the journal *Polity*, and eventually it became chapter 7 in the book that I was hoping to write.[16]

I very much liked Macalester. The chair of the Political Science department was Chuck Green, a supportive colleague who encouraged my interests in mixing methods, combining research and teaching, creating more opportunities for students to learn in a more hands-on way. In fact, he was a mentor on all these matters. I wanted to stay, but given my appointment I would have to apply for a tenure-track position if that was going to happen.

After two years, there was a search, and I applied and received the tenure-track appointment, although with four years to go before I actually received tenure. The president at Macalester was not keen on hiring me, but he relented when I agreed to these less than favorable terms. This meant that I had to end my leave from Potsdam and give up tenure there before gaining tenure at Macalester. It was a risky move, but I did it, a sign of how much I wanted to have an appointment where I could work on my scholarship.

I labored late into many nights drafting my book. I was fortunate to secure a book contract from the University of Minnesota Press (right down the street). The University of Minnesota Press was the ideal publisher for a discourse analysis of poverty research, and the executive editor, Lisa Freeman, championed my proposal with the board and assigned the book to herself as my editor. She actively advised me on the book. She even worked to improve my writing. which still needed tons of help. I would never, not even eventually, have published the book without her hard work.

At the time, I could only write if I smoked cigarettes. It was the ultimate Faustian bargain. When I smoked up a storm, the synapses would fire and the words would flow. I started to get high blood pressure (something I still have). I did not care; I was writing. I was in a flow and it felt great. I could write late into the night and into the next morning. Yet the next day was often lost in exhaustion. It did not help that I was stressed over having to earn tenure under less than welcoming conditions (although whether this added to my high blood pressure was less clear). The stress of my tenuous situation affected my teaching. Everything seemed fraught with implications. What had I done to myself, I began to ask, sometimes almost out loud.

Yet I had supportive colleagues. It was an exhilarating place in which to write. We shared a commitment to improving as scholars. We formed a writing group under the leadership of the chair of the Sociology department, Michal McCall. Michal was an incredible person in addition to being a great colleague. She had studied with Howard Becker and Norman Denzin.[17] She was creative, theoretically sophisticated, intellectually playful, and generous and kind. She had rules for our writing group. Each week we would read one person's writing and when we commented on writing in our sessions, we had to say first what we liked about the text, then what our interpretation was, and only then, at the end, what constructive criticism we would offer, and it had to be constructive. Wow! For me this was exactly what I needed: a welcoming and supportive environment where I could be helped to improve my skills.

Still, the writing was proving difficult, even as recommendations for improving my arguments and prose continued to buttress my efforts. I told one group member (Norm Rosenberg) that I found the idea of writing a whole book difficult. He responded that that was not unusual and the solution commonly pursued was to publish the book as a collection of essays. It clicked for me. I took a series of published articles and rewrote them to highlight how they all were tied together around the theme of challenging the embedded biases in the discourse that framed welfare policy research. This recommendation changed everything. From there, I wrote the first draft of the book in one year, while I continued to get feedback from the writing group.[18]

Yet I still needed help to wordsmith my awkward prose. I was looking for more shoulders on which to stand and more friends to lean on. I applied for another NEH Summer Seminar, this time in social constructionism, under the tutelage of Joel Best, the chair of Sociology at the University of Southern Illinois in Carbondale.[19] The social constructionists were making waves in sociology by showing how social problems were often constructed by social movements in ways that framed issues selectively. It was a hip seminar, with great colleagues who offered to help me edit my manuscript.

I followed the Carbondale NEH seminar on social constructionism with a sabbatical back in Madison, where I worked to complete the manuscript while I taught a doctoral seminar in social welfare policy at the La Follette Institute. That seminar was its own source of inspiration and taught me yet another lesson on the sociality of scholarship. Several of the students from that seminar actively advised me on the book, encouraging me to reshape it further. They were such good students. I remain to this day friends with several of them. One of the doctoral students, Joe Soss, became more like a colleague. I advised him on his plans for a dissertation and he commented on my writing. I eventually helped him with his dissertation and then assisted in the process of editing when Joe was converting it into a book.[20] With time, we began collaborating in publishing research together. Eventually, Rich Fording, who had followed up on my research on civil disorder and the welfare explosion for his dissertation, joined us, after I reviewed an article he was to publish in the *American Journal of Political Science*. We became a three-person research collaboration that continues to this day.[21]

My Madison Fall 1993 social welfare seminar proved to me that scholarship inevitably involves not only standing on the shoulders of others who came before us, but that often "the child is the father to the man." I have learned much from my students and continue to, providing the basis for yet another aphorism. The old saw of "publish or perish" suggests that we are required to place priority on getting our research published at the expense of focusing on our teaching responsibilities, thereby perverting the educational process for the sake of keeping our jobs. Yet, my experience suggests that this is not necessarily the case. I have most often found that my research has led to more knowledgeable instruction and my teaching has afforded opportunities to improve my scholarship. My attempts to achieve synergy in the undergraduate courses I had taken at St. Lawrence might have been primarily driven by a desire to complete my assignments more efficiently, such as by using my experience as a Government major to write about the political theorist John Stuart Mill in my Victorian Literature class. Yet the synergy I sought to achieve in combining my research and teaching was more about significantly enhancing their effectiveness, rather than just saving time.

In any case, the La Follette seminar on social welfare policy in the fall of 1993 was just the most striking example of the win-win scenario that I have seen reenacted again and again in the years since. As a result, I came to believe strongly that just as my research made me someone who had something knowledgeable to profess (in that literal sense of being a professor), engaging my students in this way made me a better scholar and a researcher. And in rare instances, some of those students have become my collaborators, and in the rarest of instances long-time collaborators.

In other words, I feel fortunate to have had the opportunity to teach wonderful students and even more fortunate to have some of these students ask to work with me on my research. What I did for this to happen is beyond me. I am just thankful to have been at the right place at the right time. I was on sabbatical visiting Madison yet again, teaching but one course. It turned out to be a seminar with really exciting students, and one of those students ended up asking to collaborate with me while on his way to becoming one of the most prominent social welfare policy scholars in the country today.[22] But it gets better: Rich Fording also approached me with the idea we should collaborate after he had finished his dissertation on the Piven and Cloward thesis. Rich is, in my mind, one of the premier political scientists studying poverty politics today. Not one, but two great political scientists asked to work with me, at a time when I did not even have tenure.

And I still don't. The stress of getting tenure at Macalester took its toll on me emotionally. I had been hired originally in the midst of a legal dispute that pitted the Political Science department and the Macalester College administration over a tenure denial. The provost had told the faculty member who was to be denied tenure that if she had not been distracted having a baby she would have gotten her dissertation done in a more timely way. The chair of the Political Science Department submitted testimony on behalf of the faculty member. It was very adversarial. The administration was keen to replace the chair, but not with his hand-picked successor—me. It was not a good situation in which to take what ended up being six years to get tenure all over again (the last four years without tenure at my previous institution, after having given up the lifeline of a leave from my tenured position at Potsdam). Given the stress associated with this situation, I was not always effective in the undergraduate classroom. My evaluations in those courses, especially the introductory course, were not always strong. There were other issues about my behavior at the time that did not reflect well on me, and I still regret that deeply.

In any case, I was denied tenure in the spring of 1995. Yet, I was not the only one affected by this adversarial situation. Another member of the Political Science department was also denied tenure that year. We were 0 for 2. Actually, 0 for 3, since the woman whose lawsuit about her tenure denial was granted two-years' paid leave as part of a settlement but chose not to invoke the option to come up for tenure again. Really, 0 for 4, since another member of the department chose to leave for a visiting position elsewhere rather than come up for tenure with the chilly climate in place. (The rumor around the college was that no one had received tenure in Political Science in decades, so it might have been 0 for a whole bunch.)

The atmosphere was toxic, and not just for faculty coming up for tenure. The lawsuit had created a serious conflict. By the time of my denial, the provost was out and already back to being a professor; and the president was a few months from being let go himself. The president would run into me at 30th Street Station at Philadelphia in 2006, eleven years after I left Macalester. He was glad to see me, wanted to see our house, and seemed relieved we were doing so well at Bryn Mawr and Haverford (where Joan works). I ended up taking him to the Haverford College Holiday Party. By coincidence, he had been member of the faculty and provost at Haverford before becoming president at Macalester. He was a much-welcomed surprise guest. We all had a good time. By then, bygones were bygones.

Yet the time of the denial was an intense moment for me and my family. Where would we go, and what would happen to me and my career? Joan and I went for a walk in the Minnesota cold. But even then, I had options. Fortunately, I had just recently been offered a visiting appointment in the Political Science department at the University of Hawai'i in Manoa, main campus located in Honolulu just above Waikiki. So come the spring, we moved across the world to that wonderful place and that great school, where I would hold a visiting position in Political Science while running a policy research center in the School of Social Work.

In Hawai'i, I taught doctoral students in a theoretically vibrant Political Science department. As part of the responsibilities associated with my appointment, I was expected to work with the School of Social Work to try to better connect research and policy advocacy. I published policy briefs on social welfare issues, testified before the state legislature, and advised Governor Ben Cayetano about changes in welfare policy. At the same time, I was tapped by the state director at the Department of Human Services in Hawai'i to chair a task force on General Assistance (the main program of cash assistance for people who do not qualify for anything else). I also worked with a human services coalition to resist cutbacks in social services that were being imposed given the economic slowdown in the state at the time. I wrote a series of op-eds in the *Honolulu Advertiser* on the cutbacks and eventually on the imposition of the 1996 welfare reform legislation that got enacted in Washington, D.C., which posed a real threat to poor families in the state. I persuaded a private foundation to fund my efforts to help welfare recipients prepare testimony that would put a human face on the cutbacks. I was very busy combining research and advocacy and enjoyed the opportunity to apply the theories about the subject and put them into practice.

I stayed at Hawai'i for two years as a visitor, until I was hired as a visiting professor by the Graduate School of Social Work and Social Research at Bryn Mawr College, in 1997. I have remained a visiting professor at Bryn Mawr since then, still without tenure and evidently without any prospect of ever being granted it. For whatever reasons, once I became a visiting professor, I seemed stuck in that track. I gave up the tenure I had at Potsdam, never to get it back. All for the opportunity to pursue my scholarship. And with the help of many people, I did just that. I have regrets; but I have had a great career as well. I found my voice and learned how to express it. I got my wish.

Yet, I could have never done it without help. Scholarship can be a solitary vocation. The "life of the mind" suggests a contemplative existence. Yet, in reality, scholarship is profoundly social. It grows best from being in a vibrant intellectual community, and it ultimately serves to reinvigorate that community. Standing on the shoulders of those who came before, leaning on colleagues for the support necessary to improve our craft and complete our work, and learning from the very students we teach, all contribute to making us the scholars we ultimately become. No man is an island unto himself, and scholarship is a profoundly social process best conducted in dialogue with others.

WORDS OF WELFARE

I finally finished my book, and it was published in the summer of 1995.[23] I was so pleased. I wrote a book! It was something that I had thought would never happen. And once again, just as something significant in my life occurred it was almost immediately overtaken by events. I was now living in Honolulu, Hawai'i, getting ready to teach two graduate courses in my new department: Reimagining the Public Sphere and Political Data Analysis (a mixed methods course)—ever the polyglot. Just as the semester was to begin, the doctors called from New Jersey to tell me that my mother was dying of the cancer we had been hoping was in remission. I flew back with my younger son, while my wife took our older son to start at Reed College.

My mother was in a near-coma. I walked in, kissed her, and she awoke to my handing her a copy of the book. She opened it to see that it was dedicated to her. She held it to her chest, kissed me back, and returned to sleeping. She did not wake again until several days later, when my wife Joan walked into the room and she instantly awoke to kiss Joan, only to fall back to sleep, never to wake again. My Mom passed away about a week later. It was remarkable to see her awake those two times. In death, life reveals its mysteries. I now saw death in my Mom's passing as I had never considered it, and I wondered all the more what she had implicitly told me, in her courageous actions, about life. The contradictions continued to pile up, hidden in plain sight, experienced in real time. As sad as I was, in the end I was glad I had published my book in time for her to see it.

The book did well. In 1996, it was chosen to receive the Michael Harrington Award from the American Political Science Association for the best work published in the prior year to promote social change. It was quite an honor for me, for a number of reasons. The first thing I thought when receiving word of the award was that I had actually met Michael Harrington when I was an undergraduate and what an honor it had been then to get to sit and talk with him (even if that included my committing the faux pas of mentioning his *Playboy* article in mixed company). The second thing I thought was that Frances knew Michael Harrington very well and was his colleague at CUNY and she probably nominated my book for the award. But I never dared to ask her, because I preferred to keep it the way it was. I was content not knowing. It was perfect just as it was. *Words of Welfare* was chosen by a committee to receive the Harrington Award, and that was all I needed to know.

The book went to a second printing in fourteen months (I was counting). It was extensively cited (I did not count). In any case, I thought it was dumb luck, meaning both parts of that expression. Given everything that had happened, I thought I was really both, dumb and lucky. No more tenure, but published thanks to the good fortune of meeting and working with so many great people.

Nonetheless, as was always my case, I could not entirely enjoy the success of the book. I knew where it had weaknesses in the writing and I felt various readers knew it too. Oh God, that scared me so. Even after it won the award, I could shudder at the thought that people were actually reading the book. It felt embarrassing that my tortured prose was seen by the reading public. My contradictory impulses were at work once more. I wanted my book to be read but worried that people would notice its writing lapses. When Joe Soss told me his wonderful wife Kira was reading the book, I got really scared. Now smart people who were themselves social welfare activists and researchers were reading the book, and they were people who did not help me draft it. They were less invested in it, I thought, and will feel more freedom to rightly criticize its weaknesses without knowing the parts we agonized over. Joe later told me Kira thought the book was good; I was relieved. Then I thought: Kira is a friend. Back and forth. Eventually, I concluded I had to do better and that was the only solution. I had to keep writing. To explain what I had already written (as I am doing still with this memoir).

My good colleague Rogers Smith once said to me: "That's what we all do; we keep writing trying to get it right!" That helped to know I was not alone. But with time, I may have set the record for publishing one book after another on the same topic, reflecting my burning need to finally get it right. I am prolific; I recognize that. Is that a good thing? In the end, it could indeed be that this memoir is yet another attempt to get it right—by explaining myself, perhaps I can clarify what it was I was trying to say and why. The twist this time is that maybe knowing who I am makes clearer what I am trying to say. That's the hope, I think. If not, what's next? In any case, I keep trying and am most appreciative to have the chance to get better at what I do, to refine my craft, to strive to contribute. I really could not ask for more.

My ambivalence about the book aside, *Words of Welfare* seemed at the time to strike a chord with its full frontal critique on the discourse of poverty research. The book argued that welfare policy research was mired in a debilitating discourse reflective of its ties to the structure of power in our society. Given how most of the research at IRP and elsewhere was funded, the research reflected a reformist perspective that tended to elide important questions about why the poor were poor. The book examines a number of issues, including the drawing of the poverty line, the measurement of the homeless, the estimation of the long-term welfare dependent population, the controversy over the antipoverty effects of welfare spending, the role of racism in perpetuating poverty, the feminization of poverty, and other issues. A key part of the argument was that welfare policy research was embedded in what I called a top-down economistic-therapeutic-managerial (ETM) discourse that reinscribed the demonization of the poor as deficient. More simply, welfare policy research was tacitly preoccupied with studying individual behavior as the primary focus for understanding why the poor were poor. As result, structural issues of concerning the perpetuation of class, race, and gender hierarchies of privilege and disadvantage remained unexamined by mainstream poverty research. The best way to counteract these embedded biases was to narrate welfare policy research from a bottom-up perspective that allowed for understanding the problems of welfare and poverty from the point of view of those most directly affected by the policies.

A number of researchers enacted my recommendation. Taryn Lindhorst and Julia Padgett did just this in their award-winning analysis of domestic violence clients, emphasizing:

> [The bottom-up perspective highlighted] the subjective, narrative, and situated nature of experience. Much welfare policy research assumes a managerial perspective that has limited relevance to the day-to-day problems confronting women who rely on the social welfare safety net. Examining policy implementation processes through the bottom-up lens refocuses attention on the accounts of those who have the least access and power in the discourses concerning welfare policy.[24]

Ann Tickamyer and colleagues noted the power of a bottom-up analysis for challenging the myopia of a top-down perspective that looks at poverty as a problem to be managed rather than solved. They emphasized that welfare policy often is designed to prod recipients to change their behavior but is framed in ways that are insensitive to how policy looks and feels for the people who are affected by it. They were particularly eloquent in highlighting the embedded economistic biases of the mainstream top-down discourse:

> Welfare policy in the United States, like much other public policy, is guided by economic models that assume a rational calculus of cost and benefit for both the macro level impacts of programs and their individual beneficiaries. Thus, most policy implicitly or explicitly incorporates a behavioral model that assumes that individual actors operate as rational entities to calculate self-interest or utility and act accordingly. In this view, policy and programs should be designed to encourage policy goals through the pursuit of individual self-interest. Yet, recent critics of the welfare system have focused on the perceived failures of past programs and policies to incorporate and promote core societal values, such as economic independence and self-sufficiency, in such a way that they encourage the pursuit of these goals. Efforts to reorganize the welfare system explicitly use the sanctions and incentives of a behavioral model to promote policy objectives.

> [Our bottom-up approach examines] the behavioral assumptions embedded in political discourse on this topic and shows how the voices of women on welfare illustrate the underlying contradictions in the way policy is politically justified and implemented. The views of focus groups of welfare recipients in four rural Appalachian Ohio counties demonstrate the disparities between the top-down goals of welfare policy and the bottom-up perceptions of their outcomes. . . .
>
> If those who design welfare policies are to democratize the process of interpreting needs, welfare participants must be positioned not merely as clients but as citizens. As welfare reform moves into the evaluation phase, evaluators of policies have a second opportunity to consider this bottom-up perspective. Making welfare reform successful requires that one's status as a client not be conceived as antithetical to one's status as a democratic citizen—that clients become participants, not merely spectators in the shaping of their futures.[25]

In this example, as in *Words of Welfare*, a bottom-up discourse narrates welfare receipt as something motivated by more than simply economic incentives (contrary to much of mainstream welfare policy research). Single mothers on welfare often are thinking in terms of providing care for their children and family bonds that may override responding to economic incentives and penalties. These can be for ethical, cultural, or other value-based reasons, or they may be dictated by the perception of what is more important for long-term survival. The bottom-up approach is therefore an important counter to the insensitivity of the top-down perspective and the limited knowledge it can provide in this case. And it can be in many others as well, especially when a top-down perspective is a tool used more to govern the poor rather than to empower clients.

DO I HAVE TO PAINT A PICTURE?

The child is indeed a father to the man. My research is undoubtedly informed by how my students receive it. As I was drafting this manuscript, a doctoral student talked to me about his research. (It should be noted that for years, although a women's college, Bryn Mawr College has admitted men to graduate study.) His dissertation involves studying the debate over Gender Identity Disorder (GID). As part of a discussion about his dissertation, he recently told me the meaning of the expression, "Do I have to paint a picture?" In the context of the GID debate, this expression has come to mean: How much do you need to know about someone in order to understand what they are trying to say?[26] The argument is that people should not have to be identified in gendered terms just to be heard and understood. I agree.

Yet, to turn it around, this memoir is designed to help understand why I wrote what I wrote and the way I wrote it, so as to better understand what it means to me and perhaps then what it might mean more clearly for those who have read what I wrote before and now. For myself, telling my story about how I worked to become the scholar I became helps me better understand what I was doing and why and for what effect. It also helps me understand the process by which I got to do it.

In other words, I might not have an ambiguous gender, but I sure was ambivalent about my work and at times ambiguous in my arguments. Telling my story has been clarifying; it has been therapeutic. Painting my picture, or better yet, putting myself in the picture I was drawing helps contextualize that effort.

In this chapter, we find that I was very lucky as I struggled to make a scholarly contribution. I was lucky to have had great mentors and great friends and colleagues, as well as great students, some of whom also became great friends and colleagues. I learned from them all and without them I would have never written one book, let alone any of the eleven other books I have published since 1995 (in recent years, without smoking my brains out)!

SIX

THEORY AND PRACTICE

Research and the Court

Even before I finished *Words of Welfare*, I was already interested in applying its thesis about the discourse of welfare policy research to my own empirical investigations. I did not want to just critique welfare policy research; I wanted to enact an alternative. I wanted to apply the thesis of the book specifically to quantitative analyses to show that even the more scientifically oriented type of research that tested for statistical relationships about poverty and social welfare could be done in ways not mortgaged to the biases of a top-down, economistic-therapeutic-managerial (ETM) perspective.

WELFARE MIGRATION

I found an issue easily. At the time, debates were heating up about the old shibboleth of "welfare migration."[1] There were metaphors flying all over the place related to the idea that poor people were consciously and intentionally moving from one state to another specifically to get higher welfare benefits.[2] The discourse was definitely its own issue. State policymakers were expressing concern that they needed to act so that their states would not become "welfare magnets" that attracted more poor just because they happen to have relatively higher benefits than other states, especially those nearby. Others feared that such talk would lead to a "race to the bottom," where states would cut benefits only to see others follow suit, forcing further cuts to avoid having relatively higher benefits that continued to attract the poor. The image of a cat chasing its tail seemed to me unavoidable.

I was convinced there was a need for an analysis of the discourse and how these metaphors framed the issue in ways that reinscribed the undeservingness of the poor. I also felt it would be important to examine how these metaphors reflected a top-down ETM perspective that assumed the poor were seeking to maximize their benefits in ways that needed to be contained and managed on behalf of the interests of the state and the taxpayers. Yet I was most interested in questioning the alleged empirical facts these metaphors implied. It seemed to me that all of these metaphors were premised on assuming a supposed empirically documented reality that the poor migrated from one state to another in quest for higher benefits. I doubted it. I thought that research that was framed from a bottom-up perspective could highlight the complexities of poor people's lives and would paint a better picture than one that assumed the poor were benefit-maximizing individuals keen to get higher welfare payments to the exclusion of other concerns.[3]

It started to seem increasingly urgent that something be done to intervene in the public discourse over welfare migration. By the mid-1990s, states started getting waivers from the federal government to restrict benefits to newcomers from out of state. I wanted to collect data to analyze the issue in terms of a bottom-up discourse that highlighted an alternative understanding of the extent to which low-income families moved and why. Yet, as I recall, when I discussed this with some of my more critical-minded colleagues, some of them thought researchers should not even examine the empirical issue, because empirical research on the topic would just lend legitimacy to a canard. To some of them, to investigate empirically if in fact there were welfare migration was in effect to take seriously the idea of the self-serving welfare migrant. My colleagues feared this would just reinforce a framing of the issue of aid to the poor in tendentious ways that reinscribed the poor's undeservingness. For them, the topic came already framed; there was not another way to re-narrate it, say from the bottom up.

For others, a reframed empirical investigation might be possible, but that would only deflect attention away from the fact that even if the poor were moving from one state to another for higher benefits, the U.S. Supreme Court had already ruled years ago in the welfare rights case *Shapiro v. Thompson* (1969) that U.S. citizens had a constitutional right to travel and could not be penalized for coming into a state to receive welfare benefits. For my critical-minded colleagues, *Shapiro* had already made welfare migration a nonissue by striking down all state durational residency requirements for the receipt of welfare by outlawing provisions that discriminated against newcomers. For these colleagues, the *Shapiro* precedent invalidated the increasingly popular provisions by states that required the newly arrived applicants for welfare to receive benefits no higher than what they received in the state from where they migrated.[4]

While my colleagues had a point, it was only up to a point. The fact of the matter was that policymakers were already going basically unchallenged in sharing anecdotal stories about hordes of poor people coming into their state to get higher benefits. The mass media were starting to join in, actively reporting what I came to call these "tales of the state."[5] Everywhere I went, it seemed, in Minnesota or Wisconsin, even later in Hawai'i of all places, there was a running stream of reports on the scourge of "welfare migration." Shortly after arriving in each place where I went to teach, I would turn on the television and there would be a report about how the poor were moving there to get welfare benefits. I am not kidding you. It was as though the myth of welfare migration migrated with me, coming to reside wherever I happened to settle. This suggested to me that this tale of the state was ongoing everywhere and I just showed up to catch the latest installment each time we moved. There needed to be some push back at the empirical level. Simply pointing out that welfare recipients had a constitutional right to move around and get higher benefits was not going to cut it with this kind of demonizing political discourse circulating ever more virulently. There was instead a need to question the presumed reality or at least to renarrate it in ways that provided more insight into the extent to which welfare recipients moved, where, and why.

The need for empirical research that was done from an alternative perspective was actually increasing. Soon the discourse was going to a whole other level. Policymakers were starting to offer half-baked statistics from poorly designed studies hurriedly put together to buttress the anecdotal evidence as pure fact. I remember one incident regarding the role of bad research in polluting public discourse on the issue. It stared me in the face. It occurred when I was testifying before a committee of the Minnesota State Senate on the fact that the state's failure to raise welfare benefits for some years at that point was increasing hardship for single mothers with children who relied on public assistance just to avoid starving or becoming homeless. A state senator responded to my testimony on the decline in the buying power that came from not raising welfare benefits over a number of years. Yet he replied not by discussing that topic but by citing statistics he had requested from the state's bureaucracy that allegedly showed that people were moving to Minnesota to get higher benefits. I was providing statistics on need and his response was to wave the research equivalent of a bloody red shirt. Trotting out the welfare migration symbol and wrapping it in some numbers was supposedly meaningful public discourse about whether we needed to be better supporting low-income single mothers with children.

How I got in this situation is its own tale of the state. I had been asked to testify on behalf of the group I was working with, the Mothers Union in Minneapolis. This group was getting very concerned about the decline of welfare benefits relative to increases in the cost of living. They felt that others in the Twin Cities were not sufficiently focused on this issue. In particular, they were growing alienated from one activist's efforts in particular. Cheri Honkala (the 2012 Green Party vice presidential candidate) was emerging as an effective and inspiring antipoverty activist. A single mother on welfare herself, Cheri's focus at the time was in getting poor people to take up residence in abandoned buildings (squatting, as it was then called) as a way of dramatizing the issue of poverty. The breaking point came when one mother faced the possibility of having her child taken away from her by the county child welfare unit for reasons of neglect, because she allegedly had put the child in harm's way by living in an abandoned building.[6]

The arrest was not an accident. Cheri had a penchant for organizing protests that were intentionally structured to end with people getting arrested. It was a strategy she would continue to use for years. The idea was to create a dramatic event that got reported in the mass media and could then be used not just to get people's attention but also to rally them around helping the unfortunate folks who got arrested simply because they were trying to give voice to their concerns. It made sense, for the most part. Yet Cheri also had a habit of staging events like this without informing everyone involved.

I remember she once organized a rally at the Minnesota State Capitol in St. Paul about welfare cuts and had various groups planning to attend, including Hmong refugees whose benefits were being slashed particularly hard. A few weeks earlier, I had arranged for Frances Fox Piven to come to speak at Macalester, Hamline University, and the University of Minnesota the week that the rally was going to occur. Cheri had heard Frances was going to be in town at the time of the rally and she called me. She wondered if Frances could come and speak to the event. I told her I would ask Frances, who agreed and spoke at the rally, standing on the steps of the Capitol in front of several hundred protesters. The throng applauded Frances's talk exuberantly. I thought we were done. But then one of the organizers of the rally grabbed the microphone and requested that people move inside to the rotunda of the Capitol for a sitdown demonstration. Frances and I joined with others and moved inside.

All of sudden, behind me I heard a scuffle. The Capitol police were wrangling with Cheri and several others. It started to look ominous, with the possibility of mass arrests. I had not signed us on for this I said. Plus, what about the fact that Frances was to speak at several campuses in the area in the next two days? She could not do that while in jail. I suggested we leave and we did, via a side door of the rotunda. Many others followed us out the door while the arrests were being made behind us, handcuffs and all. I guiltily chose not to look back. Now, I must say I personally have nothing against this type of tactic, but I think participants have a right to know when they are being enlisted in it. Otherwise, they can lose custody of their children, not simply miss their speaking engagements.

The leaders of the Mothers Union wanted move away from pursuing the poverty issue by relying on these protests. They wanted to get the word out about the decline in welfare benefits in some other, less problematic ways. They had heard via the grapevine (specifically, Theresa Funiciello) that I had done analyses that statistically documented the extent of the decline in buying power that came from not raising welfare benefits, and that my results showed the declines to be particularly steep in a state such as Minnesota that formerly had relatively high benefits.[7] The Mothers Union got me on the senate committee's calendar to testify.

My testimony was very cut and dried; I avoided talking about the role of a top-down, ETM discourse and how its metaphors framed poverty issues in problematic ways. It was difficult to resist laying it all out there, but I had been counseled to stick to the facts. So just forget that deep semiotic structure of deservingness. Yet in my heart and my head I recognized that this made eminent sense. I followed my marching orders dutifully, sticking to the facts. When I finished my testimony, I thought our strategy was savvy and we had put the facts out there clearly in a way that the legislators would have to take seriously.

Then the senator who was running the hearing and had introduced me responded. He proved us wrong. He couldn't care less about my facts. He had his own, but his facts were totally off topic, wrapped in a top-down, managerial, ETM discourse, designed to reinscribe otherness in the poor. His facts were about the growing numbers of recipients from out of state. They were designed to make the idea of increasing the welfare benefit seem irresponsible, that doing anything like that would just end up bringing in more self-serving, lazy people from out of state who would then soak up more of the taxpayers' hard-earned money. His facts came in a highly politicized package of bad research and were delivered in less than five minutes in a way that suggested that statistics on welfare recipients from out of state were transparently obviously related to the topic of declining real value of welfare benefits. In other words, it went without saying that talking about undeserving migrants taking welfare was, of course, directly related to the issue of welfare benefits. The whole show was simply stunning. Right there, the senator had enacted everything we needed to warn people about but did not.[8] Sticking to facts got us nowhere.

I was startled by this very public experience. My response was that the issue had to be attacked at all levels. I was convinced now more than ever that empirical research from an alternative perspective was desperately needed. We needed both theory and facts. We had to be critical as well as empirical, political as well as scholarly. We could not afford to stay above the fray and worry that if we got involved we might be legitimating ways of demonizing the poor. The kind of self-censorship that I was arguing against in *Words of Welfare* left topics such as welfare migration to the conservatives and allowed tendentiously framed bad research to go unquestioned in ways that critically shaped public discourse.[9] This was not good. I decided to do an empirical study that would be narrated critically to address how conventional poverty research discourse framed the issue in politically biased ways. I threw myself into examining welfare migration empirically, especially quantitatively, framing my analysis from the bottom-up to resist my work being assimilated to a top-down, ETM perspective that only encouraged researchers to look at welfare recipients as self-interested economistic actors looking to maximize their gains from welfare at the expense of other considerations. The goal was to help improve public discourse by offering an alternative perspective for framing the issue and then providing evidence within that alternative frame. Pie-in-the-sky maybe, but after that dressing down in public from the senator, it was now personal as well.

At the time, the interest in welfare reform was building rapidly. President Bill Clinton had championed the "end of welfare as we knew it." The Republicans in the U.S. House of Representatives had their Contract with America that called for time-limiting welfare receipt and imposing strict work requirements while receiving the cash assistance. Wisconsin had already enacted Wisconsin Works (W-2) under Governor Tommy Thompson. Interest in doing something dramatic was growing by leaps and bounds. The word was spreading. Shortly after my visit to the state senate, I got a call from a Swedish television reporter saying she was in the area and wanted to interview me about welfare reform. Why she was there, I still do not know. Minnesota and Wisconsin have deep Scandinavian roots, which might have led to news programs in countries such as Sweden to track developments in those states. Then again, U.S. welfare reform would become a persistently discussed topic in European countries as they came to debate issues of the affordability of their own welfare systems.[10]

The reporter came to my office the next day and taped our interview. She told me she had interviewed the then-speaker of the House of Representatives, Newt Gingrich, as well as Governor Tommy Thompson. She asked me to recommend a welfare recipient and I gave her the name of the leader of the Mother's Union. That made for an interesting set of interviews about welfare reform that eventually aired on Swedish TV (though I never saw the program because the tape that was sent to me was a Betamax and I never found the means to view it). This incident underscored to me that the welfare reform issue was becoming something very big. (Even people with alien technology were interested in it.)

Now I felt I needed to get my welfare migration study done soon. I remained concerned that there was no research that pushed back on the dominant narrative about greedy welfare recipients roaming around the country looking for higher benefits. The existing research took this fable as a credible hypothesis. We had to do better or we all would end up staring at legislators spouting fake statistics that reinscribed poor people's otherness and offered no credible narrative as to why low-income single mothers sought welfare benefits in or out of state. This kind of scholarly silence would just further contribute to draconian welfare reforms passing unchallenged.

Given where I lived at the time, I felt extra urgency on the welfare migration issue. Living in the upper Midwest at that time put me at the epicenter of the welfare migration panic. Both Minnesota and Wisconsin had for years been fairly liberal states regarding the provision of welfare benefits. They had tended to have relatively high benefits but largely white populations (the upper Midwest was our Europe). This social welfare liberalism perhaps was reflective of the Scandinavian roots deeply embedded in that part of the country. Those Scandinavian roots provided a strong sense of solidarity and equity, leading to support for those who were disadvantaged. Yet, over time this changed, perhaps in part because both states became increasingly concerned about an influx of low-income African American families to cities such as Minneapolis and Milwaukee. As a result, welfare migration became a huge issue in both states. There seemed to be a preoccupation with preventing "those other people" coming here to get welfare and live off our hard-earned tax dollars. Narrating the issue in this way was undermining the strong sense of solidarity that had been in place in these previously liberal states.

In retrospect, given the changing demographics, I see how welfare remains such a hot-button issue in these states in particular. By the time the campaign to retrench welfare had succeeded, I had moved away. But then one day I was asked back to the Twin Cities to appear on a pilot for a new MSN cable news show starring, of all people, former professional wrestler turned governor and now former governor turned talk show host Jesse Ventura. His show was entitled "The Arena with Jesse Ventura." My job was to debate him about welfare issues, such as the moral hazard of becoming dependent on welfare, fraud by recipients, and even welfare migration. Ventura could be liberal on some issues, but he was a reactionary when it came to welfare. On his show, the audience voted on whether you bested the governor, and if you won, your picture was posted on his "wall of fame" (some stupid corkboard). The audience sat in bleachers to simulate a wrestling arena. We debated, At the end, the audience clapped for me and then for the governor. I, of course, lost.

On the way back to the airport, I asked the limo driver if he thought the show would be successful. The driver replied: "Many people like news shows, and lots of folks watch wrestling, but I suspect people will want to get their news separate from wrestling." He was right. The show never aired. I did not even ask for a copy of that tape.

In other words, during the run-up to welfare reform, welfare recipients were being demonized right and left, and welfare migration was presented as an issue that served to reinscribe this demonization. From rumor to gossip, to news reports, to anecdotal stories, to government statistical reports, again and again the issue was narrated in a top-down discourse that positioned welfare recipients as greedy, lazy, and out to get the best benefits they could get, to the exclusion of other considerations. I wanted to conduct empirical research that could be narrated from an alternative bottom-up perspective, so as to provide a different understanding of welfare recipients, the extent to which they moved in state or out, why they migrated from one state to another, etc. At the time, welfare reform was getting support from a massive campaign to demonize the poor, welfare migrants included. I decided I had to do my study. Even before getting shut down by Jesse Ventura, I knew what I had to do. I had to use empirical research to address the mudslinging straight on. It was time to get down and dirty with the professional mudwrestler, politician types.

RE-NARRATING WELFARE MIGRATION: A STATISTICAL PROJECT

I learned from a most unlikely source that good data for tracking welfare migration was available from the Public Use Microdata Set (PUMS) of the U.S. Census. Carol Stack, the brilliant ethnographer, had come to Macalester College and spoken about her study of African Americans returning to the South.[11] At the time, she was using the PUMS to track migration patterns. An ethnographer, of all people, was the one who alerted me where to go to get good statistical data for my topic. It was just further evidence of the value of crossing disciplinary boundaries, mixing up methodological specializations, and reworking other precious distinctions in the academy.

I enlisted Gary Krueger, my good friend and colleague, a very thoughtful and creative, Madison-trained economist whose office was located one floor above mine in our social science building at Macalester. We got the data from the Census. (Back then, the data came on CDs, one for each of the ten federal regions, if you can believe it. Now you can just download the data for the whole country from the Census Web page.) We labored long and hard with the data, eventually publishing several articles over several years, culminating with an article that appeared in the *American Journal of Political Science* in 1998 co-authored with my statistically competent colleague Larry Nitz from the University of Hawai'i. By then I was at Bryn Mawr College, having left Hawai'i in 1997 and Macalester two years prior to that.

With these articles, I felt we had delivered on the promise in *Words of Welfare* to conduct a bottom-up analysis of the issue. Our articles resisted narrating the poor's migration choices in a top-down, ETM discourse that construed the poor in the narrowly economistic terms as greedy and lazy people who intentionally sought to maximize their welfare benefits to the exclusion of other concerns.[12]

At the time we published the article in the *American Journal of Political Science*, Ken Meier was the editor. He had been a supportive colleague in Madison, and was now helping me get our article published. He was improving many things at the *Journal*. He enforced deadlines for reviews and greatly shortened the turnaround time between submission and publication. He also instituted a format for abstracts at the beginning of the articles, to make it clear what the empirical focus was in each case. Each abstract comprised separate sections specifying the research question, hypothesis, method, data, findings, and conclusions. This added clarity to each piece. Yet when our article was published, our abstract looked a little funny to me. since our critical-minded, bottom-up approach did not quite fit the scientific format that all the abstracts were expected to have:

> *Theory*: Stories of welfare migration are often statistical narratives of economic rationality that portray welfare migrants as engaging in economically rational but illegitimate behavior. Three waves of scholarly studies of welfare migration can be delineated as reinforcing these stories with second-wave studies in particular providing evidence of welfare migration. Yet, it is questionable that: (1) state welfare benefits vary enough to induce welfare migration; (2) high levels of migration actually occur; and (3) the migration patterns of poor families ought to be narrated as economically rational behavior directed toward the maximization of welfare benefits.
>
> *Hypotheses*: Variation in the real value of welfare benefits is small. Welfare migration is an infrequent occurrence making for a small proportion of the total welfare budget. Better explanations narrate the migration patterns of poor families in terms other than those narrowly focused on welfare benefits.
>
> *Methods*: Data on welfare benefits and per capita income is used to assess the real value of welfare benefits. Data from the Public Use Microdata Set 5% sample of the United States Census is used to track the migration routes of poor single mothers with children.
>
> *Results*: Combined maximum benefits from Aid to Families with Dependent Children and Food Stamps are found to vary across the states only slightly more than per capita income. Approximately

> 90% of poor single mothers with children are not likely to move out-of-state over a five year period. Poor single mothers with children are not more likely to move to states with higher benefits. Narratives that account for alternative reasons, including increased safety, improved housing, better economic opportunities, and family ties, should be explored as explanations of the migration patterns of poor single mothers with children.[13]

The abstract read to me as a square peg in a round hole. We were questioning the implied biases of the dominant discourse of objectivistic welfare migration research; however, our article was framed by the abstract in a format that suggested it was just another straightforward empirical investigation. The last two sentences of the abstract, though, made the critical point: "Poor single mothers with children are not more likely to move to states with higher benefits. Narratives that account for alternative reasons, including increased safety, improved housing, better economic opportunities, and family ties, should be explored as explanations of the migration patterns of poor single mothers with children." We needed to study the topic from the bottom-up in terms of how low-income single mothers confronted their circumstances. And if we did we would find that the top-down economistic perspective misconstrued their decision calculus and led us away from considering alternative factors affecting their decisions to move in or out of state.

The article garnered a lot of attention, some good, some bad. One colleague joked that it was my swan song to empirical science. Others were keen to use our study as providing hard evidence to push back against the attempts to reestablish residencies requirements. Civil rights lawyers were particularly interested.

There were others who were more querulous. Steven Wasby, a courts and constitution scholar who had come to SUNY-Albany after my graduating, wrote me a letter saying that as much as he was impressed with our empirical research, we blew the citation of the *Shapiro v. Thompson* case where the U.S. Supreme originally struck down durational residency requirements. He noted we had incorrectly stated that the decision had specified that the Ninth Amendment to the Constitution included an implied right to travel. That was wrong; the decision does not specify where in the Constitution there is an implied right to travel. Instead, the decision simply asserted there was one. Oops! Wasby wrote to me that perhaps Albany should rescind my PhD! Gosh, that was cruel. Just for a footnote? Maybe footnotes are more important than I thought. (The worst part of this reminder about my inattentiveness was that a colleague who had read a draft of the paper had told me I had to delete the reference to the Ninth Amendment and I had forgotten to do that. Evidently, I was still prone to lapsing into cluelessness as I worked to publish my work in a timely way.) So it seems that I still needed to find a way to improve the quality of my work while keeping it relevant to ongoing political struggles.

Nonetheless, mistakes and all, the phone kept ringing. Next, Joel Handler called me. He remains to this day a leader in the field of legal aid for the poor.[14] He had been contacted by the American Civil Liberties Union (ACLU) and the National Organization of Women's Legal Defense Fund. They were preparing the case that would go to the U.S. Supreme Court to challenge the new option given states under the 1996 welfare reform law to reinstitute the kind of residency requirements that had been struck down with *Shapiro v. Thompson* in 1969. The Personal Responsibility and Work Opportunity Reconciliation Act of 1996 (PRWORA), aka welfare reform, gave states the option to impose residency requirements that said that a recipient who had lived in the state for less than two years could receive benefits no higher than those she had received in her prior state of residence if the benefits in the prior state were below the benefit level of the current state. This kind of durational residency requirement was designed to discourage recipients from moving to another state to get higher benefits.

What was Congress thinking by reinstituting a practice that had been ruled by the Court as violating an implied constitutional right to travel? Perhaps people in Congress thought that *Shapiro* only struck down state bans on receiving any assistance but not laws that provided for a lower benefit. Yet a close reading of *Shapiro* indicated that the Court's decision had actually struck down all durational residency requirements of any kind for the receipt of welfare. Perhaps people in Congress were thinking that since PRWORA abolished Aid to Families with Dependent Children (AFDC) and replaced it with Temporary Assistance for Needy Families (TANF) the old decision did not apply. In any case, the Supreme Court took the case, and now briefs were being prepared.

Joel had been asked by the ACLU and NOW welfare rights lawyers involved in the case to draft an *amicus curiae* (Friend of the Court) brief that reviewed the empirical research on the issue of welfare migration. Joel decided that my work was at the center of the empirical debate and wanted me to co-author a brief with him and then have social scientists knowledgeable on the topic co-sign it. We did that, and got more than forty social scientists to sign on.[15] Joel, it turns out, is not just a brilliant leader in our field; he is a warm and generous person who thoughtfully includes others in his efforts in ways that are nothing less than touching. It was at this point that I learned that Joel was also from Newark. This came up when I had asked why he had recruited a lawyer from Newark to be our counsel of record for our Social Scientists' Friend of the Court Brief. I thought that was incredibly thoughtful. Ever loyal, Joel remembered where we came from and made that a tacit part of our efforts.

Next, Joel helped spread the word by co-authoring with my Madison mentor Linda Gordon a piece about the case in the *Nation* magazine.[16] In that piece, they drew from the research we had reported on in the brief. In particular, they noted one important finding. In an article I had published with Joe Soss, we had estimated that even in those limited instances when a low-income single mother moved to a higher benefit state she lost about 62 percent of the increase in welfare benefits due to higher housing costs.[17] In the piece in the *Nation*, Handler and Gordon explained that not only did citizens have the constitutional right to move from one state to another and still receive welfare as needed, low-income single mothers most often did not move to higher benefit states when leaving one state for another; and when they did, they lost sixty-two cents of each dollar of increased welfare benefits due to increased housing costs. There was no footnote, but the reference was unmistakably to our original research. No one else had made that estimate. In fact, all of the statistical estimates cited (but not footnoted) in the article came from the brief and were based on my research with Joe and others that I had published previously.

I was delighted. While I did not become a footnote, something better happened. I had become "research" itself. The article called it "recent studies," but the only research being discussed was mine. Wow, I was all of research! From my perspective, the article was studded with funny locutions: "recent studies," "actual migration figures," "a national study," "nationally," etc. All of these global terms referred to my work, mostly my work with Joe. The way I looked at it was that I was honored to stand in for the "truth."

Yet that kind of slippage from my research to what had to be taken as the "truth" also caught me up short. I knew better than most that there was room for debate over my findings, even as we confirmed them across a number of investigations. I could not but question this kind of phraseology, which implied to me that what I had found was what everyone would find. It showed to me the limitations of editorial writing. Footnotes served not just to credit the work of people like me but to specify the specific sources, and therefore the limits, of the facts being cited. I was not all research; my findings were not all that conclusive.

Nonetheless, I enjoyed seeing all of it. I had now become what we might call an "un-footnote." In any case, my research with others was contributing to the good cause of increasing access to needed welfare benefits. And that was what mattered, not whether I was a footnote or not.

The case we were pushing on the Supreme Court highlighted that this was no mere academic issue. It was a case where human need was great and relief was urgently needed for hundreds of thousands of single mothers in the United States who were being actively discriminated against. The two women represented in the case stood for many others. We understood that; so did they. Each of these two courageous women was both moving home to California while extricating herself from an abusive relationship. If they were forced to get the lower benefit that reflected what they would have gotten in the states where they had lived previously, they could not afford to live in the California communities where they relocated. The cost of housing was too high. Welfare benefits, even at the low level recipients got, were an important women's resource for combating domestic violence. The idea that these were selfish, lazy women simply seeking higher benefits was far off the mark, and it was depressing to think that policy was being enforced in ways that were so ignorant of their situation. It could make you cry thinking just how obtuse was welfare policy, just how tone-deaf it was, clueless to its myopia, dismissive of these women's legitimate needs. Our research was designed to offer evidence from a perspective that was more sensitively attuned to how these women experienced welfare policy's limitations.

On January 13, 1999, the day of the oral arguments, I went with others to the Court. I dragged along Joan and our two kids, the oldest graduating from college, the other in high school. But it turned out to be not just important but fun. We sensed this as the drama unfolded before our eyes. Let's put it this way: attending the arguments of a Supreme Court case is great free entertainment available in our nation's capital. In this case, watching the exchange between the lawyers and the justices was nothing less than riveting. We were totally engaged and so, it seemed, were everyone else in the packed courtroom.

Why was it so entertaining? We, admittedly, had a vested interest in an important case. Yet part of it is due to the fact that the U.S. Supreme Court is just so much theatre. The justices take themselves very seriously. To start, they appear from behind curtains. It reminded me of my sixth grade class play. And those robes! Further, the presentations were delivered like onstage dialogues. A lawyer starts to present and the justices immediately interrupt, and the back-and-forth continues for a half-hour and then they turn to the poor soul representing the other side, who then has to undergo the same sort of grilling. Costumes, curtains, and dialogue; what more could you ask for? And it is free. And it matters! You should check it out.

What was most impressive was the quality of the performances. The lawyers, of course, were prepared. Yet what surprised me was that the justices knew the welfare migration case inside and out. Unbelievably, they were also familiar with the empirical research. I concluded they were all well briefed. But there was more. They knew that people were paying attention to everything they said. Associate Justice Ruth Bader Ginsburg seemed to have a soundbite prepared: "Citizens get to choose their states; but states do not get to choose their citizens!" Wow! You could campaign on that. Maybe she was.

Not everything that happened that day at the Court was reassuring. Associate Justice Clarence Thomas performed true to form (as others had warned me) and slept through most of the questioning (as I was saddened to see). Yet, at the same time, Associate Justice Antonin Scalia, I am convinced, winked directly at me when he stated: "Everyone knows welfare recipients move from one state to another to get higher benefits." That might have been too much alertness on my part.

In the end, Scalia voted with the majority to overturn durational residency requirements (probably on freedom of mobility grounds anticipating some kind of "business-as-person" logic, or some such extension of our argument in the case for a constitutional right to mobility), while Thomas awoke at some point to go back and write a dissent (on "I don't trust welfare cheats" grounds or something like that). Yet, overall, I was most pleased that the arguments seemed to go our way. Later, at the headquarters for the American Civil Liberties Union, the lawyers, the researchers, and our friends and supporters all celebrated. The justices had grilled the lawyers representing California more critically than they had ours. We were thinking we might win. We had to wait until the decision was handed down, sometime in the spring.

In May, the decision was finally announced while Joan and I were attending our older son's commencement at Reed College. We had won, seven to two. I found out when a reporter from National Public Radio called to interview me about the role of the research in the process. It turns out the role was minimal at best. The justices, it seems, prefer to base their decisions on legal principle, not social science evidence. We made it into a footnote in the majority opinion written by Associate Justice Ginsburg that said the financial burden on the states should not be a consideration since the research (there it was again) had shown the welfare migration was a minor phenomenon.[18] The opinion stated:

> The Solicitor General also suggests that we should recognize the congressional concern addressed in the legislative history of PRWORA that the "States might engage in a 'race to the bottom' in setting the benefit levels in their TANF . . . programs." Again, it is difficult to see why that concern should be any greater under TANF than under AFDC. The evidence reviewed by the District Court indicates that the savings resulting from the discriminatory

> policy, if spread equitably throughout the entire program, would have only a miniscule impact on benefit levels. Indeed, as one of the legislators apparently interpreted this concern, it would logically prompt the States to reduce benefit levels sufficiently "to encourage emigration of benefit recipients." But speculation about such an unlikely eventuality provides no basis for upholding § 11450.03.[19]

It was all a big deal for me. I had worked with others to do research that mattered. If you stop and think about it, welfare rights are a big deal. They can be a critical lifeline for many women. Our society seemed not to see it that way, but we narrated our research that way and our findings played some small part in the effort to get the Court to stand up for those women and their ability to exercise their fundamental rights as U.S. citizens. On the day my older son graduated from college, a reporter from public radio called, giving us an extra reason to celebrate.

REVISITING SCHRAM, NITZ, AND KRUEGER

The case might have ended it, but in social science, once a hobbyhorse has been created people keep riding it long after playtime is over. The issue of whether we and others had appropriately measured welfare migration continued long after the question was moot. The piece that was most critical of my work in this area was published by Michael Bailey in the *American Political Science Review*. It was painful to see such a critique on such a highly visible disciplinary stage. Bailey rightly pointed out that our statistical analyses were not the most sophisticated. He was keen to focus on the limitations in our simplified statistical models tracking the migration patterns of low-income single mothers. He was especially critical of the paper I had co-authored with Larry Nitz and Gary Krueger that had appeared in the *American Journal of Political Science* a year before the *Sanez* decision was handed down.[20] Bailey even had a section of his article entitled "Revisiting Schram, Nitz and Krueger." Nothing like having someone put your name up in lights (neon-flashing), just in case anyone missed the point of the critique.

Yet Bailey's more sophisticated analysis showed only a marginal welfare magnet effect. More importantly, his major finding corroborated my argument, stated in several articles, that when low-income single mothers moved out of state it was most often for reasons unrelated to maximizing welfare benefits and instead addressed such matters as reestablishing family ties in a time of need. In his conclusions, Bailey wrote of his findings:

> The results validate prior indications that family ties fundamentally influence residential choice. In all specifications, birth state effects

> are huge. These effects dwarf welfare effects, supporting Schram, Nitz, and Krueger's (1998, 228) rejection of narratives in which poor single mothers narrow-mindedly and illegitimately—if economically rationally—flock to states with higher benefits. These results imply that poor single mothers are as likely—or even more likely to move home as everyone else. But more importantly for the vast literature on welfare and migration, the results also indicate that welfare benefits exert a nontrivial effect on state residential choice.[21]

So it turns out we were unsophisticated but largely right. I can live with that. I agree that we need to refine our techniques and always try to improve our methods. Yet, we should not be preoccupied with technique as an end in itself. In fact, when you think about it, is this not the major concern about social science today? The social sciences have a tendency to become overly enamored with technique at the expense of paying attention to relating research to people's lives in ways that can make a difference. We should conduct our research while there is still a chance that it will relate to the policy deliberations concerning the subject we are investigating. Yes, some issues come around again. Welfare migration will probably be back on the congressional agenda in the next twenty years. But why continue to pick at it right after the U.S. Supreme Court has disposed of the issue?

For me, the central issue is that we need to do a better job connecting our research to our politics in ways that make a difference. I am glad that we can refine our techniques (especially when they prove I am still right), but I would rather be unsophisticated in ways that are both right and politically effective than just to refine my technique irrespective of what is going on in the world. Social science can be related to society in ways that matter, and we need to think more about how to do that.

My work on welfare migration grew out of an incident in the political arena and was focused on contributing to public discourse. I tried to make my investigations relevant to ongoing political deliberations. In the process of completing my work in a timely way, I admittedly rushed things and made some mistakes; however, our research overall was basically sound and was taken seriously by those involved in public deliberations.

Further, we conducted the research in ways that were attentive to political biases, and sought to anticipate its political uses. We narrated our empirical investigations from the bottom up, in ways that were sensitive to how the people directly affected by welfare policy experienced it. As a result, our work added evidence that was being neglected by researchers who, thinking they were being objective, narrated their statistical analyses from a top-down perspective that saw the poor in selective terms as strictly out to maximize their returns from receiving welfare. Our research helped shed light on how welfare was an important "women's resource" needed by women who were seeking support in times of need, such as when extricating themselves from an abusive relationship. Our politically attuned and politically timed work was part of the political effort to ensure that low-income single mothers with children were able to exercise their constitutional rights as citizens. It might not have been research conducted in the most sophisticated ways, but it was research that mattered.

SEVEN

IS ANYBODY LISTENING?

Testifying before Congress

Social scientists turn out to be only part of the troubled equation relating thought to action, theory to practice, research to policy. Even when they try to connect, not all their fellow human beings out there in the real world are open to hearing what they have to say. Some of those fellow human beings are policymakers who pretend to care about what research says but often really do not. I had good reason to believe this from everything I had read for years, but then one day I got to study the problem up close. Five years after welfare reform had been enacted, I was asked to testify before Congress about its effects.

In 1996, after years of debate about whether there were too many people on welfare, the critics of the system got their wish when President Bill Clinton signed into law the Personal Responsibility and Work Opportunity Reconciliation Act (PRWORA). It abolished the main cash assistance program for the poor—Aid to Families with Dependent Children (AFDC), originally enacted during the Great Depression, as part of the Social Security Act of 1935. Welfare reform essentially ended the entitlement to welfare for low-income families with children. Most of the families receiving welfare were the poorest of the poor and were headed by single mothers. What the law actually did was replace AFDC with a block grant program—Temporary Assistance for Needy Families (TANF)—that states could use in a variety of ways, but with a catch: they had to meet quotas in moving recipients off the welfare rolls and into jobs or face financial penalties. The law put in place time limits for the receipt of cash assistance from TANF, as well as work requirements for those receiving assistance, sanctions (i.e., financial penalties) for failure to comply with welfare-to-work rules, and a variety of other policies and procedures, all designed to send a strong signal that the poor should practice personal responsibility by not relying on welfare and instead provide for themselves as much as possible by taking whatever jobs the economy made available, even if those jobs left them poor (which is what happens most of the time).[1]

Enacted when the economy was strong, welfare reform came on line as the rolls declined rapidly. Between 1994 and 2008, the number of AFDC/TANF recipients in the United States declined by about 72 percent.[2] While this decline had been widely trumpeted as a sign of the reform's success in ending welfare dependency by getting recipients to leave the welfare rolls for work, there is strong evidence that the reform law has greatly reduced access to assistance by families that need it.[3] Between 1994 and 2005, the percentage of TANF-eligible families receiving aid from the program decreased from 84 percent to only 40 percent.[4] This figure is undoubtedly lower since the onset of the Great Recession. There have been growing rates of poverty that increased the number of families that need assistance but there has also been a lack of growth (and even a continued decline in many states) in the TANF rolls. In addition, there has been increasing concern over the expanding population of "disconnected" mothers, defined as the percentage of mothers who report themselves as neither working nor receiving welfare. According to some estimates, the size of this population doubled between the mid-1990s and mid-2000s and now stands at 20–25 percent (depending on the precise definition) of all low-income women.[5]

Welfare reform had abolished the welfare entitlement and imposed time limits, work requirements, and other restrictions on access to aid. In fact, welfare reform basically resulted in Clinton's getting to deliver on his 1992 campaign promise to "end welfare as we know it," by shifting away from cash assistance as the main form of aid and focusing more of the expenditures on services designed to promote work.[6] In fact, given that TANF was a block grant that states could use in a variety of ways, by 2000 more than half the TANF block grants monies going to all the states were being spent on services other than cash assistance to the poor.[7] Most of those services were associated with moving welfare recipients into jobs as quickly as possible. Welfare policy had moved from providing cash aid to needy families with children to disciplining the heads of those families (mostly single mothers) to make sure they took even the most meager-paying jobs.

By 2012, state legislators all across the country were in full pursuit of demonizing anyone who dared to take cash assistance. The economic fallout of the Great Recession of 2008–09 continued to roil the public, and policymakers were quick to find scapegoats to blame for why the economy continued to stagnate. The old reliable welfare queen was trotted out again and again in state after state. This time, the idea was that many welfare recipients were not just cheats but drug users who were illegitimately draining off public resources that could be used to jump-start the economy (probably in the form of even more tax cuts than the ones under presidents Ronald Reagan and George W. Bush that had starved the federal government of needed funding).

Bill after bill was submitted to require drug testing of applicants (even though welfare recipients who use illicit drugs are as rare as those imagined illegal voters these same legislators were now pointing to in order to impose voting restrictions that also disproportionately disadvantage the poor).[8] A state legislator in Wisconsin proposed a bill stating that single parenting was a form of child abuse and calling for a public education campaign to prevent it.[9] Rick Santorum, the former U.S. Senator from Pennsylvania and in 2012 a candidate for the Republican presidential nomination, reiterated his long-standing wish to require paternity testing of the children of all mothers who apply for welfare. Then there was the Mitt Romney presidential campaign advertisement that flat-out lied in claiming that the Obama administration was gutting work requirements and letting welfare recipients just stay at home and "they send you a check." The Romney campaign consistently used language that suggested that Obama was coddling the poor who refused to play by the white, middle-class rules of work and family.[10]

So it was that the country was once again easily caught up in a competition to scapegoat the poor as a source of our economic woes, this time in the aftermath of the Great Recession of 2008–09. The focus on welfare seemed a throwback, but then again it was proving to be the old standby for fanning the flames of racial resentment that played on the worst stereotypes. A temporary extension of welfare reform passed through the gridlocked Congress during early 2012, but it prohibited recipients from accessing benefits from ATM machines located near liquor stores and gambling operations (as if recipients drank and gambled at high rates, which they do not). All this worst kind of demonization went on while states did nothing about declining benefits and the declining number of poor families that could access even those meager benefits. Tim Casey, a leading expert on welfare reform wrote: "Benefit amounts are far below the official poverty level in every state and only 28% of poverty in the state with the median benefit amount. The number of children receiving TANF is now less than 25% of the number of poor children."[11]

From my perspective, the main problem at the time I was asked to testify was how welfare policy discourse framed the issue (that is, so that we would view only some aspects of the welfare picture and not others). Welfare policy discourse has for the last few decades been mired in a preoccupation with ending "dependency" rather than focusing on the underlying problem of poverty. Since the 1970s, welfare policy discourse has presented the issue so that people on welfare are visible within the picture frame but nature and causes of the poverty that has forced them to rely on government assistance have been framed out of the picture. The result is an image of the problem that suggests that the recipients themselves, who are trapped in a welfare system that does nothing to encourage them to change their attitudes and behavior so that they might become self-sufficient, are the cause of their own distress. The frame has emerged from what was known for a long time as the "culture of poverty" argument, and it now dominates welfare policy discourse.[12]

Given my experience testifying before the state senate in Minnesota a few years earlier, I knew that if I were going to testify before Congress about the effects of welfare reform, I was not going to just dump a bunch of facts on the table for a congressional committee to choose to consider or ignore. Instead, I was committed to first questioning the prevailing frame of welfare policy discourse that, then as now, focused on reducing dependency irrespective of whether that effort would increase poverty for many families.

At the time, Joe Soss and I had just completed an article about framing in welfare policy discourse.[13] We argued that, beginning in the 1970s, various policy actors had begun to offer a new frame for viewing the issue. Once the welfare rolls had grown in the 1960s, and in particular after African Americans had begun to receive assistance in greater numbers, conservatives in particular had commenced a campaign to change the terms of debate on welfare. The issue was no longer poverty, but instead, the real problem, they argued, was what they called "welfare dependency." This argument built on the idea that there was a culture of poverty that sapped poor people of their motivation to become self-sufficient and focused on how the welfare system actually reinforced that lack of motivation. In other words, the poor were poor not because they lacked money but because welfare was sapping them of their motivation. They had become "dependent" on welfare in ways that made them incapable of focusing on becoming self-sufficient via participation in the job market.

The focus on dependency medicalized the issue. Welfare dependency was to be seen as akin to chemical dependency. As a result, the dependency frame brought forth its own therapeutic locutions. Welfare recipients were suffering the economic equivalent of addiction, for which the logical response was not to give them more money but to treat them for that addiction. Proposals for reform were framed to make welfare the policy equivalent of a twelve-step program, where recipients were taught how to take the steps necessary to become economically self-sufficient.[14] The vocabulary of a changing welfare policy discourse reframed the issue in ways that suggested specific changes in policy and programming that shifted toward treating recipients for their medicalized condition. Instead of money, what recipients needed was treatment, in the form of counseling, classes, monitoring, and a step-by-step process that encouraged them to leave welfare and get a job.

The dependency frame proved to be powerful, in part at least because it was backed by powerful interests. Beginning in the 1970s, economic conservatives led by a coalition of business lobbies adopted this argument into their efforts to turn back the welfare state and reassert the priority of the market. Particular business interests had specific material goals: by pushing the poor out of welfare and into low-wage work, employers hoped to lighten their tax burden and, more important, prevent tight labor markets from enhancing the bargaining position of labor or pushing wages upward. Their coalition gained important allies when moral conservatives entered the fray representing a broader countermovement against changes in gender and race relations, consumption patterns, and sexual and familial norms that they saw as evidence of moral decline. The new frame was championed far and wide by both economic and moral conservatives. Throughout the 1980s and 1990s, foundations, with funds supplied by donors from both conservative camps, promoted a string of influential critics whose books charged that welfare encouraged perverse behavioral choices, flouted the obligations of citizenship, and undermined the voluntarism of civil society.[15] Soon, such critics were joined by government officials who saw political capital to be gained by attacking federal welfare programs and shifting control over welfare resources to the state level. The frame stuck when liberals were forced to defend an unpopular program that they themselves perceived as inadequate, and as a result failed to establish a positive alternative to the dependency frame for debating the future shape of welfare policy. By the 1990s, the push to end welfare dependency had become bipartisan.

The discourse of welfare dependency framed the issue in ways that inevitably affected how research was conducted. The dependency frame implied that if the problem was that people were too dependent on welfare, then the solution was to get them to leave. As a result, government and foundation funding ended up disproportionately going to what were called "leaver studies," which tracked people who left welfare. The research focus on "leavers" followed from discourse that framed the issue as one of reducing dependency on welfare rather than eliminating poverty. Joe Soss and I had argued that this selective dependency framing with a focus on getting people off welfare led researchers away from studying what happened to the people who were being denied access to welfare. Nobody was really pursuing what could have been called "arriver studies." As result, the research assumed from the onset that the key explanation for the decline in the number of recipients was derived from people leaving, not from people not arriving. Eventually, we would discover that this was not true, and in fact with time the number of families eligible but not receiving assistance would mushroom along with the number of families that were mired in "deep" poverty (i.e., below one-half the poverty line).

The frame of welfare dependency led to a biased focus on getting those currently on welfare to leave, when in fact it was at least as important to track what happened to those people who did not get onto the welfare rolls, even though they needed to. More and more of them were being forced into deep poverty because they could not access needed assistance. Now we know better. Then, I only knew that the frame was biased and allowed us to tell only part of the story, in ways that I suspected made welfare reform look like the success it really was not. If I were going to appear before Congress to testify on welfare reform, I wanted my testimony to highlight this fundamental flaw in the research-policy connection.

A MINOR DISTRACTION FROM THE MODEST PROPOSAL

When welfare reform was enacted in 1996, it was authorized for five years, so that in 2001, it was up for reauthorization. The initial congressional hearing on reauthorization was scheduled in the U.S. House of Representatives for the Committee on Education and the Workforce, to be held by the Subcommittee on 21st Century Competitiveness. (It was a funny-sounding name for a congressional committee. To me, it was difficult to believe that a committee in Congress actually had a campaign slogan for a name. Then again, Congress largely conducts its business in ways that first and foremost facilitate its members getting reelected, as political scientists long ago astutely pointed out.[16])

I was contacted by Wendy Mink, a prominent scholar on welfare policy who was working to help her mother Rep. Patsy Mink (D-HI), my former congressperson, recruit witnesses for the hearing. Wendy asked if I could testify and I agreed. At the time, I was preparing to give the keynote address at a conference in Tampere, Finland, on narrative and public policy. (By no coincidence, I was talking about framing in welfare policy discourse, but this time focused on the role of images.) Almost immediately after I responded to the e-mail request asking me to testify, Wendy wrote to say that the hearing might have to be postponed, though she did not say why. I was soon to find out. It was afternoon in Finland but morning on the east coast of the United States. The date was September 11. Quickly, people were talking. A colleague said I should go to a television. I saw the second plane go into the South Tower of New York City's World Trade Center. Oh God, I thought, what the hell is happening!

Many crazy things were said that day and the next, whether when I was trying to contact my wife back in Pennsylvania (phone operators in Finland do not normally speak English) or in conversation with colleagues. The most perplexing was when a colleague from Israel approached me after my talk about racial imagery in welfare policy discourse (see next chapter) and, rather than comment on my talk, blurted out: "Now you know how we feel!" Maybe she was right, but all I was feeling was numbness. I was not fully present, and was not interested in bonding with anyone over how we shared being targeted by terrorists.

Trying to get home proved to be still another encounter with my Jewishness. At first, I could not fly to Heathrow, outside of London, to connect with a US Airways flight to Philadelphia. Then, after an extra few days of delay, I was told that I could catch a flight home. I flew to Heathrow and immediately was told there were no flights going to Philadelphia at all. A woman from US Airways took me aside and said that there was seating available on a flight to Kennedy International Airport, since many people were refusing to risk flying to New York after what had happened. At first, I was not sure whether she was talking straight with me. She wore a US Airways uniform but was behind a British Airways desk. I asked if she was with US Airways and she said: "We nicked their booths." This did not help since I did not know what "nicked" meant (and when I did find out, I found that it is not legal). Yet I said I was game, and she took me to the gate. On the plane, I discovered that most of the passengers of the mostly empty plane were Hasidic, Ultra-Orthodox Jews seeking to get home to Brooklyn. The folks around me were very friendly but did not really say much of anything to me during the flight other than the usual "excuse me" to get by and such. Yet, as the plane began its approach to the airstrip, everyone held out their hands to hold. I was not a big fan of the Ultra-Orthodox and their politics concerning Israel (they seemed to me to be active in doing whatever they could do to drive the politics of that country far to the right). Yet what was I to do on this day, just post-9/11? I hesitated and then clasped others' hands in unison, as we descended to the ground bonded now as politically strange bedfellows. We landed safely.

The next challenge was to get home to Philadelphia. I got a seat on a van going to the Philadelphia airport, and the driver offered to drop me downtown, where Joan could pick me up. The eight or so of us on the van were strangers to each other, and no one spoke a word until we were crossing the Verrazano Bridge that connects Staten Island to New Jersey. As we looked out the side windows of the van, we could see Ground Zero, the smoke still pumping up from the hole in the ground in a massive plume that arced high in the sky and bent over until it hit the horizon, as if the smoke went all the way back to Europe from where I had just come. The remaining buildings at the World Trade Plaza were seared by black arched stripes, burned into them by the fires that still smoldered in the ground in front of them. Gone were the twin towers that had constituted the permanent face of lower Manhattan. The magnitude of the attacks was now palpably real, staring us right in the face. Everyone started talking at once, saying how horrible it was, where we were when it happened, whether we lost anyone there, who we were, how we were all bonded together, if only for that one moment.

Back home, Joan reiterated what she had said on the phone to me when I was still stranded in Finland: "We will never be the same!" And we are not. The country changed that day, and as a people we did as well (if not in the same way). The Patriot Act, the War on Terror, war in two countries simultaneously, from the mundane nuisance of heightened airport security to the body counts, we became a country now preoccupied with fighting a different sort of enemy that was neither a government or a people but a network of radicals in opposition to the United States and its relationship to oppressive governments in the Islamic world. Yet I agreed with the slogan of the first rallies taking issue with how the United States was responding: my grief was not a cause for war. With time, Americans would tire of waging war on multiple fronts, and we became desperate to find a better way to ensure security against terrorists while trying to be responsible members of the world community.

None of this great disturbance necessarily had to relate to the issues of poverty and welfare, but as is often the case in U.S. politics, things not related the poverty and welfare end up affecting our ability as a people to address fundamental issues of need. Just as the War on Poverty got derailed by the war in Vietnam, now the War on Terror was taking us away from continuing the fight against poverty at home. Sometimes it seemed to me that we acted as a society that wished to deny the persistence of poverty in the midst of our plenty—if not quite a people open to considering Jonathan Swift's satirical "modest proposal" to eat poor babies as a solution to poverty.[17] It was as though any distraction could take us off-course, perhaps because we have never been all that committed to staying on-course.

In the years since 9/11, the number of households living in poverty has risen, eventually at an unprecedented rate during and after the Great Recession of 2008–09,[18] as has the rate for "deep" poverty (i.e., the number of families with incomes below one-half the poverty line).[19] A major reason for these increases has been the decline in access to cash assistance from the government among families headed by someone who was not working. One group that has become the focus of growing attention is those "disconnected" mothers (who are neither working nor getting welfare).[20] Yet the country has been financially strapped fighting the War on Terror, and the federal government has had to focus on bailing out the banks and trying to restore economic stability first, such that addressing the dire need of those on the bottom of the socioeconomic order is once again a lower priority, ever to be infinitely deferred.

TESTIFYING: A QUESTION OF DISCOURSE

Back in 2001, I did not know how bad it would get (who can predict that a state legislator would want to pass a law stating that single parenting constitutes child abuse?), but I had some inkling. For this initial welfare reform reauthorization hearing, I wanted to testify to share my concern that the new restrictions of welfare reform were not the success they had been cracked up to be. Already by 9/11 the economy was slowing; but when the reauthorization hearings for welfare reform started later that month, members of Congress were not ready to seriously consider addressing the deficiencies of welfare reform. For the first few years after welfare reform was enacted, it was largely considered a success, because it had reduced the number of families on the welfare rolls.[21] I was convinced that any testimony I provided would be given marginal consideration at best. I assumed I would be an outlier. I had already written in *Words of Welfare* that poverty research was most often framed to accord with the prevailing policy discourse rather than to challenge it. Given everything I had written and experienced in trying to talk about welfare policy research to policymakers, I felt obligated to explicitly discuss the issue of framing in order to help make my testimony plausible in spite of its dissonant quality. I set about writing a different kind of "expert" testimony, one that not only offered a bunch of facts, but tried to call attention the issue of framing and why some facts (such as the reduction in the welfare rolls) were given more emphasis in the prevailing discourse while other facts (such as the reduction in the percentage of eligible families receiving assistance) did not.

On September 20, 2011, I entered the McCormack Building near the Capitol, where now extra security precautions were in place but otherwise things seemed as usual. The witnesses were put in separate side rooms for Democrats and Republicans respectively, while the hearing room audience filed in. Eventually, the members of Congress joined us. Then we took our seats and testified one after another, five witnesses in all, with just a few minutes each to summarize our written testimony.[22] Ron Haskins of the Brookings Institution spoke first. He had been the key staffer for the Republicans back when the 1996 law was written. His testimony heralded welfare reform as an overwhelming success. The other key Republican witness was Robert Rector of the conservative Heritage Foundation, who was rumored to be the author of the preamble of the welfare reform law that starts: "Marriage is the foundation of a successful society." He lauded the reform law as well, but put in a plea to now do more to promote marriage as the real solution to welfare dependency. Joel Potts, a welfare administrator from Ohio, spoke suggesting that most of the administrative problems associated with implementing the law, including families not getting food stamps, Medicaid, and child care when they went to work, had been now solved. Heather Boushey, the other Democratic Party witness, from the Economic Policy Institute, provided testimony showing that single mothers often ended up with lower net incomes when they left welfare for work.

My testimony aside, the most distinctive thing about the experience of testifying was that the members of Congress from both parties used the testimony they had solicited to stress issues they had already decided were what needed attention. Research, again, was more about rationalizing preferred approaches rather than helping policymakers to consider new concerns. You could argue that the policymakers already knew enough about welfare reform and did not need new research to tell them to think differently. But then, why had we been invited to testify? It seemed clear that we had been invited largely to affirm what had already been decided more than to influence those decisions. We experts and our research were part of a symbolic exercise, much as Murray Edelman warned me years before.[23]

As for my testimony, I started with the issue of framing and then moved to questioning the specific statistical claims made within the dominant frame focused on reducing welfare dependency rather than poverty:

> Five years after the enactment of the Personal Responsibility and Work Opportunity Reconciliation Act of 1996, that law is now widely heralded as a success. While some aspects of the law have worked for some families, many aspects have not—so much so that I would suggest that the much-heralded claim that welfare reform is a success is overrated and very much premature. A good part of the problem stems from the fact that public discourse has in a questionable way shifted the frame of reference from poverty to dependency. As a result, reductions in welfare caseloads are misleadingly seen as the primary measure of success when poverty remains the pressing issue.
>
> Some analysts have claimed that it is critical to prevent single mothers with children from "staying at home and doing nothing." Others have stressed the importance of treating welfare dependency like an "addiction." Yet, the focus on reducing the welfare caseloads overlooks that many poor, single mothers with children are being forced into temporary, low-wage jobs such that these women remain

> poor while they come under increased strain to fulfill both their child-rearing and wage-earning responsibilities.
>
> Numerous claims have been made for the success of welfare reform that are questionable at best. There are claims that welfare reform has reduced poverty and done other wonderful things for families. I would suggest that important questions need to be asked about these claims before we can develop a clear picture of where welfare reform has taken us. Taking a critical eye to existing research helps us pose these questions.[24]

Beyond the issue that framing allowed welfare reform to be seen as a success prematurely, I introduced evidence that highlighted that not all those leaving welfare were doing well. I added evidence on systematic racial disparities in outcomes under welfare reform that I said should give us pause when assuming that the reforms were working for all the affected families. I also provided evidence from an in-depth study funded by the Robert Wood Johnson Foundation with which I was involved that welfare recipients were not always getting their food stamps, Medicaid, and child care when they went to work.

Given that my testimony differed from Haskins, Rector, and Potts on these points, Rep. Buck McKeon (R-CA), the chair of the committee, expressed concern that the experts did not agree. Haskins, in fact, felt obligated to respond in writing, which was included in the final transcript of the hearing.[25] He took issue with claims Boushey and myself made about how single mothers were faring under welfare reform.

Part of the difference, as expected, was due to how we framed our interpretations of the data. Both Boushey and I had relied heavily on a study by Kathryn Porter and Allen Dupree that showed that the poverty rates for working single mothers had not decreased from 1995 to 1999.[26] Haskins countered that this was because welfare reform had increased the number of working single mothers and many of the former welfare recipients had yet to earn enough to lift them out of poverty. The Porter and Dupree study also indicated that these women had lost government support and that the net effect in some cases was to produce no major gains in income. Haskins's response to this point was that this was what welfare reform was all about, that is, reducing dependency on the government in exchange for increasing reliance on earnings from paid employment. In other words, where some people such as Heather Boushey and myself were emphasizing that poverty remained a real issue, Haskins had framed the issue in terms of reducing dependency.

In his subsequent review of the effects of welfare reform, Robert Moffitt notes the debate over whether the improvements in income and earnings were due more to economic growth during the first five years of welfare reform or to welfare reform requiring work; and within this debate whether it was the positive incentives in effect at the time, such as the Earned Income Tax Credit and greater access to child care, that were the policies that contributed to these improvements, while the negative restrictions such as time limits, work requirements, and sanctions did very little to help boost income, earnings, and work effort. Moffitt notes that for the time period in question, the income, earnings, and work effort of single mothers improved markedly, while reductions in poverty rates for single mothers were much more modest.[27] Moffitt's overall assessment suggests that Haskins's emphasis on the positive findings was vindicated in the short term.

Yet even as he remains a supporter of welfare reform, Haskins has changed his tune and has most recently worried out loud that welfare reform continues to restrict access to assistance by those who need it to the point that it is driving down incomes and increasing poverty.[28] This gets to another major difference in the testimony back in 2001. Boushey and I were emphasizing that while welfare reform worked for some families, it was injurious to others, with as much as one-third of the single mothers not working after leaving welfare. In other words, both Heather and I were concerned about what would be eventually become an intensifying focus on the growing numbers of "disconnected" mothers (i.e., neither working nor receiving welfare), many of whose incomes left their families living in "deep poverty" (i.e., incomes below one-half the poverty line). In his review of the effects of welfare reform, Moffitt notes that these findings are based on the fact that while 60–70 percent of those leaving welfare went to work, 30–40 percent did not, suggesting that even as the reforms worked for some families they did not for others, leading to increases in the number of low-income mothers who were employed but also increases in the number of disconnected mothers living in deep poverty.[29]

Haskins had had the opportunity to anticipate this problem back when he felt the need to write a rebuttal to our testimony for the published transcript of the hearing. His retort failed to take seriously the idea that while welfare reform was working for some families it was not helping others. Haskins in fact noted that "deep" poverty had declined in 1998 and 1999. Rector's testimony noted this trend as well.[30] The trend proved to be short-lived.

What is most unfortunate about this mistake is that this is the population most likely to be directly affected by welfare reform's harshness. Most families below 100 percent of the poverty line actually have incomes too high to qualify for welfare. It is the poorest of the poor that are likely to qualify for welfare. Yet, already even in the go-go years of the booming economy of the late 1990s, when welfare reform first started to get implemented in the states, we saw evidence that there were growing numbers of families being cut off from welfare and left without any means of support. Eventually, the issue of disconnected mothers would become the central concern that it is now. In fact, people would finally start to connect the dots, and important research would suggest that welfare reform was producing more disconnected mothers who were living in "deep poverty" or even "extreme poverty" (surviving on two dollars or less in income per person per day—the World Bank's measures of global poverty).[31]

In a widely circulated 2012 report, Luke Shaefer and Kathryn Edin state:

> Welfare reform . . . combined with changes to other means-tested public programs that have raised the benefits of work for low income households, has been followed by a dramatic decline in cash assistance caseloads, from an average of 12.3 million recipients per month in 1996 to 4.4 million in June 2011; only 1.1 million of these beneficiaries are adults. . . . [W]e estimate that, as of the beginning of 2011, about 1.46 million U.S. households with about 2.8 million children were surviving on $2 or less in income per person per day in a given month. This constitutes almost 20 percent of all nonelderly households with children living in poverty. About 866,000 households appear to live in extreme poverty across a full calendar quarter. The prevalence of extreme poverty rose sharply between 1996 and 2011 [from 636,000 to 1.46 million households]. This growth has been concentrated among those groups that were most affected by the 1996 welfare reform. Despite the presence of a substantial in-kind safety net, a significant number of households with children continue to slip through the cracks. And it is unclear how households with no cash income—either from work, government programs, assets, friends, family members, or informal sources—are getting by even if they do manage to claim some form of in-kind benefit.[32]

Therefore, over the long haul, welfare reform might have been promoting work, but its restrictiveness was also reducing access to assistance by those who needed it, with the result that it produced increases in extreme poverty, and at an accelerating rate with the onset of the Great Recession, when welfare reform's restrictiveness persisted only to prove to be exceptionally inappropriate. It seems that welfare reform's days as a success story have come to an end. The issue of what to do about increasing poverty has returned with full force. The welfare dependency frame prevented us from focusing on it, but now, given the dramatic increases in poverty, especially among disconnected single mothers, we can see that that frame had induced a myopia leaving the policy process blind to the weaknesses of welfare reform. Reframing the issue as one of poverty reduction cannot now come a moment too soon.

A STATE-TYPE THING

Back at the hearing, my other major concern was about racial disparities under welfare reform. It was, however, lightly passed over during the questioning at the hearing (race as once again the proverbial elephant in the room). At the time, I had just published the first of a series of articles documenting the racialized character of welfare implementation.[33] This work was to become an enduring focus for me over the next decade, especially in my collaboration with Joe Soss and Richard Fording. The original paper was based on a bet I made with my colleagues after I had started to make presentations that showed how the states varied in adopting options for increased restrictiveness under welfare reform regarding time limits, work requirements, sanctions, and other policy options such as imposing a family cap that denied increases in benefits for a mother who gave birth to an additional child while receiving cash assistance under the TANF program. I remember suggesting to the audience one night while speaking at the University of Western Washington that the breakdowns seemed to suggest that states with relatively large proportions of recipients who were African American seemed to have adopted the most restrictive options under welfare reform. After about a year of crunching the numbers, that initial hunch held up in multivariate analyses. Along with my collaborators, I subsequently published the findings and then reported them to Congress at the hearing.

While asking about these findings later, a reporter told me that Rector had dismissed them as just "a state-type thing."[34] I am not sure what he meant, but I think he was suggesting that it was just Southern states that chose more restrictive options and they just happen to have more African Americans on the rolls (as if that was unrelated, which it was not). Lawrence Mead added his agreement at a Brookings Institution forum on the issue of state flexibility under TANF a few months later: "The Southern states, on the other hand, are doing what they've done historically and that is restricting dependency not only by low benefits but by strong sanctions and work requirements as well. That's why we tend to see a strong caseload fall in those areas."[35] For some reason, Larry, like Rector, chose not to mention the racial composition of the welfare populations in those Southern states as if it were incidental.

Yet, even though he did not challenge Mead at the Brookings forum they both participated in, Thomas Gais, along with Kent Weaver, had already provided confirmation of our basic findings in a Brookings Institution paper, in what proved to be the first of numerous studies confirming our analysis that demonstrated that the racial composition of the welfare rolls in the states was the major predictor of state policy restrictiveness (even if you controlled for whether a state was in the South, thereby disconfirming the Rector and Mead dismissal).[36]

The issue of race loomed large for me now. Working with Joe Soss and Richard Fording, I started to think that the entire process surrounding welfare reform was thoroughly racialized from top to bottom, including the national government's enactment of welfare reform, the states' implementation of it, the role of local service providers, the behavior of frontline workers and the effects on clients.[37] Given the history of race in welfare policy in the United States, it should not have been surprising, but it needed study before we could be sure what the role of race precisely was and how it operated to influence welfare policy decision making throughout the system. While Congress and conservative researchers did not want to talk about it, I did.

EIGHT

CALLING OUT RACIAL BIAS

Images, Words, and Numbers

"Sandy, I am ashamed of you! I thought you would know better than to put a picture of a black woman on the cover of your book. Everyone knows that most people on welfare are white!" (See Fig. 8.1.) That's what a colleague said to me after I handed her a copy of my new book back in 2000.[1] A smart, passionate advocate for the oppressed, she was not alone in her disappointment with the cover image. The week before, when I was speaking at a conference in honor of Frances Fox Piven at the University of Oregon in Eugene, another colleague stuck a Post-it note on a copy of a flyer for the book that read: "The book sounds great, but the cover will reinforce stereotypes." Evidently, I was still the ever-naive one, assuming unreflectively what others had more critically dissected. They were saying that I should have known better. But actually, I did, as I will explain.

So it was that, even as I was starting to focus on producing statistical analyses on racial bias in welfare policymaking, people were calling me out as complicit in perpetuating those biases. It was not as though I did not have warning. The issue of racial imagery had been haunting me for some time. The year before, at the eleventh hour, I had removed an image of an African American woman from the cover of a volume on welfare reform I was co-editing. (It was, literally, late at night when I decided I had to e-mail the publisher to stop the printing of the cover.) The book was printed with a perfectly blank, black cover, because it was too late to find another picture. I might have been clueless, but every once in a while I would have an epiphany (if you could call it that).[2] Yet that actually might have been the right move then, because the image was overly stark in its depiction, implying a kind of desperate helplessness—a picture does indeed speak a thousand words, and sometimes the wrong ones.

Figure 8.1. Putting a Black Face on Welfare (Source: http://www.amazon.com/After-Welfare-Culture-Postindustrial-Social/dp/0814797555)

I was learning that the issue of "putting a black face on welfare" is more complicated than my colleagues were suggesting.[3] In fact, I felt that this issue merited more thorough scrutiny, rather than leaving the clichés that were circulating to go unexamined. I decided I had to make that my next topic for study. I was starting to think that the Left needed to be challenged as well as the Right to address the issues of race and welfare forthrightly, rather than continuing to sweep them under the rug with unquestioned nostrums of political correctness. I felt we had to turn the lens back on ourselves, the advocates for the poor, to examine how our nonuse as well as our use of images made us complicit in reinforcing racism in welfare policy discourse. By the next year I was ready. In fact, the presentation I was giving on 9/11 in Finland was about race imagery in welfare policy discourse.

My main interest at the time was in continuing to pursue in more depth how welfare policy discourse was racially encoded in ways that had profoundly detrimental consequences for both determining what policies were enacted and how the clients most directly affected by those policies were treated. In particular, there was good reason to think that there was some kind of virulent feedback loop whereby an implicitly racially encoded welfare policy discourse reinforced preexisting racist attitudes in ways that led to persistent denial about the sources of black poverty and what to do about it. Our policies re-coded racism. They were complicit in further demonizing African Americans who lived in poverty, and made it that much harder to enact welfare policy in the future that could effectively attack poverty that afflicted low-income families of all races and ethnicities. We were stuck in a racist rut. And not talking about it, out of fear of offending people on all sides, did no good. At least, this was my opening position.

The flap over the book cover had pushed me to add images to the equation. Yet, even within this focus, my main concern was of the same as my colleagues': that racial imagery tapped into prevailing biases about how those "other" people were not playing by white middle-class rules of work and family and therefore deserved to be treated more harshly until they got with the program and started acting responsibly. In this way, welfare came to punish all poor on the assumption they were, mostly, black people who were not playing by white middle-class rules of work and family.

Nonetheless, the way folks responded to the image I put on the cover of my book got me thinking that the story was more complicated. Using images of African American women in reference to welfare policy might thoughtlessly allow racial stereotypes to recirculate, but it also highlighted that something more was going on than people simply letting the pictures do the talking for them. In other words, if you were to stop and think about it, what was really so wrong about using the image of black woman to frame a discussion of welfare policy? I mean, it might have been wrong, but then again, what, specifically, was so wrong about it? How was it wrong? And, also, how and when might it be right?

A number of points immediately began to jump out for me. First, let's assume that it is indeed wrong to use images of African American women when referring to welfare because they remind people of deeply embedded racist stereotypes that insist that African Americans are lazy and sexually promiscuous, which is why they are on welfare. The result is that people continue to think negatively of welfare as an irresponsible giveaway to undeserving, low-income African Americans. In fact, belief in the laziness stereotype and belief in the sexual promiscuity stereotype are major predictors of whether someone in the U.S. adult population supports paternalist welfare reform.[4] So it stands to reason that using an image of an African American woman for the cover of a book on welfare might tap into those stereotypes in ways that tar both African Americans and welfare with a highly stigmatizing brush. Yet for any image to enact this double whammy, people have to interpret the picture. A picture does not dictate that when we associate race with welfare we always assume that those are undeserving people who need to be disciplined so that they will begin to practice personal responsibility like white middle-class people. A picture could not do that on its own. For this interpretation to occur, we have to allow ourselves to invoke, consciously or not, prevailing racist stereotypes about women on welfare. Rather than just putting it all on the pictures, we should acknowledge our own role in interpreting the images. This raises the issue of what precisely our role interpreting these images of black women is and to what extent does that make us complicit in reinforcing racial biases?

Second, there was a more serious problem: my colleague was wrong. It simply was not true that most people on welfare were whites. That was just something people liked to say for a long time, but the fact of the matter is that it was no longer true in the post–welfare reform era. It might have been true once but this statistical claim was now so dated as to be unhelpful. It amounted to no more than an unsupported assertion that covered over the issue that welfare reform had racially disparate effects and imposed far greater hardships on nonwhites than whites. Not talking about the increase in the percentage of welfare recipients who were black was simply whitewashing this issue. Ironically, not seeing the current welfare population as disproportionately black helped to avoid talking about the role of racism in perpetuating poverty for black single mothers.

It is true that my research with Joe Soss and Richard Fording demonstrated that welfare reform's restrictions were more likely to be imposed on African Americans in part because they were more likely than whites to receive welfare in states that adopted the strictest versions of time limits, work requirements, sanctions, family caps, etc.[5] Nonetheless, in the early years of welfare reform, whites seemed to have more options in the face of the new restrictions and were leaving welfare at a faster rate than either African Americans or Latinos. The net result was that African Americans had become the largest group receiving cash assistance under the Temporary Assistance for Needy Families program (TANF), and nonwhites (African Americans and Latinos not identifying as white) had become a majority of all recipients. In 2001, when the issue arose for me, the U.S. government reported the racial distribution for all active families as: 30.1 percent whites,

39 percent African American, 26 percent Hispanic (of any race), 2.1 percent Asian, 1.3 percent Native American, 0.8 percent Other, and 0.7 percent Unknown.[6] In other words, even though welfare reform's strictest policies were more likely to affect nonwhites compared to whites, the shrinking welfare rolls now had more nonwhites on them than whites. These data suggested that welfare reform was leaving the nonwhite population behind, trapped in an increasingly punitive welfare system.

I understand why it was important to highlight that low-income white single mothers receive welfare just like low-income nonwhites. We have an obligation to fight the vicious canard that only blacks are poor, for it reinforces the idea that poverty is caused not by economic disadvantage but culture or other factors specific to race. To insist that most welfare recipients are white stems from the laudable goal of discouraging people from seeing those who rely on public assistance as different from the rest of the population instead of just regular folks who need help. I agree with that sentiment and think it is as important to emphasize as ever. In fact, it is always important to remind people that the overwhelming majority of all poor people (most of whom are not on welfare) are white.[7] Yet it did no good to fall into the mistake of continuing to insist they were a majority of welfare recipients after welfare reform had made that no longer the case.

To insist that most welfare recipients were white was an anachronism that was factually incorrect. And factual misstatements are never helpful when trying to connect research to policy, or truth to power, as the old saying goes. This is a common problem in that statistics often get to have a career of their own, circulating in unquestioned ways in public discourse, much like unsubstantiated rumors, with one person passing on what they've heard or read from another source, without finding out whether that statistic has any grounding in fact.[8]

Yet in this case, this unsubstantiated statistic was circulating too close to home. It was not just colleagues but even invited public speakers that were insisting to student audiences that most welfare recipients were white and that we should emphasize that in the name of not demonizing them as these "other" people. Around the time I was dealing with the book cover issue, we invited to campus a member of the Kensington Welfare Rights Union to speak about the issues of poverty and welfare from the perspective of people who had gone through the system. The presentation was very interesting and even poignant, but then there was this hiccup where it morphed into citing unsubstantiated claims that welfare recipients had the same racial and ethnic breakdown as the general population. This was taking the issue to a wholly new level. The welfare population does not mirror the racial and ethnic breakdown of the general population, and pretending otherwise is not just wrong but unhelpful.

Although I agree that welfare recipients must be seen as regular people and not stigmatized as deviants, we need to do this in a way that is attentive to the facts of the situation and to explain those facts responsibly. Only then will we be able to begin to address the issues of poverty and welfare effectively. If knowledge were power and the facts were going to help us make better public policy, it would be good to get our facts straight. But people were not doing that. What really troubled me was that we were not pointing out that under welfare reform the dwindling welfare population was now more likely comprised of nonwhites, and as a result, this silence was leading us away from discussing an important topic that required critical scrutiny. Why was this happening and what were the effects? More poignantly, what were the consequences of inaccurately insisting that most welfare recipients were white? Could this lead us away from addressing the deficiencies of welfare reform that were themselves the result of racial bias? In other words, could there be both good and bad in putting a black face on welfare?

PUTTING A BLACK FACE ON WELFARE: THE BAD

I was attending the multicultural seminar for faculty at Brown University in the summer of 2000 when the picture of New Jersey's Governor Christine Todd Whitman frisking an African American male appeared in the *New York Times*[9] (see Fig. 8.2). The photo surfaced as evidence in the trial of New Jersey state troopers accused of racial profiling in the shooting of several young black men on the New Jersey Turnpike. The defense introduced the photo to suggest that racial profiling was condoned from the governor's office on down. The picture shows the governor, dressed all in white, smiling while frisking an innocent black man. As a result, the case against the state troopers was eventually dismissed.[10] The photo not only suggested that that Governor Whitman thought it was just fine to pull over at random a black youth to be frisked for no apparent reason, but it also reinscribed the canard that most young black males are criminals. An image was created that reinforced racial bias. The governor was caught reenacting the demonization of black men, which suggested that we should continue to single them out for punitive treatment. Putting a black face on crime was, in this case, doing absolutely no good for clarifying the issue in the public's mind. Given the seminar I was attending and the time I was attending it, I was ideally placed for considering the issues raised by this photo taken back in my home state.

Why would the governor agree to be photographed in this way? It might be that gender was imbricated with race in a diabolical fashion. The governor was a moderate Republican woman who could have used increased

Figure 8.2. Erasing Your Gender on the Back of a Black Man (Source: http://en.wikipedia.org/wiki/File:Whitman%26rolax.jpg)

support from the more hardcore conservatives in her party. A photograph of her frisking a black youth might have improved her image by depicting her as being tougher on crime than her gender implied. If that was what motivated her to go along with the photo op, then she was, essentially, erasing her gender on the back of a black male for her own political gain and at his personal expense, with the added charge of reinforcing racial bias among those who looked at the image. Christie Whitman got to become a white man, if just for a photographic moment.

Yet, for this reinscribing of racial bias to happen, the image had to be interpreted by people who already were vulnerable to allowing racial biases to affect how they responded to it. In other words, the picture could not do it by itself. Instead, racial profiling had to be something people were already prone to before viewing the image in ways that confirmed their expectations that black men were especially likely to be committing crimes. Frederick Schauer rightly suggests that we as humans inevitably use categories to classify people based on probabilities of how they are apt to behave.[11] Yet he also rightly suggests that that does not justify assuming all black men are criminals, or that it is acceptable to randomly pull over black men, or that it is acceptable to detain black men at rates well above their crime rates. In other words, to overuse a category beyond what probabilities suggest is to treat members of that category as if they were all equally defined by it. That would be unjustified racial profiling (which is what some police do). People who interpret all images of blacks as suggesting they are prone to committing crimes is just plain racist. When used to interpret images, that racism is what makes those images vulnerable to misuse. It is not the image by itself that does the dirty deed.

Not all people will misuse such images, and some people will actually use the image in opposite ways, to suggest alternative understandings of what is being depicted. Paul de Man once defined reading as supplying what is missing to a text.[12] Texts are inert until they are read; reading breathes life into them, making them interpretable through the very act in the moment when they are interpreted. The net result is that each reading supplies its own narration, making the idea of one objective reading of any text unattainable and the definitive meaning of any text something that is infinitely deferred and ultimately undecidable. The same is true with pictures. Pictures are nothing until they are seen. What we see is an act of visualization, as multivalent and polyoptic as texts are undecidable. Every picture produces as many visualizations as there are people to see it.

Take the picture I wanted to put on a book cover but did not because at the last minute I decided it was too vulnerable to being interpreted in ways that reinscribed the demonization of African American women on welfare (see Fig. 8.3). Upon reflection, I had decided that the picture merited consideration for discussing the very problem I now am revisiting. Let me reiterate my analysis. The woman depicted in the picture had been removed from the welfare rolls in 1997 for failure to comply with welfare-to-work rules. She lost all income support, to the point that she was reduced to cooking family meals on an outdoor grill. In the picture, she sits outdoors and stares blankly away from the camera while her teenage son looks on. She seems to be an enigma, for she does not defend herself or appeal for a hearing regarding her treatment. Her inscrutability creates doubts in our

Figure 8.3. Visualizing the Welfare Queen (Source: http://www.washingtonpost.com/wp-srv/politics/special/welfare/stories/wf032398.htm)

minds, allowing some of us to decide that she is incorrigible. Her passivity becomes a form of active defiance. Her black face is a blank slate on which those who are so predisposed allow a prejudicial welfare dependency discourse to write its stigmatizing story. Her body language is therefore not of her own making, but a discourse that reads her a certain way. Simply being there, in poverty, in the backyard, cooking on the grill, her passivity becomes a willful chosen dependency. Without knowing anything about her, her hopes, or her dreams, she becomes for those of us inclined to read her so as the very embodiment of the welfare queen.

And so it is that the viewing subject must interpret the viewed object before any racialized image gets to be used to reinscribe the story of the black welfare queen. It is not just the images but how preexisting racial biases circulating in the culture get queued by these images, so that when they are activated they can influence interpretations that then reinforce a racist understanding of why African Americans are more likely to rely on welfare than whites. Yet, if we are keen to how these cultural biases can influence us, if we resist the atrophying of consciousness, then we can reject the racist interpretations they suggest, and we do not have to be so vulnerable to having these images reinscribe the prevalent stigmatizing story of who uses welfare and why. Our job in the service of a postracist society is to be ever vigilant and resist these sorts of interpretations of racial imagery associated with welfare. When we do that, we in fact might actually find such images helpful.

PUTTING A BLACK FACE ON WELFARE: THE GOOD

How can racial imagery about welfare actually be a good thing? Well, it depends. Images designed to tendentiously depict African Americans and other nonwhites as lazy and promiscuous women who are irresponsibly using welfare to fund a deviant lifestyle are not helpful by definition. But most images are not so strident in their depictions. Instead, more porously interpretable images can actually prove to be helpful if we are prepared to provide constructive alternative interpretations. Take the image in Fig. 8.1.

The image in Figure 8.1 ended up on the cover of one of my books.[13] The editors thought it was a more positive image than the one in Figure 8.3, so they approved it. The African American woman depicted is on a bus, but she is no longer in the back (as in the pre–Civil Rights Act South); she is working (adorned with gloves and work clothes); she stares into the camera (as if not ashamed). This image offers the possibility of these more positive characterizations. Yet these are not the positive features of the image that I want to emphasize. Instead, the positive, for me, goes back to the issue of recognizing that there are now under welfare reform more nonwhites than whites on welfare. This is an issue that should not be swept under the rug as if it were an embarrassing fact that might undo efforts to create greater sympathy for welfare-reliant mothers on the grounds that "they" are just like "us."

If we overlook the racial composition of the welfare population, we are overlooking the extent to which nonwhites confront extra barriers imposed on them by the broader society, racial discrimination in accessing jobs in particular. It is obtuse to suggest that this is not a real factor confronting nonwhite welfare recipients. Whitewashing the welfare population leads us to avoid acknowledging that racial disadvantage is still a serious structural impediment operating in our society, which prevents the socioeconomic advancement of low-income nonwhite folks who are struggling to escape poverty and the welfare system. It remains the case that we may need to take account of race in order to eventually get beyond it, including accounting for how nonwhite welfare recipients confront additional racial barriers in their struggle to escape poverty.[14] By putting a black face on welfare in a sensitive and thoughtful way, we can begin to do that.

FOR NOW: THE NEW JIM CROW

Yet there is no denying that racialized imagery, words, and numbers continue to get bandied about in political discourse in ways that work to denigrate low-income African Americans and, to a lesser extent, other nonwhites. In particular, the prevailing discourse that depicts black males as thugs is a continuing assault on our collective and individual sensibilities. From their profiling by cops to their demonization in political discourse, the black male is reinscribed with otherness in less than helpful ways that have helped legitimate their mass incarceration. Their depiction as the dangerous other continues to wreak havoc on their lives, their families, and their communities. And their mass incarceration cycles back to operate as its own symbol serving to rationalize that not doing anything more constructive to address their ongoing marginalization.

I know a lot more about this than before. In 2011, I sat on the Harrington book award committee (probably because my first book, *Words of Welfare*, had been selected for the award in 1996). I nominated a book that ended up winning the award: *The New Jim Crow*, by Michelle Alexander.[15] I was incredibly moved by the book. It reads like truth serum, saying what many of us (including even the author herself, as she poignantly reports) may have previously been reluctant to think, let alone say out loud, but also, implicitly at least, sense probably to be true: that racism is why we in the United States continue to create new ways to punish the inner city black poor just for being who they are—i.e., people who are systematically denigrated and demonized by the racialized thinking that influences our social welfare deliberations. After rereading the book, I know Alexander's formula for making this truth serum effective: the narrative is so honest, so unpretentious, so highly readable, and so convincing. With her own memoir-like style of writing, she makes her analysis personal in ways that are hard to dismiss and which deserve detailed examination, for it highlights the persistent power of racialized images, words, and numbers even today in our post–civil rights society to rationalize the continued subordination of a significant subpopulation in our society.

Alexander states that she personally long avoided confronting this simple truth, even as it kept staring her in the face. It was not an immediate recognition for her; instead it was something she hoped was not true, especially as an African American woman growing up in the post–civil rights society. She so wanted to believe we were now beyond the old racism of the past. And maybe we are, but it turns out that that does not mean that we are now beyond racism. Instead, it just means we have moved to a new racism, a more implicit racism, one that more stealthily relies on racially coded imagery to infiltrate our thinking and public policies. As an idealistic young civil rights lawyer, Alexander resisted until she finally was forced to stare back at the truth her black clients and neighbors showed her about how society was treating them. She reluctantly came to realize that even in post–civil rights America most of us refuse to see the role that racism continues to play in structuring the allocation of life chances in our society, especially the role of race in the treatment of that substantial portion of poor black men who end up with criminal records that make them essentially unemployable and often strip of them of basic political rights, including especially the right to vote (thereby making it ever harder for them to work with others to change this unjust situation).

Alexander's historical account pivots on the 1980s, when through get-tough criminal justice policies, emanating first and foremost from the War on Drugs, black men started getting locked up at unprecedentedly high rates and increasingly became a disposable population facing the prospect of life bereft of economic opportunities and without basic political rights. Alexander notes that when she came out of law school she refused to see the disproportionate imprisonment of young black men as anything more than the product of their making bad choices in our newly established post–civil rights society. Yet life intruded, and a series of incidents drove home to her that race played a big role in determining how precariously these men were positioned in the social order, making them vulnerable to marginalized status that involved engaging in activities (such as participating in the drug trade) that were increasingly categorized as deserving the most punitive treatment.

Alexander confesses that she came to appreciate how she herself, even as an idealistic young lawyer, did nonetheless partake of the racialized outlook that had come to dominate society's view of black crime. Although she had chosen to become a civil rights lawyer working on employment discrimination, she realized that when it came to thinking about the growing rates of incarceration of black men starting in the 1980s, she was part of the problem by not allowing herself to see that these men had been systematically set up via a not entirely unconscious set of decisions to racialize the issues of deviance, crime, and drug use and to use race to justify the harshest penalties as the primary response.

In other words, the disproportionate imprisonment of black men was not what economists call mere "statistical discrimination" (i.e., purely the result of the fact that black men were more likely to commit more crimes). Instead, this disproportionate rate of incarceration had to be the systematic result of racially biased decisions by political elites to manage what had become a disposable population in the most punitive way possible. And it was the systematic result of racialized thinking (blacks are more deviant) that discouraged efforts to assist black communities and resulted in racialized outcomes (black men are more likely to be shut out of legitimate labor markets and less likely to be deserving of basic political rights, such as voting).

In other words, racialized thinking was a self-fulfilling prophecy that produced the very result that it assumed in the beginning. This personal story tells us that we are all vulnerable to being in denial about how the

United States keeps reinventing ways to avoid addressing the inequities created by racism and are in even more denial about the facts that we allow racism to prevent us from doing anything about it other than single out the black poor for systematic punishment for the poverty they suffer due to their increased marginalization. We instead use that racial bias as a way of legitimating not only neglect of the social issues it colors (such as poverty) but also the very punitive policies to manage the consequences of those festering problems (most especially by criminalizing the poor for their poverty and then stripping them of political rights to do anything about it). As hard as it is to believe, this New Jim Crow, as Alexander calls the new system of racialized punishment, may be worse than Old Jim Crow (the system of racial apartheid that prevailed in the South circa 1880–1950).

What is most disconcerting is that all of this is happening most often without invoking race explicitly, through policies such as three strikes you're out, mandatory sentencing, levying adult charges on juveniles, offering tougher penalties for crack relative to powder cocaine, felony disenfranchisement, and other ostensibly race-neutral but actually race-coded policies. These punitive criminal justice policies are the product of the way prevailing racial stereotypes infiltrate our thinking to justify the creation of a disposable population, then to criminalize resultant behaviors, and finally to aggressively punish people for those behaviors. The implicit reference is the black drug dealer and the crack whore with the crack baby: all black, all the time, in the mass media–manipulated consciousness of the white mass public. To the degree that we, consciously or unconsciously, allow these racial stereotypes to influence our thinking, they can become the basis for not acting in supportive ways to redress the racial inequities that persist, and even in some cases to intensify them in the face of social and economic change. The net result is that we are way beyond the "benign neglect" that Daniel Patrick Moynihan cynically advised President Nixon to follow as a policy for race relations after the civil rights movement peaked. We live in an era of the New Jim Crow, a new regime for using race to first create and then manage the inequity our political economy fosters and needs. When will we learn to see race for what it is: the tool of subordination that makes our capitalist system go round?! We might learn this critical, if basic, insight, if we read and reread this important book.

At some level of consciousness, including implicit biases, but also at times explicit ones as well, we all at times are vulnerable to relying on race to avoid addressing the structural inequities of our market-centered society,which have devastated inner-city black communities. If we do not resist the atrophying of consciousness that comes with participating in the dominant discourse, we can end up relying on race to excuse the worst forms of neglect and the even worse forms of malign treatment, especially by the police and others who make and implement criminal justice policy.

In the wake of imploding manual labor job markets and the rise of mass unemployment in this population, we neither turned to public policies to improve the human capital of black youth through education and training nor embarked on a massive job creation effort to ensure that once they became employable there would be jobs for them to take. Instead, we allowed race to be the pretext for neglecting the problem; then, when a black market in drugs and other illegal activities became a flash point in political discourse, we criminalized that behavior while continuing to neglect the poverty of the participants in that underground economy. (They don't call it a "black" market for nothing!) As a result, we moved to a program of mass incarceration, while promulgating such tough policies regarding the non-rights of ex-felons that the black men swept up in this system would have no hope of ever achieving membership in mainstream society even after being released from prison.

We need to confront the distinct possibility that we have chosen mass incarceration of black men in particular as a systematic way of dealing with their becoming a disposable population that has been passed over by the changing political-economic system. The punitive turn to penalizing drug use with imprisonment was not a social, political, or economic necessity; instead, it was a choice elites made and then championed. They achieved mass public support by using racialized imagery to legitimate this draconian approach to punishing deviant behavior. The mass incarceration of black men was meant to be a way to manage marginalization of an identifiable population as an alternative to addressing their needs in more supportive ways that might lead to their integration into mainstream society. Yet the problem is compounded. The mass incarceration of so many black men becomes its own political spectacle serving to symbolize the undeservingness of low-income African Americans more generally.[16]

Alternatives to the prevailing racially biased understanding of the problem are possible but being ignored. The prevalence of racialized thinking has led to ignoring the direct connection of the drug culture to the implosion of manual labor markets. Racism has reinforced misunderstandings about the relationship of crime to unemployment and made it easier to imagine that blacks are more likely to engage in criminal activity as a result of their just being different in ways that were specific to them, their background, or their culture. In other words, they could take legitimate jobs but choose not to, preferring the drug trade instead. Yet, it turns out that blacks do not commit crimes at higher rates than whites at given levels of unemployment. For instance, it is not that black men are preternaturally more criminal; it is that they are more likely to be unemployed. And their unemployment is not the result of some inborn laziness, as another prominent stereotype suggests. Instead, their higher level of unemployment is the result of nondecisions at the highest levels of government that have allowed the changing economy to bypass segregated, black, inner-city, poor neighborhoods. Systematic disinvestment in schools and jobs for those communities has been furthered by allowing race to influence the neglect reflected in educational and jobs policy. And resistance to integration, which allowed for the increased concentration of poverty along racialized lines, helped to further facilitate this neglect. As a result, it is difficult to see that race is not constitutive of the sources of the problems of higher poverty rates in segregated black communities and the corresponding higher rates of crime.

Eventually, we need to confront how race affects the implementation of the carceral system itself, which has grown up to manage the resulting problems born of white neglect. Police profiling, it turns out, involves more explicit race bias of the older sort, further compounding the racialization of criminal justice policy implementation that is born more of the newer implicit race-coded, but not explicitly racialized, discourse. Either way, once young black men come within the crosshairs of policing, the cops are all too frequently more than willing to act on the most biased of assumptions. It seems that the implicit racism of public policy creates opportunities for the exercise of explicit forms of racism. It is as if the self-fulfilling prophecy of racism creates a basis for reenacting it all over again.

Yet even if we become self-aware and seek to bring the madness to a halt, we quickly see that the New Jim Crow system becomes self-reinforcing on multiple levels: (1) black men with criminal records are made permanently unemployable, leaving them little choice but to return to the underground economy of illicit behavior in ways that increasingly ensure they recidivate back into prison; (2) black youth increasingly have little choice but to embrace the identity of the street tough as the only option that garners respect among peers and offers some prospect of economic advancement; and (3) police and other officials are encouraged to profile young black men in ways that only increase their chances of being singled out for criminalization. The New Jim Crow now runs of its own accord, and even if we want to stop it, we will find it hard to shut down. The difficulties of reversing this shift to a new system of exclusion are compounded by our stripping away of political rights from those with criminal records, including most prominently felony disenfranchisement laws. Those most directly affected are basically powerless to participate in producing the needed political change.

Even arguments about the expense of mass incarceration fall on deaf ears. Part of the reason, I would add, is that while it costs more to imprison than employ the black poor that get caught up in the get-tough criminal justice system, it probably costs less than creating decent jobs for the all black poor that need work. Mass incarceration is expensive but probably not as expensive as mass employment in good-paying jobs on the scale that is needed. Be that as it may, I am prepared to concede that mass incarceration is not a rational policy on any level.

In the end, I agree with Alexander when she concludes by rejecting incremental tinkering and instead calls for a mass social movement to rise up to call out the racist character of this new system of exclusion. Alexander has actually toyed with her own "Crisis Strategy," à la Piven and Cloward's proposal that if the poor exercised their rights to welfare it would overload the system and force change to something better.[17] Alexander has written:

> After years as a civil rights lawyer, I rarely find myself speechless. But some questions a woman I know posed during a phone conversation one recent evening gave me pause: "What would happen if we organized thousands, even hundreds of thousands, of people charged with crimes to refuse to play the game, to refuse to plea out? What if they all insisted on their Sixth Amendment right to trial? Couldn't we bring the whole system to a halt just like that?" Could she be serious about organizing people, on a large scale, to refuse to plea-bargain when charged with a crime? . . . [I]n this era of mass incarceration—when our nation's prison population has quintupled in a few decades partly as a result of the war on drugs and the "get tough" movement—these rights are, for the overwhelming majority of people hauled into courtrooms across America, theoretical. More than 90 percent of criminal cases are never tried before a jury. Most people charged with crimes forfeit their constitutional rights and plead guilty. In the race to incarcerate, politicians champion stiff sentences for nearly all crimes, including harsh mandatory minimum sentences and three-strikes laws; the result is a dramatic power shift, from judges to prosecutors. The Supreme Court ruled in 1978 that threatening someone with life imprisonment for a minor crime in an effort to induce him to forfeit a jury trial did not violate his Sixth Amendment right to trial. Thirteen years later, in *Harmelin v. Michigan*, the court ruled that life imprisonment for a first-time drug offense did not violate the Eighth Amendment's ban on cruel and unusual punishment. No wonder, then, that most people waive their rights. If everyone charged with crimes suddenly exercised his constitutional rights, there would not be enough judges, lawyers or prison cells to deal with the ensuing tsunami of litigation. Not everyone would have to join for the revolt to have an impact; as the legal scholar Angela J. Davis noted, "if the number of people

> exercising their trial rights suddenly doubled or tripled in some jurisdictions, it would create chaos." Mass protest would force a public conversation that, to date, we have been content to avoid. People should understand that simply exercising their rights would shake the foundations of our justice system which works only so long as we accept its terms. As you know, another brutal system of racial and social control once prevailed in this country, and it never would have ended if some people weren't willing to risk their lives. It would be nice if reasoned argument would do, but as we've seen that's just not the case. So maybe, just maybe, if we truly want to end this system, some of us will have to risk our lives.[18]

I am not sure that is the way to go in this case, but I agree that any effort must be substantial, for the mass incarceration of black men is part of a broader shift toward a more disciplinary approach to managing the poverty population more generally and involves changes in social welfare as well as criminal justice policy.[19] This juggernaut needs to be confronted head on as the new way of perpetuating that old moral scourge staining our nation's reputation: the color line still systematically works to promote marginalization that leads to mass immiseration. And today the massive numbers of African American men ensnarled in the criminal justice system is its own political spectacle serving to not just marginalize low-income blacks but in the process also to rationalize that marginalization.

All of this is to say that Michelle Alexander's life experiences, including the evolution in her thinking growing up African American, female, and becoming a civil rights lawyer, have taught her to see clearly the continuing role of the state in reproducing invidious racial distinctions. Reading Alexander prompts me to think that when you get right down to it, race is not something that is exogenous to state power. While race is associated with skin color, it is not specific to it. It is, instead, an artifact of state power. It is a quintessential example, with class and gender, of what Michel Foucault calls governmentality, defined as the state creating populations and then disciplining people to populate those populations. Further, it is a practice of the state that to varying degrees we all end up being implicated in reproducing.[20] State power, like all power, is better seen not as something we do or possess but rather as something in which may we partake, by sharing with others what is given to us, in ways that affect us more than we can affect them. The state creates race for purposes of ordering populations, and then its treatment of the people who have been raced in these ways serves to reinforce that racialized order in whose reproduction we all participate.

Today, no better example exists of how the state reproduces the racial order it has established than how the state treats the poor, including the welfare poor as well as those ensnarled in the criminal justice system, where in either case programs impose discipline for failure to act white regarding work and family values, with the result that those so disciplined end up serving as reminders of how "those other people" are not like "us." Both the welfare and criminal justice ends of the emerging disciplinary regime involve state practices that result in race making. The neoliberal-paternalist regime of poverty management is a constellation of state practices that reproduce the racialization of the population while simultaneously rationalizing the inequities the racialized social order produces.

Alexander's life story is one in which she has learned firsthand about the criminal justice end of this system of race making. She has learned all too well how the push to mass incarceration has been facilitated by state-sanctioned racialized thinking that disproportionately affects nonwhites in ways that end up legitimating the very same racial distinctions the state originally put in play. From Alexander's bottom-up perspective, working on the front lines with people swept up in the dragnet of the criminal justice system, she has personally witnessed the horrors of racism perpetrated by that system, even as we claim today to be living in a color-blind, post–civil rights society. Her personal stories are a strong foundation for highlighting what is wrong with the racialized disciplinary regime and provide a basis for resisting it. Her memoir-like approach to educating us about the New Jim Crow is more than edifying. It makes explicit what is hidden in plain sight. Her willingness to peel back the scales on her eyes and see the horror of this state-sanctioned system of race making staring her in the face is, by itself, nothing less than inspiring.

NINE

THE DEEP SEMIOTIC STRUCTURE OF DESERVINGNESS

Enduring Identities in Dependency Discourse

Reading the works of others was convincing me that racialized thinking in our post–civil rights society was basically, as I have suggested, "hidden in plain sight."[1] It was just beneath the surface, available to be tapped, triggered by verbal or visual cues circulating in the culture, often regardless of whether we wanted to think in racialized terms or not. We were becoming a society where there was "racism without racists."[2] My study of welfare policy discourse had convinced me that its implicitly racialized character had made it impossible to get most white Americans to consider what was wrong with welfare reform.[3] In their view, it was not wrong to expect those "other" people to adhere to the principles of work and family. It was as though we implicitly assumed this was not about race, even if it was.

Therefore, it had become clear to me that it was important to call out the role of identity in social welfare policy. And it was important for people who were identified as "other" to get to tell their stories about how they experienced that marginalization. I wanted to continue to promote a bottom-up view of social welfare policy, where the people most directly affected by these policies got to give voice to their subordination.[4] In fact, you could say that a memoir approach to understanding the racialized system for managing the poor had its place. Just as this memoir tries to provide background on why I wrote what I wrote over time, other memoirs could help promote understanding of how the people caught up in the disciplinary regime for managing poverty had come to do what they did.[5] As the old feminist consciousness-raising motto suggested, the personal was political. We needed to know in personal terms how those people being "othered" by the racialized regime experienced their subordination.

My interest in discourse had been developing for some time. It had started when I spent a sabbatical year at the University of Wisconsin in 1986–87 and was mentored by Murray Edelman, who in many ways was a 1960s pathbreaker in pointing others down the road to the study of political discourse. Now I was finally starting to put the pieces of the puzzle together to develop my own theory to explain the persistence of the victim-blaming discourse trained on welfare recipients. By the early 1990s, I was increasingly convinced that personal identity itself had to be understood in relationship to discourse. We needed to examine how we articulated understandings of ourselves and others in relation to the language we used to talk about ourselves as people with identities. In the oft-repeated refrain among contemporary social theorists, we needed to understand that "the discourse spoke us as much as we spoke it."[6]

In other words, a memoir-like approach (such as the one I am taking in this book) risked making us misunderstand what was going on as if we as individuals simply made personal choices independent of broader structures, such as social institutions.[7] Taking this auto-critique further, I would suggest that a memoir-like approach also risked ignoring the underlying discourse that positioned individuals and identified them in relationship to other people. I was, therefore, interested in the role of discourse in perpetuating the subordination of marginal populations in our society.

The focus on discourse highlighted for me the fact that there were key categories for discussing welfare policy that actually went beyond race (even if they had come to be racialized). My study of historical texts on welfare policy convinced me that most white Americans had always been skeptical about providing public assistance to the poor regardless of their color.[8] When it came to providing public assistance to needy families, it was clear: we were not Sweden. I began to think that the most fundamental aspect of welfare policy discourse in the United States was that it worked to reinscribe an invidious distinction between those who "earned" benefits and those who were getting "handouts." There existed what I would eventually come to call a "deep semiotic structure of deservingness" that was embedded in welfare policy discourse and reinscribed an invidious distinction between those who deserved support from the government and those who did not.[9]

In other words, as time went on, I started to take a semiotic approach to the issue.[10] By semiotic, I mean the use of semiotics, which is, technically, the study of signs. Semiotics focuses on signs as opposed to symbols or signals (the other two of the three main ways of communicating via discourse). Signals, like traffic signals, are limited in the interpretations they allow: red is stop, green is go. Symbols are at the other extreme and are the most porous and open to interpretation. Signs are in between, not as prismatic as symbols but more open to interpretation than signals. Semiotics focuses on how signs operate to create fundamental distinctions that structure the ways we interpret the world, as when welfare policy discourse reinscribes a tendentious divide between the deserving and undeserving poor.

It came to me that signals were an effective way to understand this division between the deserving and undeserving poor when I read Jack Balkin's book *Culture Software*.[11] The semiotic approach to the study of social phenomena starts with the assumption that the culture of any society is at its base grounded in an interpretive grid or a structure of intelligibility that informs the discourses we use to express our understandings of ourselves, our relationships to each other and the world around us. The interpretive grid or structure of intelligibility is comprised of interrelated binary distinctions that operate as codes communicating fundamental distinctions about what is natural and cultural, good and bad, moral and immoral, rational and emotional, and so on.

Therefore, semiotics emphasizes the ways deeply sedimented binaries or dichotomies serve as the basic codes for structuring the making of meaning in any particular social order. For Balkin, these binary codes operate as "cultural software" that provides a set of "nested oppositions," trading on each other in a form of intertextuality to create hierarchies that privilege one side of a particular binary at the expense of the other. These codes are not epiphenomenal but central in providing the basis for narratives we use to make sense of social relations writ large.

Semiotics probably appealed to me as a lapsed structuralist who was not entirely, but surely partially, taken with poststructuralism. Structuralism emphasized deeply embedded structures, such as the underlying structure of binaries that structured our thinking. I found that very appealing, even if the free play of signifiers that poststructuralism celebrated offered the hope for radical re-visionings of how we made sense of ourselves. Yet, at the same time, I sensed that the semiotic approach to culture therefore enables us to go beyond a structural analysis of the means by which society is organized in ways that constrain social choices and actions to show that emerging from these structural conditions there is an interpretive grid that informs, mediates, and constitutes our social relations. For instance, Jeffrey Alexander, in writing about election campaigns in the United States, has effectively highlighted the power of the underlying coded binaries that form the basis of a culture:

> Difference is a semiotic truism, but it is also one of the major strategies of politics. As campaigns work the binaries, they try to simplify the meaning of every issue that comes up, bringing it into semiotic alignment, on one side or the other of the great divide. Everything must be made clean or dirty, and, whenever

> possible, the newly pure and polluted folded into the narrative arc of historical transformation. This spinning machine comes to an end on 4th November, when the act of voting allows a purging catharsis, a spitting out of the negative, and a transformation of the individual into the collective will. Until that day, politics is about creating difference, not overcoming it. The principal strategy for protecting the purity of your candidate's image is to categorize the other candidate in polluted ways. If we are to be coded as clean and democratic, he must be made dirty in the litany of tried and true, antidemocratic themes. If we are to be narrated as heroic, he must become a villain.[12]

As for elections, so it is for social welfare policy. Since the Social Security Act of 1935, the United States has had a two-tier system of distributing cash benefits.[13] The top tier consists of the nationally administered social insurance programs, including, most prominently, Social Security retirement benefits for the elderly; the bottom tier is comprised of the state-administered public assistance programs for the poor, including what is commonly called welfare, in particular the Temporary Assistance for Needy Families (TANF) program. The top-tier programs are federally funded, with benefits that adjust to the cost of living, and recipients are generally not stigmatized for receiving their benefits, but rather characterized as deserving, often on the assumption that they earned those benefits by virtue of participation in the labor force by either themselves or the head of their family. Bottom-tier programs are funded in part or whole by states, with low benefits that are not adjusted for the cost of living, and recipients are often stigmatized as undeserving because they did not earn their benefits through work. For years, this tiered system has operated to reinscribe an invidious distinction between recipients of the different programs.

In the literature on public policy, the theory of policy feedback suggests that policies do not just reflect politics but also circle back to affect our political attitudes and behaviors.[14] This is a good way to characterize how the tiered system of social provision has worked to reinscribe this longstanding distinction between the deserving and undeserving poor. The poor who get welfare are undeserving because they are not like the elderly who earned their benefits by working. Joe Soss and I published an article in 2009 that showed that even after welfare reform forced TANF recipients to work they still were seen as undeserving in the eyes of many citizens, perhaps because requiring them to work only reinforced the assumption that they had not been working before they were required to do so.[15] The assumption is, unfortunately, often wrong, since welfare recipients for years have frequently been combining welfare and wages.[16] Yet facts rarely have affected the extent to which people allow unexamined stereotypes to affect their attitude toward those "other" people who are allegedly not playing by white, middle-class rules. Welfare recipients, both white and nonwhite, frequently do not conform to stereotype. Yet that did not matter, since it seemed that the tiered system of social provision was feeding back and reinforcing mass attitudes about the poor. The very design of the welfare state was helping to perpetuate what seemed to me to be a longstanding semiotic structure of deservingness.[17]

HOW IT WORKS

I was a structuralist who was also a poststructuralist. Further, I was still an empirical researcher who used statistics to demonstrate the facts of a problem, even as I was a discourse analyst who showed that we relied on an underlying system of signification to make sense of what we took to be the facts of the social reality we were examining. My bipolar, schizoid approach to the study of race, poverty, and welfare was increasingly rationalized for me as "mixed methods." I saw valued added by combining different approaches, or at least swapping one out for the other when it proved beneficial at any point in time, depending on the audience and the problem in question.

By the late 1990s, I was a frustrated empiricist who was greatly discouraged that no matter how we used statistics to point out the myths associated with poverty and welfare, people kept insisting that the welfare poor were these underserving "other" people who were not playing by white, middle-class rules of work and family. The 1996 welfare reform law came to be seen as successful simply because its enactment was followed by an acceleration in the decline in the number of welfare recipients (which actually had started with an uptick in the economy in the early 1990s). No amount of empirical research that highlighted the real conditions of the poor and the need for social assistance seemed to matter. As a result, I became interested in the mechanism by which this deeply embedded invidious distinction repeatedly got reiterated and reimposed on the poor as undeserving. I started to think about the relationship of narrative to discourse more seriously than previously (and in ways that led me to semiotics).

My rethinking of narrative as distinct from discourse involved learning to "read between the lines."[18] I say "read between the lines" because discourse had come to mean to me the unsaid more than the said: it is that unsaid underlying structure of intelligibility that creates a referential context for deriving meaning from what is said. As Barry Laga clarifies: "[B]y 'discourse,' I mean not only the way we use language, but also the assumptions, attitudes, values, beliefs, and hierarchies that are attached to way language is used. [The] task is to show how a text functions within a discourse or show how a text attempts to negotiate among competing discourses."[19] Just as Jacques Lacan could effectively suggest that the unconscious is structured like a language, discourse is in significant part like the unconscious, hidden in plain sight, available to be referenced, even if not explicitly so.[20]

In this rendering, discourse is different than narrative. Narratives are the surface textual representations of actions and events, while discourse is the underlying interpretive context for making sense of those surface narratives. Consciously or not, we inevitably rely on the underlying discourse for interpreting the implicit understandings that are only suggested by the explicit, surface narratives. Just as we rely on implicit understandings to interpret nonverbal cues, we rely on the structure of intelligibility associated with any discourse to connect the dots in any narrative. Narratives are potent with meaning in ways that only discourse can reveal. To focus on the explicit narrative at the expense of the implicit discourse is, metaphorically speaking, to miss the forest for the trees.

An example of the relationship of the unsaid discourse to the said narrative comes from film. In criticizing reviews of Stanley Kubrick's film *Barry Lyndon*, Michael Klein distinguishes between discourse and narrative:

> There seems to be an expectation, virtually prescriptive, that the core of the film should reside in the narrative, in the sequence of events and point of view of the main characters. However Kubrick's modernist perspective is somewhat different. While the events do shape the characters' lives, they are relatively neutral, incomplete signs. The characters are devoid of self-consciousness. The total configuration of visual and aural signs (including the music and the voiceover), that is the discourse, defines and determines our response to and comprehension of the events. . . . The discourse is ironic and analytic (places the characters and events in a larger perspective); it also engages our sympathy (defines value and meaning). A discourse is a configuration of [s]igns . . . that over-determines the narrative.[21]

When examining the underlying discourse, we see that even the tried-and-true distinctions regarding what is natural versus cultural, or what is reason versus emotion, or even male versus female, practice their own intertexuality: each claims to refer to a real binary, but in fact its ability to reference the real world is infinitely deferred, and these distinctions only end up referring to other distinctions. It is like finding out that behind the curtain there is no real Wizard of Oz, just some old man. The foundation is actually made of sand; the cat chases its tail; any attempt to get to the origin of it all is frustrated by the continuous reference to another distinction.

When we try to explain a distinction between two words, we must use other distinctions to clarify. We never get to ground that distinction in a definitive way in the world of objective material reality, whether it is to distinguish what is natural from what is cultural, what is rational from what is emotional, or even what is essentially male from what is female (even if the last distinction suggests we can come close—i.e., do genitalia really define the difference between male and female?). There is no terra firma on which we can base our use of words to reference real things objectively understood. (I know this can be infuriating; but then again I did not make the world. I only report on it. Don't blame the messenger.) The alleged fundamental distinctions regarding what is real refer not to objective reality but instead only to each other, one binary to the next endlessly, never quite getting to anchor their particular distinctions in the material world. Our access to the real world is ineliminably intertextual.

I eventually saw everything as intertextual: I was now deep into discourse analysis, well beyond my earlier forays. Yet, to say *intertextual* may sound too obscure, so let me explain. Take something centrally related to our topic: the historically privileged citizen-subject of Western, liberal political discourse—the rational, autonomous, self-sufficient male. He actually emerges out of the intertextuality of nested oppositions that suggests that women are more emotional than men because they are more tied to humans' biological nature due to their childbearing capacities. The relevance for critiquing welfare policy discourse is acute. For instance, this kind of demystification helps question the dichotomy of structure and agency that lies problematically at the base of the still-hegemonic, Western, liberal-capitalist political discourse that assumes at its foundation the independent, self-sufficient, autonomous citizen-subject—for example, a male breadwinner—who is therefore to be privileged over those subjectivities that imply dependency and an inability to act for oneself on one's own terms—for example, a female welfare recipient.

Questioning the implied subjectivities of all policy discourses is in fact political work that is critical. At the center of the imaginaries of most policy discourses is the implied subject of that policy: the policy identity assumed to be reflective of the citizen-subject who is the target of that policy, be he or she citizen, taxpayer, worker, voter, business owner, homeowner, welfare recipient, retiree, illegal immigrant, ex-con, terrorist, green consumer, hedge fund manager, and so on. The implied subject position so defined by any one particular public policy is the quintessential example of how policy discourse operates by creating an unsaid, assumed reference point to which the ostensible metaphors of the surface narrative of any policy gesture (see Table 9.1).

Table 9.1

Surface Level:
Narrative (often including a story of how a policy problem and its solution came to be)
Framing Metaphors (always present in any policy narrative referencing an underlying discourse for making sense of the narrative and its story)
Underlying Structure:
Discourse (comprised of critical distinctions for making sense of particular policy narratives)
Subjectivities (key distinctions that reference why some identities are to be privileged in a policy narrative)

Heuristically, it can be argued that there is value in suggesting that there are levels of policy discourse, much like the idea that there are levels of consciousness. On the surface, there are key framing metaphors embedded in any policy narrative that point to an underlying discourse that provides reference points for making meaning from the framing metaphors and the ostensible narratives with which they are associated.

As Deborah Stone has insightfully noted, policy narratives often tell politically convenient "just so" stories, often championed most effectively by the most powerful groups active in the public policy process, that suggest why it makes sense to see a policy and its problem of concern a particular way. The policy narrative and the story it provides inevitably include framing metaphors that suggest that the saga told about a policy, its problem, and the people associated with dealing with it are analogous to other situations and characters. The context for interpreting these metaphors is that underlying structure of intelligibility, or what I am calling here the discourse, which itself relies on key binary distinctions for privileging certain practices and people.

The policy narrative and its framing metaphors rely on that discourse for implying that there is a certain type of identified citizen-subject who is assumed to be the focus of concern (either as a problem person or praiseworthy person, as, for example, in the case of welfare policy in the United States today, where such a protagonist is cited as either a demonized "welfare mother" or a "personally responsible mother," the latter designating, ironically for welfare reform, a "working mother" who assigns paid employment outside the home her top priority).

I had gone down this road before, starting with an article I published in 1993 on discourse and identity in welfare policy.[22] Frank Fischer was co-editor of the special issue of the journal that published that article, and he took an interest in my work. After my first book, *Words of Welfare* (1995), used that article as one of its chapters, we kept discussing topics related to discourse analysis in public policy studies. Frank ended up leading the group of scholars who created the journal *Critical Policy Studies*, where this type of analysis could be featured. In a recent book he has written: "Employing literary and rhetorical devices for symbolic representation, policy stories are tools of political persuasion. As strategies for depicting problems and interests, discursive devices such as synecdoches (which represent the whole by one of its parts) or metaphors (which make implied comparisons) are pervasive throughout policy stories. Such linguistic constructions are designed and introduced to convince an audience of the necessity of a political or policy action; they help identify the responsible culprits and the virtuous saviors capable of leading us to high ground."[23]

With my next book, in 2000, *After Welfare*, I had evolved to explicitly adopt a semiotic approach to these issues. Perhaps it was the latent structuralist in me, but what I found most appealing was that the semiotic approach highlighted that there is an underlying cultural interpretive grid in any society that provides the basis for the implied subjectivities of any public policy. I liked the idea that there was a structure of intelligibility that informed how we made sense of things. This structure gave rise, I thought, to basic distinctions in policy discourse that we relied one on make sense of people's identities, as good or bad, in or out, deserving or undeserving. Related questions began to form: Who are these imagined personas that inhabit any particular policy discourse? How do they get created? How do they get to act? What kind of agency do they have? What is their power over us? And how can we engage them in ways that are democratic and that enable us to make our own gestures toward a more socially just set of public arrangements? These are questions that a revitalized form of discourse analysis provokes.

As Fischer suggests, the inquiry into the discursive construction of policy identities has the potential to make a distinctive, democratizing contribution to public policy analysis. More than conventional approaches, semiotic policy analysis offers the opportunity to interrogate those assumptions about identity that are embedded in the analysis and making of public policy, thereby enabling the questionable distinctions that privilege some identities at the expense of others to be rethought and resisted. Public policy analysis can benefit from the emphasis on how discourse constructs identity.

SPOILED IDENTITY IN WELFARE POLICY DISCOURSE

With the model provided in Table 9.1, I felt I had created a window into how every policy has its "other"—its unsaid, implied citizen-subject that makes us assume that the policy is logically related to real people when in fact that other is an artifact of the policy discourse that personifies its political biases. Social welfare policy in the contemporary postindustrial United States has been shown to participate in the construction and maintenance of identity in ways that affect not just the allocation of public benefits but also economic opportunities outside of the state. Yet this is a well-established black art. Mired in old, invidious distinctions, welfare policy discourse today helps to recreate the problems of yesterday. An examination of the implied citizen-subject of welfare policy in the postreform period was quickly becoming, therefore, my object of inquiry.

History teaches us that there is a deep semiotic structure of deservingness undergirding contemporary welfare policy discourse in the United States. It is deeply embedded in the nation's roots, stretching back over two centuries. This discourse is anchored in the contrast between two central subjectivities: the deserving autonomous, self-sufficient individual and the undeserving dependent who fails to exhibit the independence assumed to be central in the making of the liberal citizen, who can be counted on to act for himself or herself (see Table 9.2).

Table 9.2

Surface Level:
The Welfare Dependency Narrative (including stories of how relying on welfare is an addiction, means you are a bad mother, makes you a bad role model, etc.)
Dependency, Personal Responsibility, Self-Sufficiency as Key Welfare Policy Metaphors (these framing metaphors suggest that accepting welfare is to be understood by referencing an underlying discourse that connects welfare reliance to other denigrated practices)
Underlying Structure:
Welfare Reform Discourse (comprised of critical distinctions for making sense of welfare reform narratives: active/passive, independent/dependent, work/care, etc.)
Subjectivities (identities to be privileged in the welfare reform narrative: the self-sufficient, autonomous subject)

These two central subjectivities not only anchor how we approach thinking about the public realm generally but also serve to create a basis for questioning whether to extend aid to the needy. We can see this in the debates about welfare that have historically informed welfare policy discourse in the United States. From before the time Thomas Malthus wrote his infamous *Essays on the Principles of Population* in 1798 in England to after Charles Murray reiterated those arguments in *Losing Ground* in 1984 in the United States, social welfare policy discourse has been dominated by what Albert Hirschman has called the "perversity thesis."[24]

In Malthus's hands, the perversity thesis combined classical liberal economic theory with Christian morality to suggest that, contrary to the apparent reality that offering financial aid to the "poor" was a kind and charitable act of assistance, such intervention actually undermined the natural order of things and corrupted the individuals who accepted such succor, so that they lost the ability to practice self-discipline and exercise personal responsibility. The theory held that helping poor people in this way actually had perverse effects because the poor are different from other people and lack the capacity for self-discipline when it comes to issues of work and family: the poor are lazy and promiscuous. If you give them financial assistance, they will just squander it, and if you persist in helping them, they will just take society down with them. The perversity thesis has proven resilient even in the face of secularization. For well over two centuries, at varying points in time and to varying degrees, much success has come to the perversity thesis and its related cousin, the futility thesis, which maintains that "the poor" will always be with us no matter what we do.

This success testifies to the power of discourse. Arguments like the perversity thesis can be persuasive independent of historical circumstances. The facts of "welfare dependency" at any time seem far less significant than the enduring power of the perversity thesis to appeal to ingrained moralisms in Western, liberal-capitalist societies about public aid corrupting the individual and undermining the self-discipline assumed to be central in the making of the autonomous, self-sufficient, liberal citizen-subject. To accept welfare is therefore often characterized as "welfare dependency" because it is associated with undermining the autonomy and independence associated with the model type of citizen-subject we all need to become if we are to take on the subject position in the liberal public sphere. If we are all dependents, then who will be able to fulfill the role of the independent citizen free to act on his or her own accord in the public sphere, politically, socially, economically, and so on? The entire edifice of the liberal, democratic, capitalist order is built on the assumption that there are free consenting individuals who enter into economic, social, and political contracts and other arrangements. Any behaviors that suggest that we are not free or independent, but instead beholden to others, or dependent, undermine the plausibility of this assumed subjectivity and pose a risk to that order that must be resisted.

The facts of welfare dependency in this sense are always already there, ready to be materialized in quotidian practices of welfare administration that treat welfare recipients in self-fulfilling, denigrating ways. All it takes is a less than active imagination willing to interpret welfare participation unreflectively, as if it were without question a sign of personal deficiency. Sadly, the modern history of the Western world, especially in the United States and England, is replete with such instances of underutilized imagination placing whatever facts were offered about welfare use in terms of this argument about an unchanging underlying moral order. And the facts of welfare dependency are less than apparent.

By the late 1990s, as I finished *After Welfare*, I was becoming increasingly frustrated with how welfare receipt was being framed in the process of rolling out welfare reform. I shared my frustration with Joe Soss while attending a conference honoring Frances Fox Piven at the University of Oregon in late February 2000. I remember the moment. We were sitting among the very large audience at a plenary session while Jared Bernstein talked about creating more jobs (something he has continued to do ever since, given the problems of our restructuring economy). I was holding a copy of *The Nation* magazine in my hand, pointing out a discussion on the politics of numbers, and I told Joe that all the numbers the proponents of welfare reform were spouting were framed in a self-serving way, to make the policy seem to be the success it was not. The numbers implicitly traded on the assumption that welfare receipt was inherently bad and reducing the rolls in any way possible was an unalloyed good. We agreed right there to write an article pointing out that the discourse framed welfare reform as an inevitable success, irrespective of what happened to the people who got kicked off public assistance.[25]

So it was that in the runup to welfare reform in the 1990s, no amount of facts about the myths of welfare dependency did any good whatsoever in undermining the ideological juggernaut the conservative, right-wing cultural warriors had developed to impugn the already sullied image of welfare recipients as malingerers and no-'counts, that is, promiscuous women lazily living off welfare.[26] Racial bias figured prominently in the narratives that circulated among welfare reform supporters and highlighted how deeply embedded racialized definitions of who is deserving permeated policy discourse. The gender bias of the discourse was equally stunning, overlooking that the overwhelming majority of recipients of cash assistance to poor families are single mothers who are trying to handle both breadwinning and caregiving responsibilities on their own. Yet the mere recitation of factual evidence about contemporary welfare recipients was to prove woefully inadequate in the face of an argument that had endured at least since the eighteenth century and had convinced people to ignore empirical information in order to appreciate the underlying "natural order of things." And in the Western, liberal political imaginary, the underlying natural order of things was assumed to be one in which the privileged citizen-subject was the autonomous, self-sufficient, male head of a family. It was as if extending aid to black, single mothers jeopardized the perpetuation of the natural order of things and needed to be resisted.

Therefore, dependency discourse in the United States was, arguably, paradigmatic of discourse in general. It provides an exemplar of how discourse operates to make itself real. Like all discourse, it interprets symptoms to be signs of some preexisting, underlying condition that it, retroactively, identifies as always already having been there, often for reasons attributable to the characteristics or traits of some implied type of person associated with a particular identity, that is, a subjectivity. In this way, it can be said that all discourses, welfare policy or otherwise, have their "others." In semiotic fashion, discourse implies identities, both a privileged identity and an "othered," denigrated identity. In the case of welfare policy discourse, from Malthus on, dependency discourse with its perversity thesis imputes a preexisting set of pathological behaviors in a timeless way to the "poor" as an othered group comprising distinctive types of people that then in their otherness give rise to the poverty and welfare dependency that we see before us in the contemporary scene. And once we accept as real this narrated discourse of implied identities, we organize our affairs, including public policies, to address the deficiencies in the denigrated identity to the point that people so identified have almost no choice but to either capitulate to being treated on those terms or risk being marginalized further as deviants of a more difficult sort.

THE MEDICALIZED SELF

As my work on the deep semiotic structure of deservingness progressed, I became increasingly concerned about the ways welfare discourse was increasingly medicalizing welfare receipt as a sickness. Perhaps it was informed by my now working full time in a graduate program in Social Work, but this concern seemed pervasive. My colleagues shared readings with me. I learned a lot. I started thinking that there was something valid in the idea that the age-old perversity thesis was now being reincarnated in highly technocratic ways. It seemed to be retrofitted for the new forms of governance that relied heavily on a medicalized discourse to characterize the welfare poor as a deficient population in need of treatment. It increasingly became clear to me that a process of intertextuality was at work. Contemporary welfare policy discourse understands reliance on public assistance in highly medicalized terms by borrowing metaphors from other service domains that end up imputing the causes of poverty and reliance to the individual and her or his personal deficiencies. Medicalization is, arguably, the main way that welfare policy discourse today creates a stage for enacting what Michel Foucault calls governmentality, where the state is in the business of disciplining the poor to become self-disciplined citizen-subjects who will be less of burden on the rest of us in spite of the persistent poverty they endure.[27]

The medicalization of what has come to be called "welfare dependency," it seemed to me, was fast becoming a major administrative focus under the new welfare reform regime instituted in the 1990s. I see it metaphorically. It is as if the aphasia of welfare discourse prevents us from confronting the trauma of poverty, and we use euphemistic substitutes such as *welfare dependency* to paper over our complicity in perpetuating other people's destitution while simultaneously shifting the blame away from the structure of society to the individual behavior of those who are forced to live in poverty.

With this old aphasic shift taking new form, welfare dependency becomes the center of our discursive terrain dealing with how, in the contemporary parlance of our therapeutic culture, to "treat" recipients for their diseased condition of dependence on welfare. Welfare use beyond the shortest periods of time as a form of transitional aid, as, say, when a single mother relies on welfare while working through a divorce, is now considered abuse. In other words, welfare use beyond a few months is now welfare abuse, signaling the need to undergo treatment to overcome one's dependency on welfare. The dependency metaphor operates more like a metonymy in which a contiguous reference point is emphasized rather than the original object of concern. The poverty that precedes welfare dependency is ignored, and instead we are asked to focus on the reliance on welfare.

This semiotic shift is, arguably, most convenient for the rich and powerful in the United States, who increasingly need to deflect attention from the lack of upward mobility afforded to the lower classes in the ossifying and deeply unequal class structure that has emerged with the changing economy, associated with globalization, and the proliferation of low-wage jobs as the only recourse to subsistence for many. Dependency becomes a displacement for talking about the underlying structural poverty of that economy, which our liberal, individualistic, agentistic political discourse cannot effectively address. So "welfare use," "welfare receipt," and the especially verboten "welfare taking" are all being replaced by "welfare dependency." As a result, reliance on welfare is articulated as a sign that a single mother suffers from "welfare dependency," which, like other dependencies, is something from which the client needs to be weaned with an appropriate therapeutic treatment. Under welfare reform, all applicants for assistance are screened, diagnosed, assessed, and referred for the appropriate treatment to accelerate the process by which they can overcome their vulnerability to being dependent on welfare.

Medicalization represents modernity's preference for science over religion, expressed in the growing propensity to conceive myriad personal problems in medicalized terms. It envisions the poor as sick, as opposed to bad. Yet that revised outlook comes with a price: welfare dependency is defined as the product of an individual's behavior, more than the inequities in the social structure or political economy. In this way, medicalization suggests that upward mobility is still possible. The poor are not fated to be poor; they can be cured of their ills and thereby activated to advance economically. This convenient displacement story, redirecting focus away from the structural embeddness of persistent poverty in the changing economy, serves the political interests of powerful groups invested in not having to attack those structural roots of contemporary poverty. By highlighting that the poor can be cured of their dependency on welfare, medicalizing implies that mobility is still possible, when in fact it is less than likely.

One manifestation of how medicalization implies mobility is the proliferation of "barriers" talk in welfare policy implementation. A major preoccupation in welfare reform as a new form of governance is assisting recipients to overcome "barriers" to self-sufficiency. "Barriers," contrary to the term's ostensible meaning, is most often construed under welfare reform as personal problems. Racial and sexual discrimination in the workplace or the lack of decent paying jobs is not usually acknowledged in state welfare programs as a barrier to moving from welfare to work. Instead, barriers are most often discussed as personal problems that are internal issues specific to the individual rather external conditions in society that are blocking one's advancement. As a result, more and more programming under welfare reform is concentrated on what are seen as the related conditions that give rise to welfare dependency, be they mental health issues, behavioral problems, or addictions. In the masculinized discourse of welfare reform, even children risk being referred to as barriers to work. The goal is to get single mothers to be comfortable being the breadwinner for their families, even if it means cutting back on their commitments to their children. Yet the idea of instilling a commitment to taking paid employment is couched in the terms of liberal political discourse. Self-esteem classes as well as psychological counseling have become common features of welfare-to-work programs as ways of engendering the self-confidence needed for participants to become the autonomous, self-sufficient actors assumed by liberal political discourse.

Over time, this issue enacts its own self-fulfilling prophecy. As more and more of the welfare population exits under welfare-to-work programs that require recipients to make "rapid attachment" to paid employment in the labor force, the remaining population is increasingly made up of recipients who have indeed incurred certain personal problems at high rates. For instance, it is estimated that "a growing share of [those individuals receiving] Temporary Assistance for Needy Families, which offers cash support to low-income single caregivers, is composed of individuals with mental illness, as new work requirements result in faster exits of those without mental health conditions."[28] The rate of depression among the welfare reform population has been growing for some time. This, ironically, reinforces the medicalized character of welfare dependency as if it were a real phenomenon that was in fact always already there in the first place, as if most recipients were always suffering from the illness of welfare dependency and its related medicalized conditions. Just like any good discourse, "welfare dependency" then becomes its own self-fulfilling prophecy, making itself real by manufacturing the reality that, it claims, preexisted it. Reliance on welfare comes to be seen less as an economic problem and more as a mental health issue.

Yet medicalization did not change fundamental attitudes about welfare, which remained ambivalent. Most Americans still do not in principle oppose government assistance for low-income families and in fact continued to believe that we have a collective obligation to help the poor. For instance, from the 1980s through 2009, 60 to 70 percent of Americans indicated they supported government assistance for the poor and believed government had a responsibility to guarantee every citizen food to eat and a place to sleep.[29] At the same time, most Americans also continued to believe that those in need should receive assistance only if they maintain a commitment to personal responsibility and a work ethic. The campaign against welfare dependency was successful not because it changed this mix of attitudes. Instead, its success was in reframing the issue to focus on welfare dependency as a problem that needed immediate treatment. The problem of dependency came to be seen as a major source of society's economic as well as social and cultural ills. It increasingly was framed as creating a significant drain on the economy even as it encouraged out-of-wedlock births, single parent families, and a decline in the work ethic. The dependency frame saw public assistance not as a hard-won protection *for* poor workers and their families; instead, it viewed welfare as a policy imposed *against* workers' values as well as their bank accounts.

This "us versus them" identity politics reframing of welfare has been facilitated by the fact that welfare has for a long time been depicted in the mass media using highly misleading racial terms and imagery. As a result, the public tends to exaggerate grossly the extent to which blacks received public assistance and in turn became increasingly critical of welfare as a program for poor blacks, who were seen as "other" people who were not like most white middle-class families and did not adhere to work and family values. Racial resentments and old stereotypes of black laziness became more influential in spawning growing hostility toward welfare.[30]

The reframing of the welfare issue as a problem of dependency concentrated in a black underclass has involved the policy equivalent of a Gestalt switch by which the same facts came to be seen through a new lens, leading to a different interpretation. In an earlier era, liberals had framed "troubling" behaviors among the poor as products of poverty and used images of social disorganization, especially among poor blacks, as evidence for the necessity of extending aid. The conservative campaign against welfare dependency, however, reframed these same behaviors as products of "permissive" social programs that failed to limit program usage, require work, or demand functional behavior. "Long-term dependency" became a key phrase in welfare debates, usually treated as part of a broader syndrome of underclass pathologies that included drug use, violence, crime, teen pregnancy, single motherhood, and even poverty itself. Gradually, permissiveness and dependency displaced poverty and structural barriers to advancement as the central problems that drew attention from those designing welfare policy.

The discursive turn to dependency had important political consequences. First, welfare dependency and its effects on the poor set the agenda for poverty research in the 1980s and 1990s. To distinguish myths from realities, researchers expended great effort identifying the typical duration of participation spells and the individual-level correlates of long-term program usage. Structural questions received less attention as defenders responded to critics in a debate that focused on work effort, program usage, and poor people's behaviors. Second, as dependency came to be seen as a cause of intergenerational poverty, it became a kind of synecdoche, a single part used to represent the whole tangle of problems associated with the poor. To fight dependency was, in essence, to fight a kind of substance abuse that led to unrestrained sexuality, drug problems, violent crime, civic irresponsibility, and even poverty itself.

As a synecdoche for diverse social ills, dependency became the basis for a powerful crisis narrative in the 1980s and 1990s. Critics spoke of a "crisis of dependency," often in conjunction with fellow travelers such as the "teen pregnancy crisis" and the "underclass crisis." As Murray Edelman explains, such crisis language evokes perceptions of threat, conveys the need for immediate and extraordinary action, and suggests that "now is not the time" to air dissent or seek deliberation.[31] Claims about the prevalence of long-term program usage were often overblown, and images of wholesale social disintegration depended on highly selective readings of poor people's attitudes and behaviors. But by applying the label "crisis," critics turned ambiguous trends among the poor (many of which also existed in the rest of society) into a fearsome threat to the values of "middle America."

Just as the "drug crisis" seemed to require a tough, incarceration-minded War on Drugs, the crisis of dependency called for nothing short of an assault on permissiveness. In this environment, poverty advocates who tried to direct attention toward issues other than dependency were seen as fiddling while Rome burned. Long-term program usage was viewed as a major social problem requiring a bold solution; it called for extraordinary measures, not tepid liberal palliatives. The only suitable response was to attack dependency at its root by imposing a new regime of welfare rules designed to dissuade and limit program usage, enforce work, and curb unwanted behaviors. In 1996, that is exactly what welfare reform did.

This reframing of welfare dependency as a manifestation of the pathologies of the poor, and most especially black, underclass created the political climate that led to President Bill Clinton joining with a Republican Congress to "end welfare as we know it." The result was the Personal Responsibility and Work Opportunity Reconciliation Act of 1996 that abolished the sixty-one-year-old Aid to Families with Dependent Children (AFDC) program, which had come to be an entitlement that citizens had a right to receive once determined to be eligible. In its place, states would now receive block grants under the TANF program, which could be used to provide cash assistance as AFDC did, but they had to meet quotas in moving recipients into paid employment. In addition, recipients faced work requirements, time limits, caps on benefits, and the possibility of sanctions when not complying with contracts they signed promising to take steps to leave welfare for work. The purging of the welfare rolls that had started in the early 1990s with waivers allowing states to experiment with some of these new restrictions accelerated after 1996 until the economy slowed in 2001. As a result, the number of recipients of welfare fell from 13,242,000 in 1995 to 4,076,764 by September 2009—a decline of 69.2 percent. And while welfare reform has been widely heralded as a success for this reason alone, it has resulted in most single mothers leaving to become mired in poverty (see chapter 7). These hardships have been most frequently visited on black single mothers, who are also likeliest to be forced off welfare by sanctions and to have to cycle back on if they have limited-time eligibility remaining.

Welfare was thus retrenched in no small part because of the way welfare dependency discourse had reframed this policy issue in gendered and racialized ways that portrayed welfare use as a pathology that had to be treated therapeutically. Borrowing metaphors from allied arenas of service provision laid the basis for a veritable medicalization of welfare dependency as a personal pathology that required individualized treatment as much as any other behavioral problem. With such a reframing, it became all the more difficult to see reliance on welfare as a product of structural problems in the economy or society. Public opinion was not so much changed as mobilized to support the retrenchment of welfare as the primary means by which we as a society could attack not just the scourge of welfare dependency but the cluster of pathological behaviors with which it was associated.

So it was, then, that I came to appreciate the role of discourse in framing the dominant understandings of the welfare poor as wholly "other." And not just as other, but now as a medicalized other in need to treatment for the disease of welfare dependency. Now, with the medicalized discourse of welfare dependency firmly entrenched in public deliberations about welfare use, welfare reform increasingly has turned into the social policy equivalent of a twelve-step program. Rather than a program to redistribute needed income to poor families with children, it has become a behavioral modification regime centered on getting the parents of these children to become self-disciplined so that they in turn will become self-sufficient according to ascendant work and family values. Increasingly, this behavioral modification regime is implemented via public-private partnerships in which state and local governments contract with private, often for-profit, providers to move single mothers with children off welfare and into jobs and marriages. The medicalized discourse of dependency logically calls forth new forms of governance that can practice the governmentality needed for regimenting low-income parents into the low-wage labor markets of the globalizing economy. The net result is that poverty is displaced as the persistent underlying problem that it is, and welfare policy comes to be focused ever more on reducing welfare dependency as an end in itself.

The medicalized discourse of welfare dependency may have made reliance on welfare the social policy equivalent of an addiction, thereby making welfare recipients out to be "sick" rather than "bad."[32] Yet this discursive shift did not exonerate the poor. The medicalization of welfare dependency simply reinforced the belief that most welfare recipients were passive dependents who were idle when they could have been working; and it further reinforced the idea that offering the poor aid only perversely encouraged the bad habit of idleness. In fact, in today's medicalized parlance, offering aid was characterized as "sick," as Newt Gingrich and others noted in the years just before welfare reform was adopted by the United States Congress. From this perspective, it became that much easier to believe that if welfare recipients were treated for their condition, they could be taught how to do what is right, and then they could take their place in the workforce and begin to work their way to self-sufficiency, if not quite out of poverty. Indeed, although the rolls have declined and the labor force participation rate and earnings of former adult welfare recipients are up, the underlying poverty that afflicts their families persists. The "welfare poor" have been replaced by the "working poor." And the metonymy of dependency as a product of individual choice continues to leave us in denial about the structural causes of poverty in our economic system.

THE PERSISTENCE OF THE DEEP SEMIOTIC STRUCTURE OF DESERVINGNESS

Today's welfare system trades on a discourse dedicated to making itself real by becoming its own self-fulfilling prophecy. The governmentality associated with contemporary welfare policies has been aptly described as "a political project that endeavors to create a social reality that it suggests already exists."[33] In fact, poverty governance today assumes that welfare recipients are already market actors even before they start taking paid employment. As a result, the different dimensions of their lives, from mental health issues to child-rearing responsibilities, are termed "barriers" to work that must be overcome. This reconstruction is but one element of a broader rewriting of identity that is well captured by the exhortations of a welfare "job club" instructor observed by Anna Korteweg: "No one in this room has been out of work, the way we're going to write your resume. You're working in the house, you're a taxi driver, a budget planner, you volunteer at your children's school, you're a food preparer. You're self-employed, you're not receiving the income but you're working all the time. You have been successfully and diligently working daily."[34] Welfare policy discourse repositions single mothers on welfare as proto-workers who are to prove their worth to society by taking paid employment under almost any conditions and regardless of how poor the pay. They are to be regimented into the bottom of a globalizing economy of declining wages. There, they learn to be the compliant members of that subordinate caste. Their inclusive exclusion is executed when we come to see them as no longer the "welfare poor" but now the "working poor."

In fact, the deep semiotic structure of deservingness undergirds much of contemporary U.S. politics in these transitional times. Witness the Tea Party's success in recent years in attacking the efforts of the Obama administration to aid those disadvantaged by the Great Recession or those who find even when the economy is growing that they cannot afford health insurance. The Tea Partiers have been obsessed with demonizing the unemployed and the uninsured as undeserving dependents sucking at the teat of government.[35] The Tea Party activists square the circle tying the Obama administration's attempt to aid the disadvantaged with the paranoid delusions of Glenn Beck that Barack Obama is an acolyte of Frances Fox Piven and Richard Cloward, who is bent on aiding the undeserving poor just to bankrupt America and force the country to adopt a communist form of government. As one sign read in front of the U.S. Supreme Court when the Court considered the constitutionality of the Affordable Care Act requirement to buy health insurance, "no Obamarx Care or Cloward and Piven spending."[36] The very idea of aiding those who are not working or working at jobs that do not provide health insurance is not just treated suspiciously as aiding the undeserving but is assumed to be a communist plot to undermine the American way of life where each person pulls their own weight.

As I watched the breathtaking return in the presidential campaign of 2012 to the victim-blaming discourse trained on the welfare poor, I became convinced that there is an abidingly deep semiotic structure of deservingness that undergirds U.S. political discourse. And it is not some marginal facet of our politics; it is at its structural core. It is held in reserve, available to be reinvoked as needed to push people's buttons, score political points, whip up hysteria, and mollify it with the finding of ready-made scapegoats for our economic travails and cultural anxieties.[37] In other words, the deep semiotic structure of deservingness gets reenacted again and again. It reproduces a diabolical relationship between discourse and identity demonizing people, for whom they are made out to be based on how they have been treated. This relationship between discourse and identity is older than our founding fathers, but its own origin story infinitely defers grounding our understandings of deservingness in the real world of real people and their real life circumstances. Instead, nothing more than its self-referentiality provides the basis for how we decide that "they" are not like "us," and that the "poor" need to learn to act "middle class." Symbolic shadowboxing becomes how policy discourse continually pummels the poor. Rust never sleeps and neither does the deep semiotic structure of deservingness.

TEN

THREE HEADS ARE BETTER THAN ONE

Collaboration, Mixed Methods, and Disciplining the Poor

Not everything in my life has been a perfect storm. Sometimes the stars are aligned. That is what happened when Joe Soss and Richard Fording asked if they could work with me. Why me? I was older; Joe had only taken a course with me when I was a visiting professor and Rich just happened to have studied what I wrote from afar. Dumb luck, I say. Whatever the case, it was the beginning of a great collaboration in which I got to offer ideas and they got to apply their many talents to making those ideas become a reality. It does not get much better than that. And with time, they had all the best ideas too. I often ended up being a dutiful research assistant helping to carry out whatever it was we, together, decided we needed to do. Better still.

After some time, we hit on the idea of conducting a major study of the implementation of welfare reform, tracing from how it got enacted at the national level down to how it got adopted by the states, to how local contract agencies implemented it, to how caseworkers performed, to ultimately how it affected clients. That study took about nine years to complete from its first conceptualization to the publication of the book.[1]

There is a debate, of sorts, among the three of us about when this project got started. One version of the story is that in 2002 when we were putting together an edited volume, *Race and the Politics of Welfare Reform*, we decided to conduct an in-depth study of how welfare reform was being implemented.[2] (This was, yet again, another book of mine where there was tremendous consternation about what image to put on the cover. We eventually went with a cartoon drawing of a hand holding a placard on which the title of the book was written. It implied politics more than race, though the book was about racial politics.)

Another version of when the welfare implementation project started is that we approached the idea of the project more incrementally, starting the following year at a breakfast meeting that preceded a congressional briefing, organized by the Leadership Conference on Civil Rights, about racial disparities in treatment under welfare reform. (Joe had arranged our participation in the meeting to publicize the findings from our earlier research in the edited volume, but he could not attend because, ironically, he was moving from Washington, D.C., to take a position at the University of Wisconsin-Madison, where he and I had first met when he took a course from me in 1993.) Before the briefing, Rich Fording proposed that we conduct an experiment with welfare-to-work case managers to see if they treated black clients differently than whites. I remember the meeting clearly. Besides Rich and me, my wife Joan and Wesley Bryant, a doctoral student working with me, were present. (Wesley's dissertation research involved surveying several hundred African American male youth in four different program settings to assess their levels of what Wesley and others call "internalized racism" and its relationship to their propensity to commit acts of violence. He found a high correlation in multivariate analyses. Yet he also found that youth who attended an Afrocentric charter school both had lower levels of internalized racism and were less likely to have a propensity to commit acts of violence.[3])

We all thought the experiment was a great idea. I in particular was very excited at the prospect of conducting this experiment. I taught in a school of Social Work and the idea of studying street-level bureaucrats had always been on the top of my list of things I never seemed to get done.

After the briefing, we told Joe about our idea. Yet, doing an experiment was going to be difficult, as none of us had conducted any experiments, let alone one with case managers. By experiment, we meant something specific. An experiment in this case meant a test where all factors were the same except the characteristics of the client. That way, we could isolate through what is called controlled observation whether the race of the client made a difference in treatment. We thought it would be best to conduct this test via a survey of case managers over the Internet, in which, having accessed a Web page, they read short stories or vignettes about hypothetical clients and then decided whether to penalize them (i.e., sanction them) for failure to comply with welfare-to-work rules. What the case managers would not know was that each time they went to the Web page and read the stories, the characteristics of the client would change, so that we could see if clients of different races got treated differently. Yet how would we write these stories? How would we make sure they were realistic? How would we design the Web page? What state would let us contact their case managers? How would one get this thing done? We were, pretty much, novices.

We decided to think more about how to proceed. Through a series of conferences and many e-mail exchanges, our thinking evolved to encompass a plan for a more robust study of the front lines of welfare reform, in which a survey-experiment of case managers that tested for racial bias would be just one part. Over time, as we fed off each other's excitement, we elaborated more and more ambitious plans to conduct a major study that would thoroughly examine welfare reform from its inception at the national level, to how it played out on the front lines of implementation, to how it affected clients.

We submitted a major research proposal to the National Science Foundation (NSF). We waited to hear their decision. Each of us regularly reviews for the NSF, and we were optimistic about our chances. Well, after the time we were supposed to hear had passed, I wrote to the official who had told me it was set to be evaluated. His response was that, subsequent to his telling me that it was ready for review, it was somehow decided that our proposal did not fit that section of the NSF and that it had never even been sent out for review. Months of work wasted, and no opportunity was accorded us to submit the proposal to another section.

Personally, I suspected politics. The fix was in. Why? Well, by then we had chosen the state where we wanted to conduct the in-depth frontline part of our study: Florida. The year was 2004. The governor was Jeb Bush; the president was George Bush. Was one brother going pay for a study that might make the other brother look bad? Probably not. Then again, after the paranoia subsided, I realized that neither brother probably knew about this study. Still, it seems strange that our proposal was swept under the rug and not passed on to evaluators, who might have looked on it favorably. Maybe the bureaucrats were anticipating what the brothers would want. Maybe, just maybe, I am paranoid. I have to face facts: it is not easy being me. And doing the kind of research I do only makes it worse.

We still wanted to pursue the proposal. We had worked hard on it. It represented much of what the three of us wanted to accomplish intellectually as well as politically. We wanted to collaborate so that we could mix methods, using both theory and history as well as conducting quantitative and qualitative data analysis to examine welfare reform as part of a broader shift to what we had come to call a disciplinary approach to managing the poverty population. Our study would be ambitious theoretically and empirically; it would approach the study of public policy in a more holistic and politically informed way than was often the case.

We had already made contact with officials in Florida who had agreed to allow us to study their implementation of welfare reform for that part of our larger project. Florida was widely recognized in policy circles as an innovator in implementing welfare reform.[4] The state had a decentralized system that relied on the workforce boards created by the Workforce Investment Act of 1998, and it had a state of the art performance management system to hold private, mostly for-profit contractors accountable for achieving goals to move welfare recipients into jobs. Florida was a leader in imposing sanctions to prod recipients to take whatever jobs the economy provided. It had a good level of racial and ethnic diversity, which added a critical dimension to our choosing it for our study.

We wanted to study Florida for a variety of reasons. As luck would have it, when we asked, Florida almost automatically gave us administrative data on clients for multiple years. Based on a just a few getting-to-know-each-other sessions, the folks in Florida agreed to allow us to conduct field research in selected offices of welfare-to-work agencies, to interview program officers and case managers in depth, to conduct a statewide survey of case managers, and to collect other information as well. This quick approval presented its own mystery. Why would the people running the welfare-to-work program in Florida allow us to study their operations? I am pretty sure they already knew that we had previously published research on racial bias in welfare reform. In fact, as the study eventually unfolded, when we reported to them research demonstrating racial disparities, the response was simply that they were not interested in those findings, that they were divisive, and that we should go ahead and publish that research in academic journals. It was as if they did not care that we might find racial biases manifesting themselves in the administration of welfare reform, and they were not afraid that racial disparities might be reported in academic journals since no one whose opinion they cared about would read those journals. The one thing they asked us to promise was to never report our findings in the newspapers, as that was something they did not want to wake up to read in the morning.

But why did they agree to allow us in particular to study their program? At the original meeting in Tallahassee, the key person who approved our study was impressed when Rich explained that his initial examination of the administrative data showed a wide variation in sanction rates across the twenty-four workforce regions in Florida. The heads of the state system were concerned that the different regions and their contract agencies had different understandings of what they were supposed to be doing. Also, they indicated in subsequent private discussions that they were concerned that contract agencies might be gaming the system, producing results that made them look good according to performance management indicators, but were not really doing what they were supposed to. This would turn out to be an understatement (see chapter 8 of *Disciplining the Poor*).

Personally, I think the folks in the main office wanted us to travel around the state, make contact with the frontline agencies, and by our mere presence suggest that the people at the top of the system were looking into what they were doing. In fact, everywhere we went people assumed we were from the state government and were there to check up on them. We had to continually explain that was not the case. It was as if the heads of the state system liked us because we could pose as attack dogs sniffing around looking for dirt. Given our past record as critics, we could play the part well. We made strange bedfellows, who bonded over a shared concern to find out what was happening on the frontlines. As result, in spite of political differences, we had an excellent working relationship with the folks in Florida from the beginning of the project right through to the end.

No contracts were signed; no money was exchanged; we got to do our study and they got to find out what we discovered that was happening in the different regions. It was all agreed to with a handshake. (I am not sure we actually ever shook hands; most of the folks we worked with were women, which might explain that, and we simply nodded to express that this was our arrangement.) Still, we needed money. We had to repeatedly fly there, rent cars, sleep in cheap hotels, eat bad food, use recording equipment, etc. Who would pay for all that? First, Rich got a small grant from the Poverty Research Center at his home institution at the time, the University of Kentucky. (The center would publish a number of the working papers we produced from the study.) Then Joe got some funding from the Institute for Research on Poverty at his home institution at the time, the University of Wisconsin-Madison. And I got funds from the Center on Ethnicities, Community and Social Policy, and from the faculty research fund at Bryn Mawr College. I also got key computing services staff, in the person of David Consiglio, devoted to the project for the administration of the Web-based survey/experiment, which we ended up mounting at Bryn Mawr. Still, it was not nearly enough. Mike Laracy, a program officer at the Annie E. Casey Foundation, was told about the project by contacts at Bryn Mawr, and he found us some money that ended up funding most of our shoestring budget. He said that foundations had already decided not to fund welfare reform studies anymore, that it had been declared a success and the only way he could fund us was with limited amounts out of something like an all-purpose backup fund. Yet he really wanted to do it, since he saw that the consensus on welfare reform as a success was premature. He recognized the value of our work, and we were delighted. Yet, the funding was indeed limited for what we were trying to do—about $60,000. We had to make it last for four years while we did our fieldwork. In the end, we cobbled our ambitious project together, relying on the kindnesses of strangers.

ON THE BEACH IN JANUARY

We went to Florida many times. We observed field offices, we interviewed staff at all levels, we consulted officials about the system, and we periodically checked to make sure we could still do the survey/experiment. I wanted to do that for a variety of reasons: I had never done an experiment, I wanted to study case managers, I wanted our study to succeed on all levels. I spent years going there and basically doing everything I could to make sure we could finish our study. We had so much data from so many sources that I started to become a total kvetch, insisting we could write the book years before we did. (As should be apparent by now, I am not a patient person—think about it, I am writing a memoir and I am not even retired!)

Joe and I often interviewed the same people, sometimes in groups, sometimes individually, checking to be sure we were getting it right. Each of us interviewed other folks from the system on our own. We did not have a template as much as a dialogical model for learning from our interviews till we were convinced we knew what was going on. It started with Rich conducting the interviews with the state officials both in Tallahassee and in Tampa, where the workforce officials were situated. Our interviews were designed to facilitate our own learning rather than to present opportunities for our informants to confess. While the field interviews were ongoing, Rich kept crunching the administrative data, and we all kept trying to design the statewide survey and experiment. We were triangulating 24/7.

In fact, it took us several years before we could say we finally understood the Florida system inside and out. We were trying to understand the whole system but our focus ultimately was on how and why case managers imposed sanctions on noncompliant clients. Sanctions had come to be the cardinal practice of the new disciplinary regime. All states had new sanction schedules that sought to punish recipients with benefit reductions and terminations for failure to comply with the new welfare-to-work rules under welfare reform. We wanted to understand how Florida came to use sanctions, to what effect, and whether race figured in the equation. Our prior research contrasting all the states indicated that race played a big role in determining whether a state invested in the get-tough approach of welfare reform.[5] Now the question was whether the race of the clients affected their treatment.

In order to understand sanctioning, we had to attend the same training workshops that the state provided for all its case managers. I forget where Joe went for his training. I cannot forget where I went, or when: Ft. Lauderdale in January. It was winter in Philadelphia; it was heaven in Florida. Joan and I got a room in a B&B on the beach while I attended lessons daily for a full week along with case managers from all over the state. These sessions focused on how to kick people off the welfare rolls (to put it euphemistically). I was delighted to be at the beach in the winter, but I was depressed that I was learning how to deprive poor families of needed resources.

But my Florida experience was soon to get even more disconcerting. One day, as I was driving in a low-budget rented car between interviews in a metropolitan area and a remote rural community, I was listening to talk radio (it was research, honest)! The topic was: "Have we gone too far?" And this was Florida, mind you! How could Florida go too far? As a tax haven for criminals? As the center of the illicit drug trade? As the most incarcerated state in the country? As the leader in privatizing state services? As a state that steals presidential elections? I was at loss. Driving into the swamp, I listened with perked ears.

As it turned out, the question posed by the topic referred to the fact that a sixteen-year-old had just been convicted to six years in prison for stealing a six-pack of beer from a stop-and-go. How could that be? He had used a gun, and in Florida, as in a few other states, that was one of the mandatory sentencing restrictions: use a gun in a robbery and you get six years. That helps explain mass incarceration. It also helps explain our willful ignorance about how we have come to lock up so many people. Six years for a six-pack for a sixteen-year-old? What are we doing to ourselves? Even talk radio was starting to ask the question. I was listening (while driving). Florida was thinking about just how punitive it had become. It was a start, if only that.

Whether it involved sanctions training in the most beautiful town in the world or talk radio openly reflecting on punitive criminal justice policies, Florida was an acquired taste. Yet in Washington, D.C., it was considered the role model for welfare reform. You figure out whether Congress was looking through the wrong end of the telescope. All I can say is there is nothing like field research to clear that up.

THE EXPERIMENT

The most experimental thing about the experiment in our study was the fact that we were doing it. None of us had ever done one. We each had taught research methods, including experimental design. Yet at first it seemed like the old saying: Those who can do, those who can't . . . teach! We got enormous help from friends and colleagues who instructed us on many levels, from sample size, to questionnaire design, to Web page construction. We read textbooks and consulted the literature. We spent several years just thinking the whole thing through. It was its own learning experience. In the meantime, we continued the analysis of the administrative data and the field interviews, leaving the survey/experiment for when we were finally ready.

The day came in December 2006, when Florida officials sent an official electronic memo to all workforce regions indicating an Internet link for case managers to use to complete the survey. Over the next month, case managers across the state completed the survey. Then we started to analyze the results. Linda Houser, a doctoral student in Social Work at Bryn Mawr, worked with David Consiglio to get the data set for analysis. She eventually became a co-author of the paper reporting the results of the experiment.[6] The results confirmed racial bias.

Yet, given that our collaboration was founded in good part on wanting to demonstrate the power of mixing methods and using different types of data to confirm findings, we wanted to use the administrative data to see if we could triangulate our results showing racial disparities in treatment of clients. Further, scholars such as Troy Duster were at the time pointing out the need to confirm experimental findings in hypothetical situations with other data from the real world.[7] We developed a statistical analysis to model the experimental findings in the administrative data on clients. Once we agreed on the models, the rest of us waited to hear the results from Rich. One day in 2007, as I was out jogging, my cell phone rang. It was Rich, reporting that our key finding—that African Americans were more likely than whites to get sanctioned when they already had a prior sanction—was confirmed in the administrative data. It was great to hear on one level, sad on another.

The experimental data showed what real case managers were thinking about hypothetical clients. The administrative data could not show what case managers were thinking but showed what actually happened to real clients. Together they confirmed that black clients were more likely to be sanctioned than white clients, especially when the black client had a prior sanction that served as a cue triggering a reminder of the prevailing stereotype of those "other" people who were not playing by white middle-class rules and were more likely to be lazy. And these findings held up even when the case manager was an African American woman herself. It was as if the prevailing stereotypes circulated silently in the culture, hidden in plain sight, not consciously being relied on until a marker presented itself, triggering the reminder of that racial stereotype, and the black client would be more likely to get singled out for punishment. And this was true regardless of the race of the case manager. In the post–civil rights society, there could be racism without racists, and the welfare system reenacted it of its own accord.[8]

Our findings were published in the featured article of the June 2009 issue of the *American Sociological Review* (see footnote 6 in this chapter). I had not published an article in that journal since 1983, the last time I had submitted an article there, when Pat Turbett and I had co-authored our analysis on the Piven and Cloward thesis (see footnote 23 in chapter 4). Yet what was most remarkable was that the study even got done, let alone published. At first we had not been sure how to actually do an experiment. Then we were not sure the State of Florida would let us do it. Next, we had no idea if it would work. And last, we wondered if our findings could be triangulated. The stars had aligned and we had produced serious evidence from a collaborative mixed-methods study that racial bias was deeply embedded in the welfare system in the very ways I have been trying to explain in this book. My personal history and my intellectual trajectory had merged.

A THEORETICAL DISPUTE

The idea that I would be nowhere without my relationships to other people was about to get very complicated. While conducting our research for the book, I had been developing a correspondence with the sociologist Loïc Wacquant, who was also studying how poverty governance was changing. His argument was that the United States relied on racism to move to a more punitive system for managing the poverty problem in ways that had disproportionate negative impact upon low-income African Americans. We were moving from a system of "regulating the poor," as Frances Fox Piven and Richard Cloward called it in their monumental 1971 book of that title, to a system of "punishing the poor," which became the title of Wacquant's 2009 book.[9]

For Wacquant, this shift in poverty governance was most dramatically represented by the explosion in incarceration rates, especially among African American males, over the last thirty years, largely due to the heightened penalties that came with the War on Drugs. Wacquant argued that a neoliberal-paternalist philosophy about the way to treat the poor informed this shift. For Wacquant, neoliberalism meant greater reliance on the market and less support from the government, and paternalism meant that for those who could not make it in the market-centered society the result was, essentially, lockdown if you strayed from the path of the straight and narrow.

I was very much taken with Wacquant's perspective and told him so. We corresponded about my interest in developing the neoliberal-paternalist framework for our project. Over time, though, Joe, Rich, and I developed our own understanding of neoliberal paternalism, drawing more from Wacquant's Berkeley colleague in Political Science, Wendy Brown.[10] My relationship with Wacquant soured somewhat when I pointed out these differences in published articles.[11] I had stood on someone's shoulders, but now it looked as though I had come to kill the father (putting aside the fact that Wacquant is considerably younger than me).

What can I say? Things happen, minds change, thinking evolves, I thought about it, and in the end I came to a different conclusion. Yes, at first I simply wanted to use Wacquant's version of neoliberal paternalism for theorizing the philosophy that informed the shift in poverty governance. Yet, over time, continued discussion with my collaborators became its own theoretical seminar where we read and debated just what neoliberalism and paternalism meant to us and how we saw them interacting to provide the philosophy that informed the shift in poverty management that was unfolding before our eyes. In the end, we saw that this philosophical conjuncture was, centrally, about what Michel Foucault called "governmentality," or the policies of the state designed to get citizens to be self-disciplining subjects who anticipated how to behave in the ways sought by the people authorized to maintain the social order. In fact, I had already made this sort of Foucaldian argument in several of my prior books on welfare.[12]

We had already by 2007 decided to title our book *Disciplining the Poor,* in contrast to both Regulating and Punishing the Poor. In the first chapter, we lay out the areas in which we agree with what Wacquant argues and we show that much of what Piven and Cloward articulated remains compelling as a perspective for understanding the role and function of welfare in our contemporary political economy. Yet we aim to demonstrate how a system of disciplining the poor has been put in place, with welfare reform at its center. For us, the system largely operates to get the poor to accept their plight at the bottom of the socioeconomic system and to be willing to take the lowest paying jobs. Yet it does this not by simply punishing deviant behavior by those who fail to go along; instead, the regime of poverty governance in place today operates primarily to discipline the poor by using both incentives and penalties to inculcate market-compliant behavior. The new regime is focused on teaching the poor to be good citizen-workers who accept the need to eke out their existence from the low-wage, temporary work available in the globalizing economy.

I have tried to learn from others, such as Wacquant, while benefiting from their support. Sometimes it has led me to find my own voice (even with collaborators). It is what makes intellectual life rewarding: you learn, and then, after a certain point, you teach as well. It is all part of the process and I am honored to get to participate.

THREE HEADS ARE BETTER THAN ONE

Our book was published in late 2011. In January 2012 the first of several scheduled conference roundtables about the book was held, where welfare policy scholars got to critique it. On the day of that first roundtable, I had lunch with a former student, who had gone on to earn a PhD in Political Science, concentrating his studies in political theory of a very philosophical sort. Yet he was also someone who had maintained an interest in using theory to think about public policy. He gave up college teaching to take high-level appointments in the federal bureaucracy researching key issues of social welfare policy. I am very proud of him, as I am of all my students with whom I have worked closely. When we met for lunch that day, he had just finished reading the published book in anticipation of our meeting. As we met, he said: "Well, I guess three heads are better than one!"

I like that. It is what we had hoped would be recognized as part of our scholarly contribution: that different scholars with different theoretical and methodological skills can work together to combine different forms of analysis to produce a more robust understanding of their chosen topic. It is actually rare. Social science scholarship has for some time been widely recognized as becoming overspecialized, such that different forms of analysis talk past each other.[13] *Disciplining the Poor* is written to, first and foremost, contribute to the scholarship on how we as a society treat the poor, and in particular the persistently troubling role of race in influencing that treatment. Yet it is also written to be a contribution to thinking about ways to do such work that are more interdisciplinary, more willing to go beyond sectarian differences in method, and more willing to combine the uses of theory and history with different forms of empirical analysis. It might take collaborating with others to get it done, but then again, that's the fun of it.

And collaborating can make your scholarship better. *Disciplining the Poor* was selected in 2012 for the Michael Harrington Award from the New Political Science section of the American Political Science Association (making me the first scholar to author two books selected for that prize). It also was tapped shortly after that for the Oliver Cromwell Cox Award for 2012 from the American Sociological Association, as the best book contributing to the elimination of racism. Then, around the same time, I got word that I had been named the 2012 recipient of the Charles McCoy Career Achievement Award, also from the New Political Science section. The Caucus for a New Political Science had been created in the 1960s by leftist political scientists, such as Frances Fox Piven, who were pushing for the American Political Science Association to be more politically engaged and address contemporary issues such as civil rights and the war in Vietnam. I had joined while still in graduate school in the early 1970s. My first book, *Words of Welfare*, had won the Harrington Best Book Award back in 1996, and now again the section was recognizing my work big time. I cannot help but think the collaboration had something to do with not just winning the Harrington Best Book Award for a second time but also being tapped for the McCoy Career Achievement Award. Here is my McCoy acceptance speech:

> I am honored to be selected as the 2012 recipient of the Charles McCoy Career Achievement Award. Charles McCoy was one of my heroes back when I first joined the Caucus as a graduate student in 1975. I actually joined the American Political Science Association thinking that it was an organization led by people like

> Frances Fox Piven and Murray Edelman, who the Caucus would run as candidates to oppose what Charles McCoy called the "apolitical politics of political science." (I loved that phrase, it resonated so deeply for me as an alienated graduate student.) I attended the annual meeting in 1975 in San Francisco thinking folks like them were in charge. Chagrined, I still stuck with the organization while continuing to try to learn as much as I could from Edelman, Piven and her husband Richard Cloward. They in fact became my mentors. I continued to be mentored by Joe Zimmerman and Jack Gunnell from SUNY/Albany but Piven and Cloward and Murray Edelman intensified my education greatly in politically protean ways. In fact, I have spent a good part of my professional life studying what they wrote, listening to their counsel and trying to follow through on their ideas. Evidently someone noticed. Not that I was shy about it. I wrote and wrote trying to emulate the level of insight and analysis they offered in ways that would matter publicly and politically, sometimes with more success than others. More recently, I have collaborated, often with former students. My collaboration with Joe Soss and Richard Fording now spans more than a decade. I stood on shoulders of mentors and leaned on the shoulders of my students. I was no scholarly island unto himself, we can be sure of that. Be it what it is, I am delighted that my colleagues want to recognize what I have done as a member of this scholarly community. I am humbled as much as I am honored. I will now re-dedicate myself to trying even harder to make scholarship that matters politically.

I am still (and will be always) standing on shoulders of my mentors and leaning on the shoulders of my students. The spillover effects of collaborating are, more than ever, apparent to me. Three heads are indeed better than one!

ELEVEN

MOVING ON

Turning to Europe

By 2011, I had been traveling on and off to Europe for about a decade to speak about welfare reform in the United States. I started to notice a pattern. Audiences in Europe (mostly faculty and students, but also government officials and activists) often treated my presentations as horror stories from a land that time forgot. It seemed to me that their interest in what I had to say was more than academic. In questions posed to me, I could hear that they did not just want to know about my subject, but they were also engaged by the sheer scariness of it. How could Americans treat their disadvantaged fellow citizens as I described? Yet this was more than schadenfreude. What was most frightening for my European audiences was the idea that welfare reform as I was describing it might become some kind of zombie starting to make its way from the United States to Europe. Now, that was really frightening! Each time I went to speak in Europe, this kind of anxious response seemed to bring an extra charge to my presentations. Colleagues would share with me their concerns that political leaders in their countries were plotting to Americanize their welfare system and make it more consonant with the neoliberal-paternalist regime that I described. They worried out loud about this possibility and consistently asked me how to stop it (as if I had experience stopping what I had just described, which had in fact become a reality in the United States). Instead, all I could do was worry with them.

With time, the questions changed to comments noting that in fact the zombie of U.S. welfare reform had already made it ashore in Europe and was now working to change the nature of public assistance to the European poor. Now the frightened person was me. For years, I had taught what the textbooks said about the U.S. welfare state, namely, that it was a welfare state laggard that trailed European countries in aiding the poor but in time it would catch up, our welfare state would mature, there would be a convergence of systems and the United States would become more like Europe. It was a hopeful story, which reassured me and my students that if we kept at it we could do better in the way we treated the economically marginalized. But what I was hearing now was the reverse: rather than the United States becoming like Europe, Europe was starting to become more like the United States. Great! Going to Europe was starting to sap me of what little optimism I had that we could improve the U.S. system of social provision. How would that be possible if the welfare states of Europe were starting to use our more restrictive approach as a model for managing the poor?[1]

While my continual visits to Europe were transforming me into the academic equivalent of a horror show, I started to get connected to an incredibly rich network of scholars who were pursuing this issue with great intent. This was perhaps the most exciting part of this new chapter in my career. It was through this network that I became aware that European scholars were increasingly worried about the extent to which policymakers, from the European Union down to the local level, were at first thinking about and then actually emulating significant aspects of the neoliberal-paternalist regime of poverty governance that was being rolled out in the United States. Eventually, I would learn a term to describe this relatively rapid adoption of policies from one country to another. Jamie Peck, one of the leading scholars on the shift to a neoliberal-paternalist approach to restructuring the state, called it "fast-track global social policy."[2]

I first heard about the Americanization of European welfare policy when I spoke in Ireland. My good friend and former fellow graduate student Carl Swidorski was living for a semester in Ireland while he taught as a visiting professor at the University College of Cork. The students at Cork who were studying U.S. politics seemed well versed in the subject, even though it did not involve their country. Carl is a great teacher, but there was something more, I suspect: Europeans tend to be more interested in the United States than we are in them. It was not just the students, though. During that visit, I met with Social Work faculty who were preoccupied with how social services in Ireland were being Americanized. For example, where previously they had taught students how to help clients seeking public housing exercise their rights to assistance, now their instruction had more to do with policing and surveilling tenants in public housing to make sure they were in compliance with rules for residency. For them, the Americanization of social services was represented by the shift from being housing tenant organizers to being housing tenant monitors.

I had spoken in Finland on 9/11, and the same concerns about Americanization had been voiced by social workers there. I heard more about the Americanization of European welfare policy shortly after that when I was back in the United States to address a conference on welfare policy at Boalt Hall—the law school at the University of California, Berkeley. Joel Handler was also speaking, and he presented on his research at the time on the topic. He eventually published this work as a book, which highlighted European welfare systems' move toward implementing sanctions (and other practices) as labor activation schemes designed to get recipients to leave welfare for work, in ways that reflected the changes associated with U.S. welfare reform.[3]

In 2007, I was invited to Norway, to speak to social workers at the Oslo University College. Ivar Lodemel was doing work on labor activation schemes in Europe.[4] He recruited me in a European Union–funded research strand on the Nordic model of the welfare state. I met many interesting researchers from a number of Scandinavian countries. In 2010, I was asked to be a visiting professor at the University of Strasbourg, in France, where Vincent DuBois was conducting an ethnographic study of case managers' implementation of welfare-to-work requirements.[5] In 2011, I was off to the University of Aarhus, where Marie Østergaard Møller was doing work on case managers.[6] She had been introduced to my work by Deborah Stone, who was a recurring visiting professor at Aarhus. That was followed in 2012 by, first, delivering a presentation, and then teaching a course, at Johannes Kepler University in Linz, Austria, where Bettina Leibetseder was doing comparative work on labor activation in different European countries.[7]

There were many topics to study in this new landscape. In a few places, I proposed bringing the implicit racism experiment with Florida case managers over to see if it had applicability in Europe. My concern was that Europeans, for all their talk about multiculturalism, were having trouble walking the walk. In country after country there was increasing resentment concerning Muslim immigrants in particular, whether they were from Turkey or Somalia or elsewhere. People were increasingly complaining about having to provide welfare for immigrants. The solidarity that undergirded the European welfare states, in the Nordic countries in particular, was under stress in the face of growing religious and ethnic diversity wrought by the increasing influx of immigrants.

It all came together when I presented the experimental results in Aarhus. A doctoral student, Emily Beck (who is actually a U.S. citizen getting her PhD in Political Science from Columbia University), was studying Muslim immigration in Denmark. She and Marie Østergaard Møller were recruited by Deborah to consider conducting the experiment there. I was eager to participate. They told some chilling stories about how the Danes in particular were having a difficult time with Muslim immigration (estimated to be about 3–4 percent of the population, with as much as 40 percent of the Muslim immigrants asylum seekers, largely from the Middle East).

Turks are the largest group of Muslim immigrants in Denmark, comprising approximately 12 percent all foreigners living there.[8]

The policy context for discrimination against Muslims in the Danish welfare system had been building for some time, beginning with the enactment of the Integration Act of 1999. Ulf Hedetoft, an expert on immigration in Denmark, has written:

> On its introduction in 1999, the Integration Act became the object of intense public debate, partly because it contained a monthly integration allowance, which was considerably lower than the corresponding welfare benefits Danes receive in comparable social situations. The United Nations High Commissioner for Refugees (UNHCR), among others, found it to be a case of negative discrimination and unequal treatment of foreigners and thus a violation of international refugee conventions, to which Denmark is a signatory. After a few months, the government backed down and withdrew this section of the act.
>
> However, when the Liberal-Conservative government took office, the reduced payment was reintroduced in a new form and under a new name ("start allowance" or "introductory allowance"), in extreme cases receivable for up to seven years. Conditions were phrased so that the law does not formally discriminate against ethnic minorities, since Danish citizens also risk being subjected to its provisions.
>
> Nevertheless, there is no doubt that the law was motivated by the considerably higher unemployment rate among ethnic minorities and a belief that lower welfare benefits might work as an incentive to look for employment more actively. The Danish People's Party [the DDP—the nativist party within the governing coalition] made it clear that, in its perspective, the objective was also to reduce the attractiveness of Denmark for potential asylum seekers, in other words to minimize the alleged pull factor for would-be "welfare scroungers." And whether or not this or other initiatives introduced to curtail immigration were responsible, the number of asylum seekers over the last five years has dropped by nearly two-thirds.[9]

The Integration Act was just the beginning of the policy changes that have reflected the growing unease Danes feel about immigration, and Muslim immigration in particular. In 2002, with the DDP now in the government, a new policy was enacted that limited family reunification policy in an attempt to prevent arranged marriages, especially between a Muslim already living in Denmark and a spouse from abroad. The new law required the partners to be at least twenty-four years of age, forcing some couples to take up residence in Sweden or elsewhere until they were old enough to be legally married and live in Denmark. The government has banned head scarves and other religious dress. There were new loyalty oaths instituted with regard to upholding "Danish principles" (i.e., Western values), which were designed to be a slap in the face of Muslims who wished to practice their particular brand of patriarchy, as opposed to the Western kind. Further, the DPP exploited the Evangelical Lutheran church's close association with the government when the DDP used its leverage as part of the governing coalition to enforce instruction in grade schools in ways that were insensitive to Muslims. This led to an increasing number of Muslim children's being placed in newly created private schools, which actually undermined what the policy allegedly was trying to achieve. Last, as required by a separate policy for immigrants, they were required to go to specific welfare case workers where they were given less generous benefits than citizens.

It has always been difficult for immigrants to become citizens in Denmark, but it has become even more so in recent years. And the government's willingness to yield to anti-immigrant hysteria now extends to tightening border controls, in direct contradiction to the Schengen area agreement with other European countries.

The actions of specific members of the government reveal the deep level of resentment and hostility toward Muslim immigrants in particular. A member of Parliament, Jesper Langballe, was convicted of hate speech when he retorted to another Islamaphobe: "Of course Lars Hedegaard should not have said that there are Muslim fathers who rape their daughters when the truth appears to be that they make due with killing their daughters [the so-called honor killings] and leave it to their uncles to rape them."[10] Another Danish politician was acquitted of hate speech charges, even though he compared Muslims to Nazis. It seemed as though Islamaphobia was taking the wheels off Denmark's solidaristic welfare state.

In this context, it is not surprising to find that unemployment rates for immigrants remain high in Denmark. While the government does not keep statistics on employment rates by religion, surveys indicate lower employment rates for foreigners generally, and Muslims in particular.[11] Employer discrimination is undoubtedly a significant factor in producing these disparities.

While Denmark is a special case, I had firsthand experience with European attitudes toward Muslim immigrants that added another layer of evidence. In discussions with colleagues outside of Denmark, I heard that people complained about Muslim youth being overly enamored with the oppositional rap culture of young African American males, preferring the music, wearing the baggy clothes, using the slang, and speaking their host country's language with an identifiable accent. The last point seemed profoundly picky, to say the least. Employers evidently expressed reluctance to hire Muslim immigrants because they "refused" to speak the language without an accent. It was too funny were it not so sad.

Once again, I could see cats chasing their tails. European countries were cutting back on welfare, instituting labor activation policies, and trying to overcome what was being called "social exclusion" by integrating immigrants into the labor force, but employers were making that more difficult to achieve. Muslim immigrants were being treated suspiciously, to the point where young people had started to internalize their marginalization, further marking them for exclusion from the labor market. In the process, religious and ethnic hostility was intensifying and even reaching the boiling point. The "integration act" seemed to be a contradiction in terms. It was what Joel Handler said it was: "The paradox of inclusion." It seemed to me that this was going nowhere fast.

There was, therefore, good reason to take seriously the idea that religious and ethnic diversity might accelerate the Americanization of European welfare states. Immigration was rending the social fabric and weakening the bonds that created the foundation of a solidaristic welfare state. Countries such as Denmark were moving increasingly toward a tiered system of social assistance along lines that divided immigrants from others. The welfare state in Denmark already had features that approximated how the welfare state in the United States was structured. Both included a tiered system in which social insurance programs were the superior programs that provided better benefits for those who were seen as deserving, while public assistance programs offered inferior benefits under tighter regulation for those who had not, supposedly, earned their benefits through work. Yet, in Denmark compared to the United States, most people could more easily qualify for the better benefits when unemployed or disabled. Now, with immigration having become an increasingly controversial issue in Denmark during the last decade, there was increased tiering, with inferior benefits for foreigners. This Americanization of European welfare in response to immigration had in fact been predicted years ago. As early as 1986, Gary Freeman had hypothesized that immigration would move Europe in the direction of the United States: "Migration has contributed to the Americanization of European welfare politics. . . . The relatively free movement of labor across national frontiers exposes the tension between closed welfare states and open economies and that, ultimately, national welfare states cannot coexist with free movement of labor."[12] Alberto Alesina and Edward Glaeser more recently have made a similar argument: "One natural implication of our conclusion that fractionalization reduces redistribution is that if Europe becomes more heterogeneous due to immigration, ethnic divisions will be used to challenge the generous welfare state."[13]

Maybe it was time for the experiment. I started thinking with colleagues about designing a study to see if Muslim immigrants were singled out for discriminatory treatment within the separate system for providing aid to immigrants. If we found results that caused concern, we had a growing network of scholars to replicate the experiment elsewhere in Europe. It looked as though I was becoming a Europeanist without knowing it. I even presented papers at the Council for European Studies two years in a row. I could not believe it. I had always been an Americanist. I studied the United States. Now I was studying racism in Europe. It seemed like the right time to be doing it. All you had to do was pick up the newspaper any day of the week to see that it was a topic that urgently needed attention. I was now connecting research to politics in a new setting.

TWELVE

MAKING IT MATTER

Real Social Science in the Neoliberal Academy

At this point in my career, I increasingly want to focus my writing on social science analyses that will connect to political struggle specifically on behalf of subordinate populations, and will do so in ways that will help them better address the sources of their oppression. I recognize that there can and should be other forms of social science and theorizing, but my part is to bring those less connected but nonetheless insightful analyses to bear on what is happening now in ways that might reduce the ongoing oppression of subordinated groups. I want to stand at the nexus of different practices, so as to get them to work together more effectively. High theory, historical analysis, empirical research, community and political struggle for change are the different streams of thought and action that I feel can productively be brought into dialogue in order to make the world a better place, even if change proceeds via one research project at a time. This is how I see my distinctive contribution. It is at this nexus that I have found my voice. I want to continue to do this kind of work whether I remain in the academy or not. I want my writing to be of a quality necessary for this ambitious project to work. I recognize that I've got my work cut out for me.

I have coined a term for this kind of activity. I call it "radical incrementalism," whereby specific interventions in political struggle promote changes that are marginal but that lay the groundwork for broader, more substantive, even transformational political change in the future.[1] I previously argued that Piven and Cloward's approach to achieving radical political change on behalf of the poor was consistent with this idea of radical incrementalism. Their famous "Crisis Strategy" combined a politics of survival with a politics of social change. It advocated signing up poor families for the welfare benefits they were eligible to collect with the idea that the campaign would overload the system, induce a crisis, and force the government to consider moving to a guaranteed income, which would be easier to administer, fairer to recipients, and which would also provide more assistance, to the point of reducing the unjustly high poverty rates that still persist in the United States. The small steps taken to get people assistance that they are or should be entitled to would lay the groundwork for larger changes. That's radical incrementalism.

I therefore not only wanted to use the best available social science to help inform political change initiatives; I wanted my research to be associated with political change efforts that would promote a radical incrementalism. This, of course, is even more ambitious because it assumes that we can always readily distinguish radical incrementalism from plain old, status quo–reinforcing incrementalism. And I think that research can help on that score as well.

So I really never wanted to be a conventional political scientist at all. In fact, I have actively sought an academic appointment in Social Work for a long time in order that my political science be more politically engaged. I taught social work students for years (usually as an adjunct) while holding appointments in Political Science departments. Finally, in 1997, I accepted an appointment in the Graduate School of Social Work and Social Research at Bryn Mawr College, where I taught courses on social theory and social policy to masters and doctoral students (while continuing to teach those topics to undergraduates in Sociology as well as Political Science). In all my courses, the focus inevitably was on how to connect theory to practice, research to policy, and truth to power.

Even with my appointment in Social Work, I remained active in Political Science, directing my energy at times to pushing the discipline to promote work that was more politically engaged. So it was, then, that I readily welcomed the Perestroika movement, as it came to be called, when it came into the profession and started to shake things up back in 2000. It was spawned by an anonymous e-mail sent to a number of political scientists late at night on October 17, 2000, complaining about the current state of the discipline, the main professional association—the American Political Science Association (APSA)—and its flagship journal, the *American Political Science Review* (APSR).[2] While the original e-mail was in good part an inchoate rant, it struck a nerve. Many people responded to it quite excitedly as a rallying cry that expressed many political scientists' disenchantment with their field. The e-mail went viral, and then a more domesticated petition-type letter was submitted to be published in the APSA's magazine *PS: Political Science & Politics*. That letter read:

Dear Colleagues:

As many of you are aware, the American Political Science Association has recently experienced an extraordinary outpouring of frustration with the current state of the *American Political Science Review,* the APSA, and the profession generally. An anonymous scholar writing as Mr. Perestroika circulated to an extensive roster of political scientists a passionate memo asking many provocative, indeed painful questions. Why do so many leaders of our profession not even read, much less submit, to the APSR? Why is purchase of the APSR made mandatory for membership, thus subsidizing a journal many find unsatisfactory, instead of permitting membership without the journal or with other journals? Why do the APSA Council and APSR editorial board seem to be chosen essentially by their predecessors? Why does the APSR and why do other prominent professional fora seem so intensively focused on technical methods, at the expense of the great, substantive political questions that actually intrigue many APSA members, as well as broader intellectual audiences?

Though some recipients may have felt uncomfortable with the anonymous authorship and the highly polemical tone of this post, nonetheless an astonishing number of scholars, from all ranks of the profession, felt impelled to announce that they, too, shared these profound dissatisfactions with the status quo. Many noted that in 1998 an APSA membership survey reportedly found that in fact a very large proportion of APSA members, to say nothing of scholars who have given up on APSA, were critical of the current condition of the APSR. A lively discussion ensued, in which scholars discussed whether the problems arose from the biases of APSR editors and APSA leaders, from more structural problems in the reviewing processes, or from problems in American intellectual and political life more broadly. Inevitably, people differed in their views. There has been, however, extensive agreement that whatever the sources of the problems, changes need to be made.

What changes? Many ideas have been explored in recent e-mail discussions. These have included: 1) permitting APSA members NOT to purchase the APSR, but rather to choose alternative journals or none at all; 2) making the selection of the APSR editorial board, the APSA Council, and basic policy decisions concerning the journal and the association more open to genuine democratic decision making by the APSA membership; 3) revising the APSR

> reviewing process to seek both to insure that some methodologies are not automatically vetoed and that most articles are of interest to a broad scholarly audience; 4) finding ways to encourage scholars who have given up on the APSR to submit their work to it once again; 5) pursuing the suggestions both for an electronic APSR and a separate journal that the association's Strategic Planning Committee has raised; 6) make the 1998 survey of attitudes toward the APSR widely available, and yet more importantly, develop mechanisms to examine regularly how satisfied political scientists are with the publications and professional activities they underwrite via their APSA dues. It is very unfortunate that deeply committed political scientists genuinely believe, whether or rightly or wrongly, that they cannot criticize the status quo safely without the cloak of anonymity. We should have regular channels through which dissent can be effectively communicated.
>
> We, the undersigned, do not represent any consensus on just why the APSR and the APSA are in the condition they are now in, nor any consensus onjust what should be done. We are also not an organized or systematically recruited group; we are simply scholars who, after discussing the Perestroika memo over the course of a few days, decided to join in this letter. We do so because we believe strongly that the profession is in danger of alienating a larger and larger number of those who should be its active members, and contributing less and less to the kinds of understanding of politics that it is our responsibility to advance. Hence we urge the APSA leadership and membership alike to look seriously at the issues raised above, to speak out on them, and to take soon the actions that emerge as most widely endorsed in the ensuing discussions.[3]

I became actively involved in Perestroika largely on behalf of the cause of helping Political Science become more connected to ongoing political struggle.[4] The movement spawned conference presentations, papers, articles, books and a sustained e-mail listserv dedicated to discussing and coordinating people's efforts to the change the discipline. I even got recruited to write a proposal to become editor of the *American Political Science Review*. Perestroika did not achieve most of its objectives, especially regarding elections of APSA officers or opening up the APSR, but otherwise it produced much good intellectual ferment, and the discipline is better off because of that. Nonetheless, the resistance was substantial and that limited Perestroika's impact.

One of starkest examples of this was that at one point the president of the association openly opposed our alternative slate, which had forced an election of council members. The president at the time called us careerists who were just self-promoters willing to undermine the advances of the profession and the association just so that we could climb over others professionally. I was hurt by this since my whole modus operandi, I thought, was to stand against careerism and for political engagement regardless of the professional consequences. Not everyone was paying close attention to my arguments. And they definitely did not know that I had struggled with this issue in my career. But we ended up doing what we could, while helping institute some changes in the profession here and there.

By the time we were being called names, some people wanted to push back on one dimension of our efforts, which involved my championing Bent Flyvbjerg as a model for conducting a more politically connected kind of social science.[5] Flyvbjerg, a Danish professor of urban planning, had himself coined the term "phronetic social science."[6] Phronetic social science was social science dedicated to promoting *phronesis*, practical wisdom, a more situated reasoning, a contextually specific knowledge that could help solve specific problems in specific settings. With his phronetic approach to research, Flyvbjerg was moving beyond the "interpretive turn," the "linguistic turn," and all the other turns away from scientistic, method-driven political science and providing his own perspective on why we should encourage a more problem-driven research. He was giving us a "practical turn."[7] As with any movement, sometimes the agenda can be pushed too far, such as suggesting that all research should have immediate practical relevance, eschew the use of abstract theories that are not immediately digestible by public policymakers, or be in service of the state.[8] Yet many political scientists of various stripes, from empirical researchers to theorists, have warmed to the idea that more efforts in the discipline should try to connect to ongoing political struggle.[9]

In his original critique of the social sciences more generally, Flyvbjerg had anticipated the two main complaints that the Perestroika movement made about Political Science: (1) mainstream research too often mistakenly sought to apply what was thought to be the methods of the natural sciences to the study of social phenomena; and (2) as result, research too often was disconnected from the goal of helping people address the problems they were confronting. Without the labels, Flyvbjerg called for problem-driven, mixed-methods research that offered contextually specific understanding of social problems in ways that helped the people being studied better address their problems.

Drawing on the Aristotelian categorization of types of knowledge, he called his approach "phronetic social science." For Aristotle, *episteme* was universal knowledge, *techne* was practical application of that knowledge in the form of technique, and *phronesis* was the practical wisdom that emerged from having an intimate familiarity with what would work and is appropriate in particular settings and circumstances. For Flyvbjerg, while the natural sciences studied a subject in the physical world that was amenable to universal models of causal laws and such, the social sciences could not produce such knowledge of the social world given its subject matter, that is, people whose subjective states of consciousness and shared understandings were not amenable to being modeled by transcontextual, universal causal models. Instead, the social sciences were better adapted to provide contextually specific knowledge that could help people address the major problems they confront in their lives. Social science could conduct research that would enhance phronesis, the practical wisdom born of an intimate familiarity with a practice that could help people act effectively in particular situations. Flora Cornish notes:

> Phronesis can be understood as part of a "turn to practice" in the social sciences. After the "linguistic" and "cultural" turns gave center-stage to symbols and meanings in human affairs, attention to practice is one way of returning materiality to social theory. Phronetic social researchers engage in detail in the complexities of the phenomena which they study, examining why things are the way they are, often uncovering undesirable workings of power, and asking how things could be improved. In so doing, they develop both practical wisdom and theoretical tools that provide lenses for problematizing and reconstructing practices in other settings. They explicitly do not strive to create general or universal theories of human behavior.[10]

While I believed that there is an important role for abstract theory and empirical testing of general propositions in Political Science, from my time as a graduate student in a school of public affairs I always seemed to be interested in making Political Science matter to the real world of politics. Maybe it was a way of keeping my identity as a 1960s radical alive. I was definitely taken with Flyvbjerg's argument. I remember that when I first read the book, I could not put it down. (The only other time this has happened in recent years was when I read Giorgio Agamben's *Homo Sacer*.[11]) I kept thinking this was the book I wanted to have written. His approach combined so many of the disparate elements I wanted to synthesize. He used theory, he was an empirical researcher, he focused on challenging power. His theoretically informed empirical investigations were designed to connect to ongoing political struggle in situated contexts so as to help challenge power in particular settings and make things better for the people struggling to address a problem.

It was all too irresistible. I felt I had to reach out to Flyvbjerg. We started communicating, then writing together. We eventually worked with Todd Landman to produce an edited volume that collected case study examples by researchers who were practicing phronetic social science. We called it "real social science."[12] It was like coining a term by claiming that what we were doing was real (compared to what was false, I guess). I knew it was a bit cheeky, I admit, but we were making a statement by demonstrating that this was really happening. People were actually doing a kind of social science that was politically connected, and it was being done in systematic and thoughtful ways, undergirded by an explicit philosophical orientation.

You could say we were helping political scientists and others think more like social workers. Or at least that was what I originally thought. By the time we published our book, I had changed my mind, entirely.

SHIPS PASSING IN THE NIGHT

I chose to teach social work. It is not something that was forced on me. I wanted to do it, eagerly. I wanted to be associated with people who were actively working to make the world a better place. I did not want to just talk about it; I wanted to help make it happen. Social workers help people every day, sometimes they even help to change the society for the better. They are in the world, not just of it. At orientation during the week before classes begin each year, I tell the incoming graduate students in Social Work that I am honored to stand before them because they are people who are choosing quite explicitly to pursue a career dedicated to helping people overcome adversity. In many respects, I am very happy I chose Social Work.

Yet I am also a critic of social work. I am, in particular, concerned about the changing organizational climate in which social work is practiced. I worry about the effect of neoliberalism's focus on marketizing the nonprofit world so that will run more like a business. I worry that social work practice in a number of areas is affected by that marketized environment. Social work is changing as it comes to be practiced consistent with neoliberalism. I worry that across various arenas social work has come to be primarily about modifying people's behavior so that the problems they confront become more manageable for us as a society, even if they remain a burden for them. Social work becomes more paternalistic as it is practiced in a neoliberal environment. It comes to involve forcing people to fit into the existing society in ways that we as a society expect, more so than accommodating those different people by changing how we as a society operate. I am concerned that neoliberalism and paternalism are working together to make social work more of a tool for maintaining the existing structure of power and the inequities it generates.[13]

I came to Social Work to get away from a Political Science that was disconnected from politics. I wanted my social science to matter. I wanted to be part of an effort to change things for the better. I wanted to speak truth to power. To push back against the existing structure of power, so as to help make change possible. I wanted to work with colleagues and students who were committed to doing just that. And many social workers I have met are what I was looking for. They themselves share with me a passion for changing the world for the better, right here and right now.

Yet in the process of coming over to Social Work, I sensed social workers going the other way, leaving the world of activism in pursuit of proving that they had the scientific skills and evidentiary foundation to underwrite the treatment, intervention, services, and programs provided by social workers. From "evidence-based practice" to "performance management," Social work seemed to be increasingly about measuring results and documenting the outcomes agencies had been told to achieve, rather than pushing to change what the outcomes should be. A kind of neoliberal instrumentalism seemed to be infiltrating social work so that it was preoccupied with proving it had the right means for preselected ends that had been chosen by other people who were perhaps less interested in promoting the well-being of clients than in keeping costs down. Maybe it was always this way, and the more I studied it, the harder it was to decide, but I was concerned that social work was a subordinate practice assimilated to the existing structure of power in society, and not the ideal place to promote significant social and political change.[14]

My relationship with Social Work started to feel like ships passing in the night. It turns out I have never been at home in Social Work, much as I have never been at home in Political Science. Forever the wandering Jew, the academic wilderness is my home, I guess. I thrive on crossing disciplinary boundaries, mixing methods, collaborating with scholars with different methodological approaches, and I am committed to merging scholarship and politics to help make the world a better place. While I was trying to find a less ivory tower in the academy, it seemed to me that social work as a field was, increasingly, interested in gaining academic legitimacy by virtue of demonstrating a scientific foundation for its various practices and programs.

Part of the reason for social work's scientization is its relationship to other professional fields, medicine and psychological counseling in particular. Over time, social workers have been increasingly employed in medical and therapeutic settings where they are expected to follow along with prescribed ways of treating clients and patients. As managed care has come to medicine and therapy, social workers increasingly have become the cost-efficient providers of counseling services of various sorts. Insurance coverage has come to be contingent on limiting treatment to what has been proven by research to be effective, and that treatment must be provided in a cost-efficient fashion in order to fit the limitations of insurance coverage. This sort of hothouse environment is an incubator for neoliberal paternalism. Organizational changes are adopted that marketize operations so that they operate more efficiently and meet cost-cutting objectives. Procedures for interacting with clients and applying treatment are instituted, in order to manage the problems of clients in efficient ways, rather pursuing a more ambitious agenda of change for them. Time-limited therapy joins with performance management systems to monitor the service providers and create a disciplinary regime focused on managing costs and containing problems. Rather than investing in people and communities as to eliminate problems, Social work increasingly involves containing costs and only managing problems. As one colleague eloquently put it, "Social work is the ambulance corps for capitalism." This was not what Jane Addams, the profession's chosen founder, wanted. In fact, Addams did not want social work to become a profession at all, fearing it would ghettoize the systems of aid in which all citizens themselves were to partake, across class lines, with mutual respect and sensitivity to difference. For her, social work was an obligation we bore as citizens. In fact, from her feminist perspective citizenship was more about relationships than rights and we should not abrogate our responsibility as citizens by delegating this work to a professional cadre that would be vulnerable to do the powerful's bidding.[15]

The center of gravity of social work has been shifting for a long time, to the point that most jobs are in areas related to providing therapy. As social work becomes assimilated to the psy-services, talking about a social work that focuses on the social roots of the problems people confront increasingly becomes anachronistic. Ships passing in the night starts to sound like dinosaurs at the disco.

My long night of being a dinosaur is coming to an end. I was hired at Bryn Mawr in Social Work in 1997 as a visiting professor and nothing has changed. Now my contract is ending, I have been a full professor, but without tenure and always with the prospect of being let go. Part of the problem, I would think, is that being a critic of one's chosen field is never the easiest way to go, especially in a field that has been spending decades trying to prove that social work is not about socialism, that it actually never was, and that it only sounds as though it was. No, social work was assimilated long ago into the emerging regime of neoliberal paternalism, and reminding people of that does not always go down well.

One story tells much of the saga. I was asked to revamp the advanced, year-long practice seminar for policy advocacy students and to teach it. I was asked to do this during my sabbatical. As a visitor who got to take sabbaticals, I was as confused as the next person. The one thing I was clear on was that I wanted to keep my job. So I did it. And then, I taught the seminar for a few years. Eventually, I wanted to go back to teaching theory and policy, largely because teaching the practice seminar for advocacy students was like trying to put a square peg in a round hole. The main problem was that the placement office had trouble finding placements for advocacy students, because they had to be placed with supervisors who had a Master's in Social Work. I guess the idea was that no one else could teach them the professional way to be a social work advocate for a cause, campaign, community or whatever. In my mind, it does not make sense there is a Social Work way to fight for social justice and if you learn to fight for social justice from anyone else you are not getting properly educated as a social work advocate or activist. This kind of proprietary preoccupation was often received by students as the ultimate affront to their common sense. They were frustrated. This kind of gatekeeping was transparently designed to make sure that only social workers trained social workers, even if it was to learn things any number of activists could teach students. Students saw through it and complained about it continually. Once it became unworkable for too many students, I went back to teaching theory and policy.

After I stopped teaching the advocacy seminar, the school hired someone else to do it. And then the syllabus changed. I taught the course essentially as a critique of the neoliberalization of social work, in which agencies were made over to assure that social service was marketized and thereby provided in ways that relied on and ultimately were accountable to a market calculus. I taught students to stand up for clients in the face of neoliberalism's refashioning one area of social practice after another into arenas for making profit. The new syllabus, however, revised the course from a critique of neoliberalism and how to resist it to a course on what neoliberalism is and how to implement it. The course went from a course that questioned neoliberalism to a course that unquestioningly taught students how to practice it. It became a how-to course, as if neoliberalism was a technique that you could learn about by going to the hardware store and renting a DVD on the topic. Neoliberalism was just the latest hammer for pounding down those pesky nails called clients. Pound them down, or cover them up, but whatever you do, try not to spend too much money in the process of helping society to pretend that it can manage the costs of poverty without actually having to pay for it. To me, it sounded like technicism in the service of social and political denial.

In fact, the argument reflected in the last sentence is what gets me into trouble. (I suspect you could sense that.) I came to practice social work as a solution and ended up studying it as a problem. I found so much resistance to the idea of being in resistance that I could not but conclude that that very reluctance to be on the outside looking in was in fact the biggest problem of social work as a profession today: It is not in resistance to power. Instead, social work is well on its way to being assimilated to power. It is about proving that human services can be provided in ways that are consonant with market objectives, in ways that enhance the marketability of clients, so as to buttress market logic and market efficiencies.

In area after area, from drug treatment to child welfare to welfare-to-work, neoliberal performance management schemes that hold accountable the increasingly preferred for-profit providers become the context for implementing research-proven techniques of treatment or intervention in the name of creating a marketized system for operating programs that seeks to compel clients to be market compliant themselves. Social work has become the handmaiden of a marketized society. Pushed to the background, like an unwanted child hidden away in a closet, is the social work that challenges the way a market-centered society puts particular populations at risk and in need of assistance. That social work that takes our huddled masses and shelters them is not expected to file performance management reports, meet quality control standards, rely on evidence-based practice, all in the name of improving the likelihood that an agency and its operations may continue to receive funding because it has efficiently produced desired outcomes for its clients in ways that are consonant with market objectives.

Now, at one level all of this is entirely understandable. Social work education is about helping people learn enough so that they can be recognized as knowledgeable professionals who are eminently employable by the same neoliberalized agencies that are asking people to competently provide treatment and services as prescribed. This is a terrain not of social workers' choosing. It is the hand they have been dealt. And many social workers openly worry that they are at risk of being implicated in a regime of problem management and containment, and continually try to strategize how to participate, subversively, in what Lisa Dodson calls the "moral underground," where they try to find ways to be just with their clients and get them the help they need in spite of the protocols in place for working with these clients.[16] Nonetheless, the challenges for moral action under neoliberal paternalism are constantly present, given where the work is being done and the ways by which it is expected to be executed. It is difficult to be in resistance to neoliberal paternalism when neoliberal paternalism is your job.

A good example came to me one day when I attended a panel discussion on reentry programs for people leaving prison. The panel was comprised of a diverse list of researchers and practitioners from a variety of fields, including Political Science and Social Work. Several models of reentry programs were presented. Social workers, students included, presented their participation in an actual reentry program, highlighting the very thorough screening, diagnosing, referring, and servicing they provided. A program administrator described the significant, if marginal, impact his reentry program had in reducing recidivism among its participants compared to other ex-felons returning to the community.[17]

But it all seemed once again a day late and a dollar short. One of the presenters from social work questioned labeling this type of programming as "reentry." How could it be called "reentry" if most of the program participants never "entered" in the first place? They had most often been part of the underground economy, convicted of drug-related crimes, served their time, and now were confronted with almost no prospects of getting a job or even qualifying for government assistance for housing, simply because they had a felony on their record. Instead, these programs were reduced to simply trying to get ex-felons to follow the rules of their probation or parole and thereby reduce the rate at which they returned to prison, especially since rule violations were the main reason people were sent back. A political scientist followed with an even more stinging indictment of these programs as rationalizing our society's mindless War on Drugs and the massive rates of incarceration it has produced. Instead of investing in people and communities, this type of intervention only served to paper over the neglect reflected in not creating decent schools and economic opportunities, which left these mostly young, black males adrift to fall into the drug trade, to end up with a felony record, and ultimately to have no prospects for escaping the poverty that they were being sent back into.

In my own mind, I added the concern that interventions such as this actually made things worse. First, most program participants failed. They ended up going back to prison. Second, when they did go back, they could feel even worse about themselves because they'd been given help and had been unable to translate that into a successful transition back into the community. Last, this type of program (that had as its main goal the neoliberal objective of simply reducing recidivism) risked rationalizing our neglect in investing in people and communities in ways that actually could help. We might be actually better off without reentry programs.

Yet we have made our bed, and now we have to sleep in it. The War on Drugs that began in the mid-1970s has sent several million folks to jail, making us the most incarcerated country in the world. Many people come out of prison every day not just unprepared to transition to a lawful existence in the community but with a felony record that makes it nearly impossible to get a job and find a place to live (the two most important predictors regarding not returning to prison).[18] In 2008 alone, more than 735,454 prisoners, some from federal but most from state prisons, were released back into society. Many recidivated. For instance, a Justice Department Bureau of Justice Statistics study of 272,111 state prisoners released in 1994 found that two-thirds of them were rearrested within three years.[19] In response, the federal government has now joined with states in trying to reduce recidivism. The Second Chance Act of 2008 expanded the federal government's role in the provision of reentry services by creating grants for states to implement prisoner reentry programs. The act authorized up to $330 million for prisoner reentry programs during fiscal years 2009 and 2010. The overwhelming majority of the spending authorization is for the operation of state and local programs. While previous reentry programs have at times been shown to produce a statistically significant reduction in recidivism rates, more often the effects have been marginal at best.[20] Putting more money into reentry programs once again should not be expected to change things.

Until we as a society stop locking up so many people and burdening them with felony records that make it nearly impossible for them to successfully transition back into society, we should not expect anything to change. If, however, reentry programs were to take place as part of a broader commitment to investing in people and communities, then we would be likely to see better results. We need to start by trying to reduce those factors that give rise to this problem in the first place. We need to invest in decent schools, create more economic opportunities in marginalized communities, stop locking up so many young people, and stop shooting ourselves in the foot by creating additional barriers that keep ex-felons from jobs, housing, and various forms of public assistance. We should let people with felony records vote. Until we start doing these things, reentry programs are of questionable value.

This demonstrates the fraught nature of social work today. Taking a clinical, "How can we help this one client?" approach has its place. Some ex-felons are helped. That is a good thing. But helped to do what, not recidivate? That's it? We need to do more and better. But achieving the other goals is much more difficult. Further, even the goal of reducing recidivism is contingent upon making other, larger changes that involve creating better educational and employment opportunities for young people in these marginalized communities. Without that we remain the ambulance corps for capitalism.

We would be better off if we ended the War on Drugs, stopped locking up so many young people of color for drug offenses, and instead started investing in them and their communities so that they might have a better future. Until that happens, we are just putting neoliberal Band-Aids on a major social problem that we as a society refuse to accept responsibility for, even though we have been complicit in creating it and now are profoundly confused as to what to do about it. Social work's role in straightening out this confusion is vexed at best. In selected instances, social workers are helping individual program participants, but they are also helping to rationalize society's reluctance to do what really must be done, if not now, then eventually, before it all becomes an even greater financial, as well as social, disaster than it is.

I went away from the panel discussion further agonized about how to fit into social work. I thought about it some more and came to another conclusion. Ultimately, the real problem for me as someone who has been trying to fit into the field is that social work is not part of the liberal arts. This was most ironic. I got what I wished for and came to regret it. I originally thought that it was a good thing that social work was not part of the liberal arts. The liberal arts, I thought, were only liberal. I want to be radical. More importantly, the liberal arts are about ideas, I wanted to be about action. Social work was, in my mind, where I could be a radical who was engaged in the world.

The bigger problem was actually me. It turns out I actually like the liberal arts. You can take the boy out of the liberal arts but you can't take the liberal arts out of the boy (even after many years, by which time he is an old man). As a man of the liberal arts, I believe in open debate, criticism, freedom of thought. Social work does not, or so it seems, given what has happened to me. This disjuncture would prove to be a bridge too far for me and social work. This liberal arts problem came to a head one day when we had a faculty meeting to discuss what students had been telling some of my colleagues. Students were saying that I was running down other forms of social work in my class. I was not sure which form of social work I, as a non-social worker, represented, but that is beside the point. Actually, it is not. I had recieved a waiver from the Council on Social Work Education (CSWE), the main accrediting body, to teach policy practice even though I did not have a Social Work degree. I got the waiver by documenting years of political activism. I even included the burning of my draft card at college during the protests against the war in Vietnam (in that large metal drum that reminded me of the one we as kids burned paper in, back in Newark). I was considered a professional because, as a draft resistor, I knew how to burn paper (although probably not as a six-year-old).

In any case, I must have been once again trying to engage the students in class on the issue of who or what was really radical and what was there about social work that actually changed society for the better, instead of just helping people cope in the face of the unjust treatment they received because of the way society was organized. I might have asked something like: Just what is so radical about couples therapy? Not that couples therapy can't be done in a radical fashion. In other words, it was not a rhetorical question. But I could see that the students thought it was. Sarcasm has its limitations (as I have learned the hard way, slowly over time).

In any case, the faculty met and we talked without naming names about how some faculty were denigrating other forms of social work and that it was sending the wrong signal to students. It was news to me that social work education was about signaling. (Signals are like traffic lights. They are one color or another. But even traffic lights have yellow, and, boy, do some drivers like to abuse the yellow. For them, yellow means: go faster. As a pedestrian who walks just about everywhere, I think that is the opposite of what yellow signals. But what do I know?) In any case, our faculty meeting was about sending clear signals to students alerting them to the fact that our school's faculty, each and every one of us, values all forms of social work practice in an unquestioning way. We all were asked to assent. We dutifully complied. It was unanimous. We all agreed: all forms of social work practice, irrespective of whatever they did, were good and we wanted to students to know that that is what we all believed, each and every one of us, even me. For me, it was like being asked to sign another loyalty oath.

What was I to do? I liked this job; I wanted to keep it. I was not about to tell the dean to "take this job and shove it." I really liked my job. I silently went along. So sad, I was ashamed of myself. After the meeting, I went to the dean. I asked: What if somebody were to believe that a particular form of social work was pure, unadulterated evil? The dean collapsed in a heap of laughter. I liked that. But now it is all water under the bridge, as the ships pass in the night, and dinosaurs stop dancing at the disco.

I had already agreed to retire. I had done that as a way to keep my job until I made it to my Medicare eligibility age. If I had not done that, I probably would have been let go years before. But I never wanted to retire. I love teaching Social Work students; I love teaching. I did not want to retire. What happens next is not entirely clear. One thing is: I like what I do, a lot. I love teaching, I love working with people to try to speak truth to power. I will not stop. I will keep writing. Now that I have finally learned how to do it, I am going to keep refining my craft, hoping it helps people think, and think about addressing the fundamental inequities around class, race, and gender that serve to structure our society in ways that deserve to be resisted.

Yet all of this takes place in a very uncertain environment. It was not just social work that was being neoliberalized. The academy itself was, as well.[21] I had been very lucky in my career, as I have indicated throughout this memoir. Better than most, I have survived the academy's more recent interest in throat cutting, let alone the more established backstabbing. Others have been thrown by the wayside. And the juggernaut called neoliberalism seems positioned to take more casualties. I am getting out with my skin intact and ready now to give full-throated voice in complaint. I will not be silenced simply by virtue of losing my position. A new chapter of politically engaged scholarship is about to begin.

CONCLUSION

A Postscript on Writing

So my story now ends (even if my life goes on). Writing this memoir has been very fulfilling, in part because as a scholar I have struggled to be understood. I always wanted to make a contribution, to share my efforts to understand things so that they would matter to other people, to students, to scholars, to political actors. At times, my arguments did not resonate, seemed confused, or were just not helpful. Writing a memoir has provided me a chance to explain myself, to have it all make sense, or at least show how it might. By showing what led me to write what I did, the way I did, I feel as though I have helped explain myself as a scholar and why I studied what I did, and why I said what I said and the way I said it. That, in itself, ended up being its own reward. I don't think I am so crazy any more!

This memoir has focused on how, first as a student, and then as a scholar, I struggled to find my voice, develop the ability to express it in writing, and ultimately do so in ways that combined scholarship and activism in a turbulent academic environment. I have told my story so others can think about how they too can overcome the insecurities and deficiencies that they fear will prevent them from succeeding academically. My story makes clear that as a student I was not a good writer. My teachers told me so. As I have detailed in this book, the problem persisted long into my academic career. This writing problem was especially acute for me as someone who wanted to communicate in the public realm in ways that might influence politics to promote policy change. Yet I was deeply committed; I smoked to write; I literally cut and pasted handwritten text together, eventually migrating to using a stapler, before finally learning to compose with a computer (because it allowed easy corrections of keyboarding mistakes).

I learned from my struggles, and I think others can too. This is what I tell students, especially incoming doctoral students. You have to want it. You have to want to do well at scholarly work or it will not happen. That desire comes first. Do not for one moment minimize the emotional dimension of doing this kind of work. It is, first and foremost, about passion. This part was always easy for me. I always wanted to do something that mattered. I was passionate about it.

Once you have made the commitment, then you have to organize your life to make it happen. You have to prioritize. Even after you do that, you have to dedicate yourself to perfecting your craft. You have to work at it. You have to be patient. You have to stick with it and watch it grow and develop as you go. It is the same process of patient, constant application whether it concerns your ability to think, to read what others have written, or most especially to write to express your own ideas.

Most importantly, the critical ingredient in all this is that you have to believe in yourself, as someone who has something distinctive to say. You have to be willing to find your own voice. It is there, you just need to listen closely to hear it under the murmur of your thoughts. You have to be willing to take the "I," just as I have done in this memoir.[1] Own it. Wear it. Use it. Tell us what you have to say, based on your own experience, in your own words, in your own way, in your own voice. Even as we come to appreciate how the discourse speaks us as much as we speak it, how our ideas are expressed in ways that can seem scripted ahead of time by the prevailing ways of understanding, we still can learn to articulate our own variations of what can be said. Barbara Kingsolver once said: "Don't try to figure out what other people want to hear from you; figure out what you have to say. It's the one and only thing you have to offer."[2] Yes, we need to recognize that we are not alone, that our ideas have numerous debts to preexisting sources, and that we need know what others have said and be prepared to tell others what we think about those ideas. But you need to tell us what you have to add. I am sure it is as distinctive as you are as a person and that distinction adds to the discourse. Just listen to yourself sometime and you will hear your own distinctive interpretations of what you are reading and experiencing. Listen to yourself closely. Then tell what you heard to others. Not only that, telling us what you think makes writing a lot easier and it makes what you have to say a lot more convincing.

I have been asked many times how I write so much. All kinds of people seemingly want to know. So I have had to think about it a lot. When a college administrator asked me, I remembered that she had said that she "did not pick social work as her profession; social work chose her." That's me and writing. I do not write books, they write me. Writing, for me, is nothing less than an agonizingly exquisite affliction. It is like a drug that takes control of me and carries me away to another place. It is its own siren call that I must unresistingly give myself over to. It is an intoxicating experience. It is its own pleasurable obsession, which insistently drives me to say what it tells me to say until I am finally done, relieved to be freed from the grasp of its singular focus. As I get older, I now actually try to avoid writing, fearful that its all-encompassing power will take me away once again, when now I would rather just stay put. But time and again, my resistance fails, and I am left to be pulled into that vortex, knowing that both the ecstasy of its enchantment and the pain of the compulsion lie before me, to be relieved only by completion. (I think you get the idea.)

Take this book. I do not know from where the idea came to compose a memoir about my career as a scholar who struggled to write. But it came. Even then, as I shared the idea with family, friends, colleagues, and students, I was more reluctant than most (other than Joan, who is really good at trying to keep me on an even kneel). Still, the idea kept coming up and coming at me, and soon it was in my head all the time. I do not know why. As I mulled it over, I still hoped to be saved from its insistence. Then, one day when I was out jogging, I literally heard the book speaking to me (spooky, I know, but literally true). It was telling me in a rather insistent voice the very beginning of this story, when I got an F in freshman English. I went home, started writing, and two months later a complete manuscript was finished. I almost never stopped to reorganize the flow of the narrative; I just dutifully recorded it. I kept listening day after day, chapter by chapter, until it was done. I did not write this book, this book wrote me. This time literally, since the narrative is about my life and my work: I was writing about my writing.

Writing this way is easier. Once you give yourself over to a narrative, you become its scribe. Some ideas, though, do take time to unpack. As my younger son once said, some files are compressed. You open them up and listen to what comes out. Your task is reduced to faithfully repeating what you are being told to say. It takes being a good listener, which is, when you think about it, its own skill, but it is different than trying to figure out what to say. So there it is: my formula for writing (for me, not necessarily for anyone else). Take the "I"; listen to yourself; find your voice; let it be heard. Take good notes.

And so it goes. I write when the ideas come, when I am moved to write, in the middle of the night, whenever. It gets easier the more you do it. For this book, the ideas never stopped coming, not for one second. It became a nuisance. I had to try hard to not listen so that I could keep teaching and grading papers while the book kept talking to me all the same.

I write differently now than before. I do not smoke ever, let alone to write. I try to write shorter sentences in most cases. I always write in an active voice. I unfailingly take the "I." I listen to what my voice is telling me to say. I am not just committed to writing; I am confident about writing. The sooner you get to this last point, the better writer you will be. It took me a long time; it need not take you so long.

The main change in my writing is that, after all these years, it is something I have done so much that I now do it automatically. It is something that comes naturally, because I have practiced it so much (meaning that it was not natural but learned, in the most profoundly basic way, by having an intimate familiarity with the actual practice of writing). I learned to write naturally by writing again and again, so that it seems second nature (which is another way of saying it is learned and not natural). In other words, I am not a natural-born writer (and wonder if anyone is). Instead, I kept learning to write to the point that it just seems as if it were natural. As my Freshman English teacher said: I would learn to write . . . eventually. That eventuality comes with practice, through repetition, with time. Well, much time has elapsed since 1967. It is about time that I am able to write. I never told anyone this (which is a really funny thing to say at the end of a memoir), but I stayed back in first grade. I was a slow learner. My learning to write is the best example I can think of that. But slow learners are not just people who are slow, they also are people who learn, if slowly. I might be slow; but I can learn. I learned to write, finally.

Writing has its own challenges. But having written something means you are not nearly done, for always next there is the editing. In fact, it turns out that editing is writing. Good writing emerges out of having the willingness to edit your work to perfection. The real secret of writing is that it can never be great without editing. In fact, good writing almost always only comes from sustained editing. Collette, who was indeed a great writer, allegedly once said: "Ninety-nine percent of good writing is editing." Now, regardless of whether she actually said it or not, this is the inner truth of good writing. Many people can spill their guts on the page, replete with ideas and insight, all in a mess. Next comes the editing, then the re-editing, then the re-re-editing, then maybe after a few more iterations comes the prose expressed in words that sing. Or so we can hope. Passionately commit yourself to the task of writing well. Organize your life so that it can happen. Take the "I." Find your voice. Let your narrative speak you as much as you speak it. Perfect your craft by repetition. But whatever you do, be prepared to edit, edit, edit. Take this memoir as a case in point. Hopefully, what I relayed here is not just a good story but also a good representation of how my writing has improved!

ACKNOWLEDGMENTS

This is personal. So it must be, given the subject matter: how others made me possible. That is the real not-so-secret secret of this story: nobody is anything without the recognition of the other. Kay Klayman was my Freshman English professor who began changing my life that day she started to teach us (in a yearlong course I will never forget). Joe Zimmerman was my dissertation advisor and Jack Gunnell my mentor in graduate school in all other respects. They are still my mentors and I appreciate their support in writing this book. Frances Fox Piven was, as always, my rock: there is no better foundation for social science today and probably ever. Joe Soss and Richard Fording, my "long-time collaborators" as one press release called them, have reinvented me and supported me in writing this memoir. Basha Silverman insisted I write it. Clay Steinman insisted I make it better than it was. Brianne Wolfe edited as always to make it get where it needed to be. Bettina Leibetseder read each chapter as it was written, asking for clarification and providing thoughtful commentary along the way. Allan Irving, Dianne Butera, Deborah Stone, Imke Meyer, Claude Heffron, Brian Caterino, Rick Fisher, Barb Fisher, Rob Schram, Ann Sisson Runyan, Jeannie Reyersbach, Tom Duffin, Michael Pfeiffer, Madelane Shane, John Tambornino, Ilene Kalish, Dan Berggren, Jodi Dean, Laura Katz Olson, Victor Wallis, Phil Neisser, Corey Shdaimah, Roland Stahl, Paul Meshejian, Roni Strier, Michael Tratner, Marc Schulz, Anne Dalke, Gail Hemmeter, Deborah Harrold, Harold Langley, Mary Osirim, Dave Osten, Ronny Valentine, Guy Feldman, Susan Paul, Sherri Levy, Lauren Miltenberger, Tracey Krulcik, Kate Thomas, Nancy Hannett, Alan Draper, Carl Swidorski, Bruce Piasecki, Frank Fischer, and Lynn Appleton added helpful comments that further pushed me to make the manuscript live up to its potential. At SUNY Press, Michael Rinella proved to be a wise and thoughtful editor who adroitly shepherd this project from manuscript to published book. The two anonymous reviewers provided constructive criticism that made the final narrative that much stronger. Michal McCall, my dearest colleague from my Macalester days on, was there at the beginning as she always was, but gone just at the end. I mourn still. Jack Schram taught me to see things in new ways. Ryan Schram continued to inspire me with his own academic career.

Joan Schram was Joan as she always is, never wavering for one moment, and without her I am nowhere. And to the many students who read this manuscript and commented on it, thank you for letting me know whether I was helping or not. Now let's see what others say.

NOTES

PREFACE

1. "AAUP Says De-Facto Tenure Should Apply for Professor at Bryn Mawr College," *Chronicle of Higher Education*, September 19, 2011.

2. See Joe Soss, Richard C. Fording, and Sanford F. Schram, *Disciplining the Poor: Neoliberal Paternalism and the Persistent Power of Race* (Chicago: University of Chicago Press, 2011).

3. See Sanford F. Schram, "The Artful Study of Not Being Governed: Methodological Pluralism and a Better Social Science for a Better World," *Common Knowledge* 18, no. 3 (2012): 528–37.

4. On the footnote issue, a more down to earth assessment is provided by James Scott (whose work represents a great example of finding your own voice regardless of what the mainstream suggests). Scott quotes his good friend Murray Edelman (who led the linguistic turn in political analysis back in the 1960s): "My dear friend at Wisconsin, Murray Edelman, who died not too long ago, had a very healthy attitude about scholarship. He said, 'It's all a compost heap. You just put down a layer of humus that helps other stuff grow. Your work will all be forgotten, but it will help stuff grow.' When you see people using your ideas, it is all part of the compost heap." James Scott, interview, in Gerardo Luis Munck and Richard Owen Snyder, *Passion, Craft, and Method in Comparative Politics* (Baltimore: Johns Hopkins University Press, 2008), 366–67.

CHAPTER ONE. HOW I HAD FOUR MAJORS IN COLLEGE

1. The memory of my cluelessness in getting Bar Mitzvahed is made vivid by the Joel and Ethan Coen film, *A Serious Man* (2009). Actually, that film says a lot about my whole life if you combine the stories in the film of the Bar Mitzvahed son and his professor father.

2. See Corey Shdaimah, Roland W. Stahl, and Sanford F. Schram, *Change Research: A Case Study on Collaborative Methods for Social Workers and Advocates* (New York: Columbia University Press, 2011).

3. See Bent Flyvbjerg, Todd Landman, and Sanford Schram, eds., *Real Social Science: Applied Phronesis* (London: Cambridge University Press, 2012).

4. Jane Hill, "Mock Spanish: A Site for the Indexical Reproduction of Racism in American English," *Language & Culture*, Symposium 2 (1995): http://languagse-culture.binghamton.edu/symposia/2/part1/index.html.

5. Friedrich Dürrenmatt, *Die Panne: Eine Noch Mögliche Geschichte* (Zurich: Diogenes Verlag, 2006 [1956]).

6. C. Wright Mills, *White Collar: The American Middle Classes* (New York: Oxford University Press, 1951).

7. The extent to which students were inspired by C. Wright Mills's writings or those other scholars is subject to some debate, see Todd Gitlin, *The Whole World Is Watching: The Mass Media and the New Left, 1965–70* (Berkeley: University of California Press, 1980), 138.

8. See Stanley Aronowitz, *Taking It Big: C. Wright Mills and the Making of Political Intellectuals* (New York: Columbian University Press, 2012).

9. James Simon Kunen, *The Strawberry Statement: Notes of a College Revolutionary* (New York: Random House, 1969). The rapid-fire cadence of the diary-like entries of this firsthand account of the Columbia University student sit-in of 1968 was just how we experienced the rush of life-changing events in those days.

10. John Kenneth Galbraith, *The Affluent Society* (New York: Houghton Mifflin, 1958).

11. Ralph Nader, *Unsafe at Any Speed* (New York: Grossman, 1965).

12. Saul Alinsky, *Reveille for Radicals* (New York: Vintage Books, 1946).

13. Michael Harrington, *The Other America* (New York: Touchstone, 1962).

14. Stokely Carmichael and Charles V. Hamilton, *Black Power: The Politics of Liberation in America* (New York: Random House, 1967).

15. Once in the course Civil War and Reconstruction, Mallam asked us to play history detectives and try to guess certain facts based on clues. As a class, we did okay and I contributed a bit. After class, I let Mallam know I had gotten one particular factoid right and he replied: "I thought any third grader would have gotten that." This retort reminded me of my ninth grade English teacher who, a few years earlier, had written at the end of my book report: "Great Expectations? Based on this writing, you don't have any?" As I have said, teachers back then were not that schooled in the importance of nurturing.

16. The arguments made by Carmichael and Hamilton in *Black Power* would continue to reverberate in the social sciences. See Michael B. Katz, *Why Don't American Cities Burn?* (Philadelphia: University of Pennsylvania Press, 2012). In chapter 3, in the section entitled "The Management of Marginalization," Katz lists various factors as to why the civil disorders of the 1960s have not recurred in spite of persistent poverty, citing Carmichael and Hamilton's argument as pointing to one significant source of political repression: "Like colonial British imperialists who kept order through the exercise of authority by indigenous leaders, powerful white American retained authority over cities through their influence on minorities elected to political office, appointed to public and social service bureaucracies, and hired in larger numbers by police forces" (88–89).

CHAPTER TWO. GOING POSTAL, GETTING DRAFTED: HOW I ENDED UP IN GRADUATE SCHOOL

1. Matthew Yglesias, *The Rent Is Too Damn High* (New York: Simon and Shuster, 2012); and Thomas J. Sugrue, *The Origins of the Urban Crisis: Race and Inequality in Postwar Detroit* (Princeton: Princeton University Press, 2005).

2. http://rci.rutgers.edu/~oldnb/MappingNJ/MAPS/UrbanPopulation.html.

3. For a penetrating blue-collar Philadelphia reading of how the Irish used African Americans to create their whiteness, see Noel Ignatiev, *How the Irish Became White* (New York: Routledge, 1996).

4. *Jewish Population in the United States 2002* (Storrs: Mandell L. Berman Institute, North American Jewish Data Bank, Center for Judaic Studies and Contemporary Jewish Life, University of Connecticut, 2002). Ironically (or not), since 1997 I have lived in another one of the most Jewish communities in the United States, Lower Merion Township in the suburbs of Philadelphia, Pennsylvania.

5. Daniel J. Elazar and Real Mintz Geffen, *The Conservative Movement in Judaism: Dilemmas and Opportunities* (Albany: State University of New York Press, 2000).

6. My father understood my situation. A few years before, when he and I went to my uncle's luncheonette one night after dinner to get some ice cream, someone from his mail route was there outside on the sidewalk with his German Shepherd. The dog jumped up and bit off my dad's left earlobe (which someone thoughtfully scooped up and gave to the medics when they arrived). My father got his ear repaired but always had a scar there to remind us to beware of the dogs.

7. "The Strike That Stunned the Country," *Time*, March 30, 1970, http://www.apwu.org/news/burrus/2007/ppdate09-2007-031907-iretdoc.pdf.

8. See Philip Rubio, *There's Always Work at the Post Office: African American Postal Workers and the Fight for Jobs, Justice, and Equality* (Chapel Hill: The University of North Carolina Press, 2010), 100.

9. U. S. Department of Justice, "Religious Objections to the Postal Service Oath of Office," Memorandum Opinion for the Vice President and General, February 2, 2005. http://www.justice.gov/olc/2005/religious-objections.pdf.

10. Rubio, *There's Always Work at the Post Office*, 104. I would never have to sign another loyalty oath, even after going to work for New York State as a faculty member in the State University of New York, where the union had won a U.S. Supreme Court case years earlier striking down the loyalty oath in place for SUNY faculty at the time. *Keyishian v. Board of Regents of the University of the State of New York* 385 U.S. 589 (1967). Yet the whole issue of loyalty oaths would, years later, blow back for me in the academy in an entirely different way. See chapter 12.

11. Ibid., 103.

12. Alix Spiegel, "What Vietnam Taught Us about Breaking Bad Habits," Boy-Cott Magazine. http://www.boycottmag.com/?p=4688.

CHAPTER THREE. HOW I LEARNED TO READ

1. John Rawls, *A Theory of Justice* (Cambridge: Harvard University Press, 1971).

2. Gabriel Kolko, *The Triumph of Conservatism: A Reinterpretation of American History, 1900–1916* (New York: The Free Press, 1963).

3. See Sanford F. Schram, "The Deep Semiotic Structure of Deservingness: Discourse and Identity in Welfare Policy," in *The Argumentative Turn Revisited*, ed. Frank Fischer and Herbert Gottweis (Durham: Duke University Press, 2012), 236–68.

4. I thought back to my graduate school days and the insightful comments of my fellow students in my first semester when reading Bonnie Honig's critique of

Rawls in *Political Theory and the Displacement of Politics* (Ithaca: Cornell University Press, 1993).

5. On "empty" pluralism, see John Dryzek's critique of my argument for methodological diversity in Political Science: John S. Dryzek, "A Pox on Perestroika, A Hex on Hegemony: Toward a Critical Political Science," in *Perestroika! The Raucous Rebellion in Political Science*, ed. Kristen Renwick Monroe (New Haven: Yale University Press, 2005), 509–25. My rejoinder relies on Keith Topper's *The Disorder of Political Inquiry* (Cambridge: Harvard University Press, 2005): Sanford F. Schram, "Taking Political Science Seriously: Mixing Methods Makes for a More Contingent but Self-Reflective Discipline," *Human Studies* 30, no. 3 (September 2007): 275–80.

6. Philip Selznick, *The TVA and the Grass Roots: A Study in the Sociology of Formal Organization* (Berkeley: University of California Press, 1949).

7. Sanford F. Schram and Brian Caterino, eds., *Making Political Science Matter: Debating Knowledge, Research and Method* (New York: New York University Press, 2006).

8. Eventually I took the advice of Slavoj Žižek, who says you need to learn to enjoy your symptom. See *Enjoy Your Symptom: Jacques Lacan in Hollywood and Out* (New York: Routledge, 2001). Lacan's symptom was having two separate families; mine was having separate methods that I wanted to combine. I stated in the preface of my first book: "The process of getting my work out to others almost always at least implicitly involved having to have to choose whether I was, for lack of better terms, a 'critic,' or a 'scientist.' Being both as much as neither did not help me with the editorial review process." See Sanford F. Schram, *Words of Welfare: The Poverty of Social Science and the Social Science of Poverty* (Minneapolis: University of Minnesota Press, 1995), xvii.

9. John G. Gunnell, *Philosophy, Science, and Political Inquiry* (Morristown, NJ: General Learning Press, 1975).

10. William E. Connolly, *Political Science and Ideology* (New York: Atherton Press, 1967).

11. Peter Winch, *The Idea of a Social Science and Its Relation to Philosophy* (London: Routledge and Kegan Paul, 1958).

12. Thomas S. Kuhn, *The Structure of Scientific Revolutions* (Chicago: University of Chicago Press, 1962).

13. The black swan references the outlier. There is reason to think that the film *Black Swan* by Darren Aronofsky at least implicitly suggests that this is not just the literal reference to that ballerina's role in Tchaikovsky's *Swan Lake*. Aronofsky's first feature length film was *Pi*, about numerology (of a Jewish-inflected sort). He is most likely well aware of the "black swan" as a term of art in probability theory associated with rare events. See Bent Flyvbjerg, *Making Social Science Matter: Why Social Inquiry Fails and How It Can Succeed Again* (Cambridge: Cambridge University Press, 2001), 77–84; and Nassim Taleb, *The Black Swan: The Impact of the Highly Improbable* (New York: Random House, 2007).

14. See Joseph F. Zimmerman, *The Federated City: Community Control in Large Cities* (New York: St. Martins Press, 1972).

15. The SUNY-Albany academic leadership was very supportive in making this possible, especially Vice President for Research and Dean of Graduate Studies Louis Salkever, who arranged my funding.

16. See Elliot A. Krause, "The Functions of a Bureaucratic Ideology: 'Citizen Participation,'" *Social Problems* 16, no. 2 (Autumn 1968): 129–43.

CHAPTER FOUR. I WENT DOWN TO THE CROSSROADS: ACTIVISM AND SCHOLARSHIP

1. Jennifer Frost, *An Interracial Movement of the Poor Community Organizing and the New Left in the 1960s* (New York; New York University Press, 2001).

2. Amiri Baraka, *Somebody Blew Up America & Other Poems* (New York: House of Nehesi Publishers, 2003). Baraka's poem raises the issue of the role of conspiracy theories in American political culture in general and among subordinated populations specifically. C. Wright Mills wrote: "To accept either view—of all history as conspiracy or of all history as drift—is to relax the effort to understand the facts of power and the ways of the powerful" (*The Power Elite* [New York: Oxford University Press, 1956], 27). In other words, while the powerful exercise disproportionate power, it is not necessarily the case that everything that happens is the result of their coordinated efforts. On the role of conspiracy theories among subordinated populations, see John Fiske, *Power Plays Power Works* (New York: Verso Press, 1993).

3. Sanford F. Schram, *Praxis for the Poor: Piven and Cloward and the Future of Social Science in Social Welfare* (New York: New York University Press, 2002).

4. Schram and Caterino, *Making Political Science Matter.*

5. See Shdaimah, Stahl, and Schram, *Change Research.*

6. Sanford F. Schram, "Elderly Policy Particularism and the New Social Services," *Social Service Review* 53, no. 1 (March 1979): 75–91.

7. See Schram, "The Artful Study of Not Being Governed," 528–37.

8. See Robert B. Hudson, ed., *The Aging in Politics: Process and Policy* (Springfield, IL: Charles C. Thomas, 1981); and Bernice Neugarten, ed., *Age or Need? Public Policies for Older People* (Pacific Palisades: Sage, 1982).

9. See Sanford F. Schram, "The Deep Semiotic Structure of Deservingness."

10. Frances Fox Piven and Richard Cloward, *Poor People's Movements: How They Succeed, Why They Fail* (New York: Pantheon, 1977).

11. The issue of co-optation in Piven and Cloward's argument about the advantages of practicing dissensus politics reinforced my interest in the concept going back to my reading of Philip Selznick, *The TVA and the Grass Roots.* The controversy over the dissensus approach of Occupy Wall Street in the fall of 2011 brought this issue to the fore for me once more. See Schram, "The Artful Study of Not Being Governed." On "Co-optation Phobia," see Todd Gitlin, *Occupy Nation: The Roots, the Spirit, and the Promise of Occupy Wall Street* (New York: It Books, 2012), 140–41.

12. Frances Fox Piven and Richard Cloward, *Regulating the Poor: The Functions of Public Welfare* (New York: Vintage 1971), 338.

13. Robert B. Albritton, "Social Amelioration through Mass Insurgency? A Reexamination of the Piven and Cloward Thesis," *American Political Science Review* 73 (1979): 1003–11; and Frances Fox Piven and Richard A. Cloward, "Electoral Instability, Civil Disorder, and Relief Rises: A Reply to Albritton," *American Political Science Review* 73 (1979): 1012–19.

14. For an in-depth examination of the idea of welfare as a secondary institution, see Schram, *Praxis for the Poor.*

15. For instance, see Eugene Durman, "Have the Poor Been Regulated? Toward a Multivariate Understanding of Welfare Growth," *Social Service Review* 47 (1973): 339–59. Also see, Sanford F. Schram, "The Praxis of Poor People's Movements: Strategy and Theory in Dissensus Politics," *Perspectives on Politics* 1, no. 4 (December 2003): 715–20.

16. Richard A. Cloward and Frances Fox Piven, "The Weight of the Poor: A Strategy to End Poverty," *The Nation* 2 (May 1966): 510–17.

17. See Felicia Kornbluh, *The Battle for Welfare Rights: Politics and Poverty in Modern America* (Philadelphia: University of Pennsylvania Press, 2007), 151.

18. *Statistical Abstract of the United States* (Washington, DC: Department of Commerce, Bureau of the Census, 1961–76).

19. William J. Collins and Robert A. Margo, "The Labor Market Effects of the 1960s Riots," NBER Working Paper No. 10243 National Bureau of Economic Research. January 2004.

20. Frances Fox Piven, *Who's Afraid of Frances Fox Piven?: The Essential Writings of the Professor Glenn Beck Loves to Hate* (New York: The New Press, 2011).

21. Piven and Cloward, "Electoral Instability," 1015–16.

22. See Schram, "The Artful Study of Not Being Governed."

23. Sanford F. Schram and J. Patrick Turbett, "Civil Disorder and the Welfare Explosion: A Two-Step Process," *American Sociological Review* (June 1983): 408–14.

24. Sanford F. Schram and J. Patrick Turbett, "The Welfare Explosion: Mass Society versus Social Control," *Social Service Review* (December 1983): 614–25.

25. Schram and Turbett, "Civil Disorder and the Welfare Explosion,"413.

26. Ira Katznelson and Mark Kesselman, *The Politics of Power: A Critical Introduction to American Government* (San Diego: Harcourt Brace Jovanovich, 1987), 310.

27. Michael B. Katz, *In the Shadow of the Poorhouse: A Social History of Welfare in America*, Tenth Anniversary Edition (New York: Basic Books, 1996), 364.

28. See Richard C. Fording, "The Conditional Effect of Violence as a Political Tactic: Mass Insurgency, Welfare Generosity, and Electoral Context in the American States," *American Journal of Political Science* 41 (1997): 1–29; and "The Political Response to Black Insurgency: A Critical Test of Competing Theories of the State," *American Political Science Review* 95 (2001): 115–31.

CHAPTER FIVE. STANDING ON SHOULDERS

1. Linda Gordon, *Pitied But Not Entitled: Single Mothers and the History of Welfare* (New York: The Free Press, 1994).

2. Lawrence M. Mead, *Beyond Entitlement: The Social Obligations of Citizenship* (New York: The Free Press, 1986).

3. Sanford F. Schram and Michael Wiseman, "Should Families Be Protected from AFDC-UP?" (Madison, WI: Institute for Research on Poverty Discussion Paper #860-88).

4. Charles Murray, *Losing Ground: American Social Policy 1950–1980* (New York: Basic Books, 1984).

5. Lawrence M. Mead, *Government Matters: Welfare Reform in Wisconsin* (Princeton: Princeton University Press, 2005).

6. Soss, Fording, and Schram, *Disciplining the Poor*. See chapter 10 for an in-depth examination of that collaboration.

7. See Lawrence M. Mead, "Scholasticism in Political Science," *Perspectives on Politics* 8, no. 2 (June 2010): 453–64.

8. Frances Fox Piven, Richard A. Cloward, Fred Block, and Barbara Ehrenreich, *The Mean Season: The Attack on the Welfare State*. (New York: Pantheon, 1987).

9. Sanford F. Schram, *Words of Welfare*.

10. Murray Edelman, *Political Language: Words That Succeed and Policies That Fail* (New York: Academic Press, 1977).

11. Linda Gordon, *Woman's Body, Woman's Right: Birth Control in America* (New York: Penguin Books, 1990).

12. Linda Gordon, *Heroes of Their Own Lives: The Politics and History of Family Violence—Boston, 1880–1960* (New York: Viking Press, 1988).

13. Murray's extensive network of former students furthered my learning. In particular, I became fast friends with Ken Hoover, and we supported each other in our insistence on mixing methods, while also become the closest of colleagues.

14. Theresa Funiciello, *The Tyranny of Kindness: Dismantling the Welfare System to End Poverty in America* (New York: The Atlantic Monthly Press, 1993).

15. Mentoring is an underdiscussed dimension of the scholarly process. The inspiration as well as the support can make a real difference. When Richard was dying in 2000, he completed a final interview about his career. Asked if anyone was doing work that could carry on what he had been doing, he responded by mentioning me as the one example he wanted to point to. It was entirely unnecessary for him to single me out among all the folks that were following in his footsteps in pursuing a radical approach to social work and fighting for social justice on behalf of the poor. He did appreciate that I was ever attentive to his advice and he appreciated my taking a politically informed approach to challenging the role of research on poverty in social work and related fields. Yet, his loyalty toward me was demonstrated most forcefully in this way: he wanted to show his support for me right to the end. Joshua Miller, "We Work Together, We Think Together, We Act Together: A Narrative Interview with Richard Cloward, Part III," *Journal of Progressive Human Services* 14, no. 1 (2003): 15–39.

16. Sanford F. Schram, "Postpositivistic Policy Analysis and the Family Support Act of 1988: Symbols at the Expense of Substance," *Polity* (Summer 1992): 633–55; and *Words of Welfare*, chapter 7, "The Real Uses of a False Dichotomy: Symbols at the Expense of Substance in Welfare Reform," 123–41.

17. Howard S. Becker and Michal M. McCall, eds., *Symbolic Interaction and Cultural Studies* (Chicago: University of Chicago Press, 1993); and George J. McCall, Michal McCall, Gerald Suttles, and Suzanne Kurth, *Friendship as a Social Institution* (New Brunswick: Transaction Publishers, 2010).

18. By coincidence, Michal and her husband Paul Meshejian moved to the Philadelphia area just before we got there in 1997, when I came to Bryn Mawr College. That way, we continued to stay good friends and support each other until Michal died in February 2012 while I was starting to write this book (which is dedicated to her).

19. Joel Best, *Social Problems* (New York: W. W. Norton, 2007).

20. Joe Soss, *Unwanted Claims: The Politics of Participation in the U.S. Welfare System* (Ann Arbor: University of Michigan Press, 2002).

21. Richard C. Fording, "The Conditional Effect of Violence as a Political Tactic: Mass Insurgency, Welfare Generosity, and Electoral Context in the American States," *American Journal of Political Science* 41 (1997): 1–29.

22. Joe Soss is currently the Cowles Professor for the Study of Public Service in the Humphrey School of Public Affairs at the University of Minnesota. Rich Fording is currently the chair of the Political Science department of the University of Alabama in Tuscaloosa.

23. Schram, *Words of Welfare*.

24. Taryn Lindhorst and Julia Padgett, "Disjunctures for Women and Frontline Workers: Implementation of the Family Violence Option," *Social Service Review* 79 (2007): 405–29.

25. Ann R. Tickamyer, Debra A. Henderson, Julie A. White, and Bradley L. Tadlock, "Voices of Welfare Reform: Bureaucratic Rationality Versus the Perceptions of Welfare Participants," *Affilia* 15 (2000): 173–92.

26. Thanks to Michael Pfeiffer for telling me about "Do I have to paint you a picture?"

CHAPTER SIX. THEORY AND PRACTICE

1. For a short history of welfare migration as an enduring anxiety in U.S. political discourse, see Sanford F. Schram and Joe Soss, "The Real Value of Welfare: Why There Is No Welfare Migration," *Politics & Society* 27, no. 1 (1999): 39–66.

2. See for instance, Dirk Johnson, "The Poor Come to Madison," *Minneapolis Star Tribune*, May 9, 1995, 4A.

3. For a good place to start for considering a bottom up perspective on why low-income single mothers move from one state to another, see Carol Stack, *Call to Home: African Americans Reclaim the Rural South* (New York: Basic Books, 1996).

4. 394 U.S. 618 (1969).

5. Sanford F. Schram and Philip T. Neisser, eds., *Tales of the State: Narrative in U.S. Politics and Public Policy* (Lanham, MD: Rowman and Littlefield, 1997).

6. Cheri Honkala, by coincidence, would end up moving to Philadelphia around the same time I did, where she founded the Kensington Welfare Rights Union, and where she continued to engage in protest actions designed to raise public awareness of the poverty issue. See David Zucchino, *The Myth of the Welfare Queen: A Pulitzer Prize-Winning Journalist's Portrait of Women on the Line* (New York: Simon and Shuster, 1999).

7. Theresa Funiciello and Sanford F. Schram, "Post-Mortem on the Deterioration of the Welfare Grant," in *The Reconstruction of Family Policy*, ed. Elaine Anderson and Richard Hula (Westport, CT: Greenwood Press, 1991), 149–64; and Schram, *Words of Welfare*, chapter 5, "Home Economists as the Real Economists," 77–97.

8. As I recall, the Minnesota State Demographer's Office had provided data that looked only at people currently receiving AFDC at the time in 1990, overlooking that the welfare population has a high turnover rate. At a minimum, it would have

been better to focus more broadly on the general population at risk, which, in the case of Aid to Families with Dependent Children, would be all poor female-headed families. See Jean Hopfensperger, "Carlson's Welfare Plan May Cut Job Program," *Minneapolis Star Tribune*, June 10, 1994, Al. For a critique of state government studies such as this one from Minnesota, see Russell L. Hanson and John T. Hartman, "Do Welfare Magnets Attract?" Discussion Paper 1028-94 (Madison: Institute for Research on Poverty, University of Wisconsin-Madison, 1994).

9. Schram, *Words of Welfare*, 20–37.

10. See Sanford F. Schram, *Welfare Discipline: Discourse, Governance, and Globalization* (Philadelphia: Temple University Press, 2006).

11. Stack, *Call to Home*.

12. Sanford F. Schram, Lawrence Nitz and Gary Krueger, "Without Cause or Effect: Reconsidering Welfare Migration as a Policy Problem," *American Journal of Political Science* 42, no. 1 (January 1998): 210–30.

13. Ibid., 210.

14. See Joel Handler and Yeheskel Hasenfeld, *Blame Welfare, Ignore Poverty and Inequality* (New York: Cambridge University Press, 2006).

15. *Brief of Social Scientists as Amici Curiae Supporting Respondents*, *Anderson v. Roe*, No. 98-97, Lawrence S. Lustberg, Counsel of Record, Submitted to the U.S. Supreme Court (October 1998).

16. Joel Handler and Linda Gordon, "Welfare's No Magnet," *The Nation* 268, no. 5 (February 8, 1999): 5–6.

17. Sanford F. Schram and Joe Soss, "Making Something out of Nothing: Welfare Reform and a New Race to the Bottom," *Publius* 28, no. 3(1998): 67–88; and "The Real Value of Welfare."

18. *Sanez v. Roe* 526 U.S. 489 (1999): "Briefs of *amici curiae* urging affirmance were filed for ACORN et al. by *Paul M. Dodyk* and *Henry A. Freedman*; for the American Bar Association by *Philip S. Anderson* and *Paul M. Smith*; for the Brennan Center for Justice at New York University School of Law et al. by *Burt Neuborne* and *Deborah Goldberg*; for Catholic Charities USA et al. by *Louis R. Cohen*; for the National Law Center on Homelessness and Poverty by *Ann E. Bushmiller*; for Sixty-six Organizations Serving Domestic Violence Survivors by *Susan Frietsche*; for Social Scientists by *Lawrence S. Lustberg*; and for William Cohen et al. by *Roderick M. Hills, Jr.*, and *Charles S. Sims*."

19. Ibid., at 510.

20. Michael A. Bailey, "Welfare Migration and the Multifaceted Decision to Move," *American Political Science Review* 99, no. 1 (February 2005): 125–35.

21. Ibid., 134.

CHAPTER SEVEN. IS ANYBODY LISTENING?

1. Jane Collins and Victoria Mayer, *Both Hands Tied: Welfare Reform and the Race to the Bottom of the Low-Wage Labor Market* (Chicago: University of Chicago Press, 2010).

2. U.S. Government Accountability Office (GAO), *Temporary Assistance for Needy Families: Fewer Eligible Families Have Received Cash Assistance Since the*

1990s, and the Recession's Impact on Caseload Varies by State (Washington, DC: GAO, 2010).

3. Sanford F. Schram and Joe Soss, "Success Stories: Welfare Reform, Policy Discourse, and the Politics of Research," *The Annals of the American Academy of Political and Social Science* 557 (September 2001): 49–65.

4. GAO, *Temporary Assistance for Needy Families.*

5. Rebecca Blank and Brian Kovak, "The Growing Problem of Disconnected Single Mothers" (Ann Arbor: National Poverty Center Working Paper Series #07-28).

6. See Charles Noble, *Ending Welfare as We Knew It: A Political History of the American Welfare State* (New York: Oxford University Press, 1998).

7. Scott Allard, *Out of Reach: Place, Poverty, and the New American Welfare State* (New Haven: Yale University Press, 2009).

8. Yamiche Alcindor, "States Consider Drug Testing Welfare Recipients," *USA Today*, February 17, 2012, http://www.usatoday.com/news/nation/story/2012-02-17/welfare-food-stamps-drug-testing-laws/53306804/1.

9. Lylah M. Alphonse, "Wisconsin Bill Claims Single Moms Cause Child Abuse by Not Being Married," *Yahoo! Shine*, March 2, 2012, http://shine.yahoo.com/parenting/wisconsin-bill-claims-single-moms-cause-child-abuse-011200419.html.

10. Charles Blow, "The Welfare Gambit," *New York Times*, August 8, 2012, http://campaignstops.blogs.nytimes.com/2012/08/08/the-welfare-gambit/.

11. Timothy Casey, "TANF Extended to September 30 with a Funding Cut and New Restrictions on Accessing Benefits" (New York: Legal Momentum, the Women's Legal Defense Fund, February 28, 2012).

12. Barbara Ehrenreich, "Rediscovering American Poverty: How We Cured 'The Culture of Poverty,' Not Poverty Itself," *TomDispatch.com*, March 15, 2012.

13. Schram and Soss, "Success Stories."

14. See Sanford F. Schram, "In the Clinic: The Medicalization of Welfare," *Social Text* 62, no. 18, 1 (Spring 2000): 81–107.

15. In particular, see Murray, *Losing Ground*; and Mead, *Beyond Entitlement.*

16. David Mayhew, *Congress: The Electoral Connection* (New Haven: Yale University Press, 2004 [1975]); Barbara Sinclair, *Unorthodox Lawmaking: New Legislative Processes in the U.S. Congress* (Washington, DC: CQ Press, 2007 [2001]); and Richard F. Fenno Jr., *Congressmen in Committees* (Boston: Little, Brown, 1973) and *Home Style: House Members in their Districts* (Boston: Little, Brown, 1978).

17. Jonathan Swift, *A Modest Proposal for Preventing the Children of Poor People From Being a Burden on Their Parents or Country, and for Making Them Beneficial to the Publick* (Seaside, OR: Watchmaker Publishing, 2010), originally published anonymously in 1729, suggesting that the Irish address their starvation by selling their babies to be eaten by the rich.

18. Annalyn Censky, "Poverty Rate Rises in America," *CNN Money*, September 13, 2011, http://money.cnn.com/2011/09/13/news/economy/poverty_rate_income/index.htm.

19. The increases in the number of people living in not just "deep" poverty (i.e., one-half the poverty line) but living in "extreme" poverty (i.e., $2 or less per person per day) were particularly acute. See H. Luke Shaefer and Kathryn Edin,

"Extreme Poverty in the United States, 1996 to 2011" Policy Brief #28 (Ann Arbor: National Poverty Center, University of Michigan, February 2012).

20. Rebecca Blank and Brian Kovak, "The Growing Problem of Disconnected Single Mothers" (Ann Arbor: National Poverty Center Working Paper Series #07-28).

21. Schram and Soss, "Success Stories," 49–50.

22. U.S. House of Representatives, Committee on Education and the Workforce, Subcommittee on 21st Century Competitiveness, *Welfare Reform: An Examination of Effects*, Hearing, September 20, 2001, 107th Cong., Serial No. 107-30 (Washington, DC: U.S. Government Printing Office, 2002), http://www.docstoc.com/docs/12493146/WELFARE-REFORM-AN-EXAMINATION-OF-EFFECTS.

23. Murray Edelman, *The Symbolic Uses of Politics* (Urbana: University of Illinois Press, 1964).

24. Schram, Testimony, *Welfare Reform: An Examination of Effects*, Hearing, September 20, 2001, 107th Cong., Serial No. 107-30, 15–34.

25. Ibid., 165–74.

26. Kathryn Porter and Allen Dupree, *Poverty Trends for Families Headed by Working Single Mothers, 1993 to 1999*. (Washington DC: Center on Budget and Policy Priorities, August 16, 2001), http://www.cbpp.org/8-16-01wel.htm.

27. Robert Moffitt, "A Primer on Welfare Reform," *Focus* 26, no. 1 (Summer-Fall 2008): 15–25.

28. On Haskins's reversal, see Inyoung Hwang, "Welfare reform in a Recession," *Medill Reports*, June 04, 2009, http://news.medill.northwestern.edu/washington/news.aspx?id=133473; also see Nancy Folbre, "Welfare Reform Revisited," *New York Times*, December 12, 2011, http://economix.blogs.nytimes.com/2011/12/12/welfare-reform-revisited/.

29. Moffitt, "A Primer on Welfare Reform," 23.

30. Rector, Testimony, *Welfare Reform: An Examination of Effects*, Hearing, September 20, 2001, 107th Cong., Serial No. 107-30, 9.

31. See Jason DeParle, "Welfare Limits Left Poor Adrift While Recession Hit," *New York Times*, April, 8, 2012, A1. In this article, Haskins offers an explicit reconsideration of his insistent position when we testified in 2001. He states: "This is the biggest problem with welfare reform, and we ought to be paying attention to it." When I pointed out the problem back in 2001 as a concern that had to be noted, he was adamant in his refusal to consider it.

32. Shaefer and Edin, "Extreme Poverty in the United States, 1996 to 2011," 1, 4.

33. Joe Soss, Sanford F. Schram, Thomas P. Vartanian, and Erin O'Brien, "Setting the Terms of Relief: Explaining State Policy Choices in the Devolution Revolution," *American Journal of Political Science* 45 (2001): 378–95.

34. Aaron Bernstein, "Tugging on a Tattered Safety Net: Stricter Rules for Government Aid Will Hurt in a Slump," *Bloomberg Business Week*, October 1, 2012, http://www.businessweek.com/magazine/content/01_40/b3751711.htm.

35. See "Welfare Reform and State Flexibility," Welfare Reform and Beyond Forum (Washington DC: Brookings Institution, June 2002), http://www.brookings.edu/events/2002/0626welfare.aspx.

36. R. Kent Weaver and Thomas Gais, "State Policy Choices under Welfare Reform," http://www.brookings.edu/ccf/CCF-Brief.aspx, Welfare Reform and Beyond Policy Brief #21(Washington, DC: Brookings Institution, April 2002), http://www.brookings.edu/papers/2002/04welfare_gais.aspx.

37. See Sanford F. Schram, Joe Soss, and Richard C. Fording, eds. *Race and the Politics of Welfare Reform* (Ann Arbor: University of Michigan Press, 2003).

CHAPTER EIGHT. CALLING OUT RACIAL BIAS

1. Schram, *After Welfare.*

2. Sanford F. Schram and Samuel Beer, eds., *Welfare Reform: A Race to the Bottom?* (Baltimore: Johns Hopkins University Press, 1999).

3. Sanford F. Schram, "Putting a Black Face on Welfare: The Good and the Bad," in *Welfare and the Politics of Welfare Reform*, ed. Sanford F. Schram, Joe Soss, and Richard C. Fording (Ann Arbor: University of Michigan Press, 2003), 196–224; and Anne Schneider and Helen Ingram, eds. *Deserving and Entitled: Social Constructions and Public Policy* (Albany: State University of New York Press, 2005), 261–89.

4. Soss, Fording, and Schram, *Disciplining the Poor*, 74–75.

5. Ibid., 136.

6. U.S. Department of Health and Human Services, Administration for Children and Families, *Temporary Assistance for Needy Families: Eighth Annual Report to Congress*, Chapter X, Background Characteristics and Financial Circumstances of TANF Recipients (Washington, DC: U.S. Government Printing Office, 2006).

7. See Nell Irvin Painter, "When Poverty was White," *New York Times*, March 26, 2012, http://www.nytimes.com/2012/03/25/opinion/sunday/when-poverty-was-white.html?_r=1&ref=opinion. Painter provides a thoughtful critique of Charles Murray's attempt to blame the declining fortunes of the white working class in recent years on the alleged decline of social mores starting the 1960s, when in fact white poverty stretches over the course of U.S. history. See Charles Murray, *Coming Apart: The State of White America, 1960–2010* (New York: Crown Forum, 2012). For an important study on white rural poverty that does not fall prey to the limitations of Murray's analysis, see Patrick Carr and Maria Kefalas, *Hollowing out the Middle: The Rural Brain Drain and What it Means for America* (Boston: Beacon Press, 2010).

8. Joel Best, *Damned Lies and Statistics: Untangling Numbers from the Media, Politicians, and Activists* (Berkeley: University of California Press, 2001).

9. This section revisits the analysis I provided in *Praxis for the Poor*, 171–85.

10. David M. Halbfinger, "Judge Dismisses Main Charges in Suit by Ex-Chief of Troopers," *New York Times*, July 6, 2000, A1; and Iver Peterson and David M. Halbfinger, *New York Times*, February 3, 2001, A1.

11. Frederick Schauer, *Profiles, Probabilities, and Stereotypes* (Cambridge: Belknap Press, 2003).

12. Paul de Man, *Resistance to Theory* (Minneapolis: University of Minnesota Press, 1986), 3–20.

13. See Schram, *After Welfare.*

14. Paul Gilroy, *Against Race: Imagining Culture beyond the Color Line* (Cambridge: Belknap Press, 2000).

15. Michelle Alexander, *The New Jim Crow: Mass Incarceration in the Age of Colorblindness* (New York: The New Press, 2010).

16. On the symbolic effects of political actions, see Edelman, *The Symbolic Uses of Politics*.

17. Cloward and Piven, "The Weight of the Poor."

18. Michelle Alexander, "Go to Trial: Crash the Justice System," *New York Times*, March 10, 2012, http://www.nytimes.com/2012/03/11/opinion/sunday/go-to-trial-crash-the-justice-system.html?_r=2&ref=opinion.

19. See Soss, Fording, and Schram, *Disciplining the Poor*.

20. See Thomas Lemke, "The Birth of Bio-Politics: Michel Foucault's Lecture at the Collège de France on Neo-Liberal Governmentality," *Economy and Society* 30, no. 27 (2001): 203.

CHAPTER NINE. THE DEEP SEMIOTIC STRUCTURE OF DESERVINGNESS

1. See Micaela di Leonardo, *Exotics at Home: Anthropologies, Others, and American Modernity* (Chicago: University of Chicago Press, 1998).

2. Eduardo Bonilla-Silva, *Racism without Racists: Color-Blind Racism and the Persistence of Racial Inequality in the United States* (Lanham, MD: Rowman and Littlefield, 2003).

3. Martin Gilens, *Why Americans Hate Welfare: Race, Media, and the Politics of Antipoverty Policy* (Chicago: University of Chicago Press, 2000).

4. Schram, *Words of Welfare*.

5. In addition to memoirs, ethnographies are important sources of bottom-up knowledge about how the disciplinary regime affects subordinate populations today. See Elijah Anderson, *Code of the Street: Decency, Violence, and the Moral Life of the Inner City* (New York: W. W. Norton, 1999); Philippe Bourgois, *In Search of Respect: Selling Crack in El Barrio* (New York: Cambridge University Press, 1995); Robert Fairbanks, *How It Works: Recovering Citizens in Post-Welfare Philadelphia* (Chicago: University of Chicago Press, 2010); and Teresa Gowan, *Hobos, Hustlers, and Backsliders: Homeless in San Francisco* (Minneapolis: University of Minnesota Press, 2011). Gowan artfully combines discourse analysis and ethnography to demonstrate convincingly how the homeless people she got to know reworked competing discourses of "sin-talk," "sick-talk" and "systems-talk" to make sense of their marginalization.

6. Stephen J. Ball, *Politics and Policymaking in Education: Explorations in Political Sociology* (New York: Routledge, 1990), 18.

7. See Judith Butler, "On Self-Referentiality: Pro and Contra," *Common Knowledge* 4, no. 2 (Fall 1995): 70–73, and "Giving an Account of Oneself," *Diacritics* 31, no. 4 (Winter 2001): 22–40, reprinted in *Giving an Account of Oneself: A Critique of Ethical Violence* (Amsterdam: Department of Philosophy, University of Amsterdam, Spinoza Lectures, April and May, 2002), where Butler states: "the 'I' cannot tell the story of its own emergence, and the conditions of its own possibility, without in some sense bearing witness to a state of affairs to which one could not have been present, prior to one's own becoming, and so narrating that which one cannot know" (27).

8. Piven and Cloward, *Regulating the Poor.*

9. Schram, "The Deep Semiotic Structure of Deservingness."

10. See Schram, *After Welfare.*

11. J. M. Balkin, *Cultural Software: A Theory of Ideology* (New Haven: Yale University Press, 2003).

12. Jeffrey Alexander, *The Performance of Politics: Obama's Victory and the Democratic Struggle for Power* (New York: Oxford University Press, 2010), 81.

13. Barbara J. Nelson, "The Origins of the Two-Channel Welfare State: Workmen's Compensation and Mother's Aid," in *Women, the State, and Welfare,* ed. Linda Gordon (Madison: University of Wisconsin Press, 1990), 123–51.

14. Joe Soss and Sanford F. Schram, "A Public Transformed? Welfare Reform as Policy Feedback," *American Political Science Review* 101, no. 1 (2007): 111–27.

15. Ibid., 111–27.

16. See Kathryn Edin and Laura Lein, *Making Ends Meet: How Single Mothers Survive Welfare and Low-Wage Work* (New York: Russell Sage Foundation, 1998).

17. Even Michael Harrington, in *The Other America,* ended up reinscribing the deep semiotic structure of deservingness by suggesting the poor had a different culture than the middle class. See Barbara Ehrenreich, "Rediscovering American Poverty: How We Cured 'The Culture of Poverty,' Not Poverty Itself," *TomDispatch.com,* March 15, 2012.

18. Martha Feldman, Kaj Sköldberg, Ruth Nicole Brown, and Debra Horner, "Making Sense of Stories: A Rhetorical Approach to Narrative Analysis," *Journal of Public Administration Research and Theory* 14, no. 2 (2004): 147–70.

19. Barry Laga, "Discourse." http://myhome.coloradomesa.edu/~blaga/Theory/Discourse.html.

20. See Slavoj Zizek, *Enjoy Your Symptom: Jacques Lacan in Hollywood and Out* (New York: Routledge, 2001).

21. Michael Klein, "Narrative and Discourse in Kubrick's Modern Tragedy," in *The English Novel and the Movies,* ed. Michael Klein and Gillian Parker (New York: Frederick Ungar, 1981), 95, 107.

22. Sanford F. Schram, "Postmodern Policy Analysis: Identity and Difference in Social Policy," *Policy Sciences* 26, no. 2 (Spring 1993): 249–70.

23. Frank Fischer, *Democracy and Expertise: Reorienting Policy Inquiry* (New York: Oxford University Press, 2009).

24. See Margaret Somers and Fred Block, "From Poverty to Perversity: Ideas, Markets, and Institutions over 200 Years of Welfare Debate," *American Sociological Review* 70 (2005): 260–87.

25. Schram and Soss, "Success Stories."

26. See Soss, Fording, and Schram, *Disciplining the Poor.*

27. See Thomas Lemke, "The Birth of Bio-Politics: Michel Foucault's Lecture at the Collège de France on Neo-Liberal Governmentality," *Economy and Society* 30, no. 2 (2001): 203.

28. Sheldon H. Danziger, Richard Frank, and Ellen Meara, "Mental Illness, Work and Income Support Programs," *American Journal of Psychiatry* 166, no. 4 (2009): 398–404.

29. Pew Research Center, "Independents Take Center Stage in Obama Era," 2009, on the Center's Web site.

30. Gilens, *Why Americans Hate Welfare*.

31. Edelman, *Political Language*.

32. Peter Conrad, *The Medicalization of Society: On the Transformation of Human Conditions into Treatable Disorders* (Baltimore: Johns Hopkins University Press, 2007).

33. Lemke, "The Birth of Bio-Politics," 203.

34. Anna Korteweg, "Welfare Reform and the Subject of the Working Mother: Get a Job, a Better Job, Then a Career," *Theory and Society* 32, no. 4 (2003): 468.

35. See Theda Skocpol and Vanessa Williamson, *The Tea Party and the Remaking of Republican Conservatism* (New York: Oxford University Press, 2011).

36. Adam Liptak, "In Court, Sharp Questions on Health Law's Mandate, *New York Times*, March 28, 2012; http://www.nytimes.com/slideshow/2012/03/27/us/20120328_SCOTUS.html?ref=us.

37. On the framing of issues by political elites to first agitate the mass public and then recreate their acquiescence for policies that elites wanted to enact in the first place, see Murray Edelman, *Politics as Symbolic Action: Mass Arousal and Quiescence* (Cambridgeshire, UK: Markham Publishing, 1971).

CHAPTER TEN. THREE HEADS ARE BETTER THAN ONE

1. See Soss, Fording, and Schram, *Disciplining the Poor*.

2. Schram, Soss, and Fording, eds., *Race and the Politics of Welfare Reform*.

3. Wesley W. Bryant, "Internalized Racism's Association with African American Male Youth's Propensity for Violence," *Journal of Black Studies* 42, no. 4 (May 2011): 690–707.

4. See Curtis C. Austin, "Testimony of President Curtis C. Austin of Workforce Florida, Inc.," Workforce Investment Act Reauthorization Hearing, Senate Committee on Health, Education, Labor and Pensions Subcommittee on Employment, Safety and Training, June 18, 2003; www.workforceflorida.com/wages/wfi/news/news_releases/testimony_austin.htm.

5. Joe Soss, Richard C. Fording, and Sanford F. Schram, "The Color of Devolution: Race, Federalism, and the Politics of Social Control," *American Journal of Political Science* 52, no. 3 (2008): 536–53.

6. Sanford F. Schram, Joe Soss, Richard C. Fording, and Linda Houser "Deciding to Discipline: Race, Choice, and Punishment at the Frontlines of Welfare Reform," *American Sociological Review* 74, no. 3 (June 2009): 398–422.

7. Troy Duster, "Introduction to Unconscious Racism Debate," *Social Psychology Quarterly* 71, no. 1 (2008): 6.

8. See Moon-Kie Jung, Joao Costa Vargas, and Eduardo Bonilla-Silva, eds., *State of White Supremacy: Racism, Governance, and the United States* (Palo Alto: Stanford University Press, 2011).

9. See Piven and Cloward, *Regulating the Poor*; and Loïc Wacquant, *Punishing the Poor: The Neoliberal Government of Social Insecurity* (Durham: Duke University Press, 2009).

10. Wendy Brown, "Neo-liberalism and the End of Liberal Democracy," *Theory and Event* 7, no. 1 (2003): 47–71; http://muse.jhu.edu/journals/theory_and_event/, and "American Nightmare: Neoliberalism, Neoconservatism, and De-democratization," *Political Theory* 34, no. 6 (2006): 690–714.

11. See Sanford F. Schram, Joe Soss, Richard Fording, and Linda Houser, "The Third Level of US Welfare Reform: Governmentality under Neoliberal Pedagogy," *Citizenship Studies* 14, no. 6 (December 2010): 739–54; and Sanford F. Schram, "Review of Loïc Wacquant, *Punishing the Poor: The Neoliberal Government of Social Insecurity* (Durham NC: Duke University Press, 2009)," *Social Service Review* 84, no. 4 (December 2010): 685–89.

12. See Schram, *Welfare Discipline*.

13. See Gabriel A. Almond, A *Discipline Divided: Schools and Sects in Political Science* (Pacific Palisades: Sage, 1989).

CHAPTER ELEVEN. MOVING ON

1. Mary Ruggie pointed out that Harold Wilensky was the first to call the United States a "welfare state laggard." See Mary Ruggie, "Rich Democracies: Political Economy, Public Policy, and Performance by Harold L. Wilensky," *Political Science Quarterly* 118, no. 2 (Summer 2003): 355–56. Wilensky actually originally called the United States a "reluctant welfare state." See Harold L. Wilensky, "The Problems and Prospects of the Welfare State," in *Industrial Society and Social Welfare*, ed. Harold L. Wilensky and Charles N. Lebeaux (New York: Free Press, 1965), xii–xxv. Also see Bruce S. Jansson, *The Reluctant Welfare State*, 4th ed. (Belmont: Wadsworth/Brooks Cole, 2001); Diane Sainsbury, *Gender, Equality, and Welfare States* (Cambridge: Cambridge University Press, 1996), 28–29; Richard Titmuss, *Essays on the Welfare State* (London: Allen and Unwin, 1958); and Gosta Esping-Andersen, *The Three Worlds of Welfare Capitalism* (New York: Polity Press, Cambridge, 1990), 2. For a more recent and thorough example of such research, see Lee Rainwater and Timothy M. Smeeding, *Poor Kids in a Rich Country: America's Children in Comparative Perspective* (New York: Russell Sage Foundation, 2003).

2. Jamie Peck, "Political Economies of Scale: Fast Policy, Interscalar Relations, and Neoliberal Workfare," *Economic Geography* 78, no. 3 (July 2002): 331–60. Also see Jay Hein, "Ideas as Exports," *American Outlook* (Summer 2002); http://www.americanoutlook.org/. Hein notes that welfare reform was in the mid-1990s a popular idea, which spread from Wisconsin to Europe, for responding to the perceived (correctly, to his mind) pressures of economic globalization. He calls this an example of an emerging "global domestic policy" discourse, where ideas circulate across the developed world. Hein's description of the Americanization of European welfare policy suggests a rationale for why that reporter from Sweden wanted to interview me back when I was living in the upper Midwest.

3. Joel Handler, *Social Citizenship and Workfare in the United States and Western Europe: The Paradox of Inclusion* (New York: Oxford University Press, 2004).

4. See Ivar Lodomel, and Helen Trickey, eds., *An Offer You Can't Refuse: Workfare in International Perspective* (Bristol: Policy Press, 2001).

5. Vincent DuBois, *The Bureaucrat and the Poor: Encounters in French Welfare Offices* (London: Ashgate, 2010).

6. Marie Østergaard Møller and Deborah Stone, "Disciplining Disability under Danish Active Labour Market Policy," *Social Policy and Administration* (2012): forthcoming.

7. Bettina Leibetseder, "Jobcentre Plus McDonaldization of Unemployment and Poverty" (Paper presented at the Social Policy Association Conference "Bigger Societies, Smaller Governments?" University of Lincoln, UK, July 4–6, 2011).

8. For specific factual claims made in this paragraph, see the U.S. Department of State, at http://www.state.gov/j/drl/rls/irf/2009/127307.htm.

9. Ulf Hedetoft, "Denmark: Integrating Immigrants into a Homogeneous Welfare State," http://www.migrationinformation.org/feature/display.cfm?ID=485.

10. Jesper Langballe, "I Confess," *Danish Free Press Society*, December 12, 2010; http://europenews.dk/en/node/38110.

11. "Islam in Denmark," http://www.euro-islam.info/country-profiles/denmark/.

12. Gary P. Freeman, "Migration and the Political Economy of the Welfare State, *The Annals* 485, no. 1 (May 1986): 51–63.

13. Alberto Alesina and Edward L. Glaeser, *Fighting Poverty in the US and Europe: A World of Difference* (Oxford: Oxford University Press, 2004), 11.

CHAPTER TWELVE. MAKING IT MATTER

1. Schram, *Praxis for the Poor*.

2. See Kristen Renwick Monroe, ed., *Perestroika!: The Raucous Rebellion in Political Science* (New Haven: Yale University Press, 2005).

3. "An Open Letter to the American Political Science Association Leadership and Members," *PS: Political Science and Politics* 33 (December 1, 2000): 735–41.

4. See Brian Caterino, "Perestroika's Last Stand," *PS: Political Science and Politics* 43 (2010): 753–54. This article penned by my collaborator and independent scholar rightly bemoans the failure of perestroikans to join with me to resist Glenn Beck's vilification of Frances Fox Piven. We ended up working with mostly nonacademics in a successful boycott that helped get Beck fired from Fox News.

5. See Schram and Caterino, eds., *Making Political Science Matter*.

6. Flyvbjerg, *Making Social Science Matter*.

7. Flora Cornish, "Social Science as Practical Wisdom: Here Come the Examples," *LSE Review of Books*; http://blogs.lse.ac.uk/lsereviewofbooks/2012/09/06/real-social-science-applied-phronesis-bent-flyvbjerg/.

8. See Robert Gallucci, "We Have to Talk: The Urgency of Dialogue Between International Relations Scholarship and Policy" (Presentation at Bryn Mawr College, September 20, 2012).

9. For instance, see Jason Frank and John Tambornino, eds., *Vocations of Political Theory* (Minneapolis: University of Minnesota Press, 2000).

10. Cornish, "Social Science as Practical Wisdom."

11. Giorgio Agamben, *Homo Sacer: Sovereign Power and Bare Life* (Stanford: Stanford University Press, 1998).

12. See Flyvbjerg, Landman, and Schram, eds., *Real Social Science*.

13. See Sanford F. Schram and Basha Silverman, "The End of Social Work: Neoliberalizing Social Policy Implementation," *Critical Policy Studies* 6, no. 2 (July 2012): 128–45.

14. See Michael Reisch and Janice Andrews, *The Road Not Taken: A History of Radical Social Work in the United States* (New York: Brunner-Routledge, 2001). This excellent book discusses the Social Work program at Bryn Mawr as once a hotbed of radicalism.

15. Jane Addams, *Democracy and Social Ethics* (Urbana: University of Illinois Press, [1902] 2002); Louise Knight, *Citizen: Jane Addams and the Struggle for Democracy* (Chicago: University of Chicago Press, 2005); "Jane Addams," *Stanford Encyclopedia of Philosophy*; http://plato.stanford.edu/entries/addams-jane/.

16. Lisa Dodson, *The Moral Underground: How Ordinary Americans Subvert an Unfair Economy* (New York: The New Press, 2009).

17. For an optimistic assessment of the largely marginal effects of reentry programs, see Nancy G. La Vigne, "Can Reentry Programs be both Effective and Cost Beneficial?" Speech to Research Policy Institute, Princeton University (Washington, DC: Urban Institute, March 5, 2010); http://www.urban.org/publications/901332.html.

18. John H. Laub and Robert J. Sampson, *Shared Beginnings, Divergent Lives: Delinquent Boys to Age 70* (Cambridge: Harvard University Press, 2003).

19. Patrick A. Langan and David J. Levin, "Recidivism of Prisoners Released in 1994," Bureau of Justice Statistics *Special Report* (Washington, DC: U.S. Department of Justice, Office of Justice Programs, NCJ-193427, June 2002).

20. David Muhlhausen, "The Second Chance Act: More Evaluations of Effectiveness Needed," Testimony before the U.S. Senate, Committee on the Judiciary July 21, 2010; http://www.heritage.org/research/testimony/second-chance-act-how-effective-are-prisoner-reentry-programs.

21. Although he does not use neoliberalism to describe the bureaucratic takeover of higher education, his book accurately describes the neoliberalization of the university. See Benjamin Ginsberg, *The Fall of the Faculty: The Rise of the All-Administrative University and Why It Matters* (New York: Oxford University Press, 2011).

CONCLUSION

1. For a recognition of the value in taking the "I," see Judith Butler, "On Self-Referentiality;" and "Giving an Account of Oneself," where she nonetheless warns that "the 'I' cannot tell the story of its own emergence, and the conditions of its own possibility, without in some sense bearing witness to a state of affairs to which one could not have been present, prior to one's own becoming, and so narrating that which one cannot know." Perhaps this is why my good friend and colleague Michael Tratner counseled me that a good memoir is not about oneself.

2. http://en.wikiquote.org/wiki/Barbara_Kingsolver.

INDEX